MICROWAVE MASTERY COOKBOOK

Now create simple and delicious microwave meals developed with your lifestyle in mind

COOK

By Carol Trench

MICROWAVE MASTERY

All inquires should be addressed to:

Mic•it Publishing, Inc.
P.O. Box 23148
Minneapolis, Minnesota 55423

International Standards Book Number: 0 - 929573 - 00 - 5

Library of Congress Catolog Card Number: 88-92029

Library of Congress Catologing-in-publication data
Trench, Carol
Microwave Mastery

Includes index.
1. Microwave Cookery. I. Carol Trench   II. Title.   III. Series.

Printed in U.S.A.

DEDICATION

To a healthy life for my family and yours!

For Terri, Mike & Bob.
Always reach out and take the risk.

THANKS

I began working on Microwave Mastery in the spring of 1986. The completion of the book was delayed nearly two years when in July of 1986 my son, Bob, who was editing and publishing the book for me, was diagnosed as having Hodgkins Disease. At that time, I stopped working on the book until he had recovered sufficiently from treatment to continue working on the book again. This book would never have been published if it were not for the help of the many people whose care and concern aided us during this difficult period in our lives. I would like to thank the following and wish them success in their continued advancement of good health:

Drs. Peggy and Manouchehr Azad
Dr. Malcolm Blumenthal
Dr. Neil Hoffman
Dr. David G. Smith

The following have made this book possible:
Cover concept & layout: Doug Hagen
Cover photography: Mark Macemon, Cy DeCosse, Incorporated
Photography assistant: Chris Wallace, Cy DeCosse, Incorporated
Food stylist: Bonnie Ellingboe
Food stylist: Mary Margaret Ness
Art direction & editing: Robert Trench
Proofreading: Janice Cauley
Proofreading: Jeanne Chiodo
Indexing: Betsy Norum
Copy editing: Jim Grimmer
Copy editing: Sue McKnight
Nutritional analysis: Margaret Reinhardt, Nutrition Plus, Inc., Minnetonka
Linotronic 300 output: Picas & Points, Minneapolis
Color separations: Spectrum, Inc, Minneapolis
Printing: Malloy Printing, Ann Arbor, Michigan
Fast typing: Cheri Trench, Sally Cassellius, Michelle Brennan
All-around help: Jenny Furuseth
All the right answers: Everyone at Cy DeCosse, Incorporated, especially Clarice Hallberg
Taste-testing of all recipes: My husband Jim, Mike, Cheri & Tommy Trench, Beret & Doug Hagen, Jenny Furuseth, Robert Trench, Teri Micaelli and all others who enjoy microcooked food.
This book was published on the following equipment:
Apple Macintosh SE
Apple LaserWriter II ntx
Linotronic 300
Aldus Pagemaker 3.0

TABLE OF CONTENTS

INTRODUCTION

Fast foods dominate today's family diet. Families have busy schedules. We eat and run, we eat mini-meals, family members eat at different times and kids are cooking more. We demand speed and convenience in our meals, but we are paying a high price in calories, sodium and fat for the foods we typically view as "fasts."

Microcooking gives new meaning to fast foods. It is nutritious, quick, energy-efficient, cool and clean. Foods prepared in microwave ovens retain nutrients, color and flavor because they cook so quickly. Many foods cook in their natural juices so no additional fats are necessary. And microcooking is simple. If you can read this book, you can do it.

The recipes in **Microwave Mastery,** from appetizers to desserts, were developed with your health and convenience in mind. Each recipe has been evaluated for calorie, fat, carbohydrate, protein and sodium content.

Microwave Mastery provides complete, easy-to-follow recipes with unique reminder symbols for cooking procedures. With this book you can become a cooker, not just a warmer, while mastering cooking in your microwave oven.

MICROCOOKING VARIABLES

All of the following can affect the cooking time and the way in which foods cook in a microwave oven:

Amount of Food: Small amounts of food cook faster than large amounts; 1 cup of water boils faster than 2 cups.

Size and Shape: Small thin slices cook faster than large thick slices. Pieces that are uniform in size are best for microcooking, but if there are differences, place larger thicker pieces toward the outside of the dish.

Density: Dense foods such as meats require a longer cooking time than porous foods such as breads or cakes.

Composition: Foods that are high in sugar, like candy, or high in fat, like bacon, or high in moisture, like vegetables, attract microwaves so they require less cooking time.

Starting Temperature: Foods at room temperature require less cooking time than foods taken directly from the refrigerator.

Power Level: Foods cooked at high power (100%) require less time than foods cooked at medium (50%) or medium low (30%).

Oven Wattage: A 600 to 700-watt oven often requires less cooking time than a 400 to 500-watt oven (compact models).

Altitude: At high altitude, cooking times may need to be increased slightly.

BASIC EQUIPMENT

Use non-metal utensils such as ovenproof glass, paper, microwaveable plastic, ceramic or china without metal parts or trim.

- 1 1/2, 2 or 3-quart casserole
- 8, 9 or 10" pie plates
- 6 and 10-oz. custard cups
- 9" round cake pan
- 2, 4 and 8-cup measures
- 8x8x2" baking dish
- 11x7x1 1/2" baking dish
- 12x8x2" baking dish
- 6 or 9-cup microwave ring mold
- microwave meat rack and dish
- microwave meat/candy thermometer
- 12" glass plate

Nice "Add-on" Equipment

- browning grill, dish or skillet
- pizza oven or grill
- microwave muffin pan
- microwave steamer
- 9-cup microwave bundt pan
- bacon rack
- tender (pressure) cooker
- microwave colander
- microwave turntable

Be sure the dishes fit into your microwave oven. If you use a turntable check to see that dishes don't hit the oven walls as they rotate.

Important: All equipment should be labeled microwave-safe. To test for use in a microwave oven:

> **Place** in a 1-cup glass measure:
> 1/2 cup water
> **Set** the dish to be tested next to 1-cup glass measure.
> **Microcook** on high for 1 minute.
> If the dish is cool to the touch after 1 minute, it is safe to use for microcooking.
> If the dish is hot, it has absorbed microwave energy and should not be used for microcooking.

OVEN WATTAGE

Important: All recipes in this book have been tested in a 600 to 700-watt oven. Microwave ovens for the home vary from 400 to 720 watts. Compact or lower-wattage ovens may require a time adjustment to give similar results as in the 600 to 700-watt ovens. Dish size and power levels may also change. Oven manufacturers usually include a cookbook or conversion chart with their compact ovens. If you are unsure of the wattage of your oven you may:
•Check the instruction manual.
•Locate the oven label.
•Try the water test:

> **Place** in a 2-cup glass measure:
> 1 cup water at room temperature
> **Microcook** on high.
> **Check** the water after 2 1/2 to 3 minutes.
> If 1 cup boils in 2 1/2 to 3 minutes = 600 to 700-watt oven
> If 1 cup boils in 3 1/4 to 4 minutes = below 600 watts

COOKING TIME

In most recipes you will find a time range for cooking. For example,

Microcook on high 3 to 5 minutes.

Cook the minimum time first and check. Cooking times are given as guidelines to doneness. Do not overcook! You can always add more time to food that is undercooked.

POWER LEVELS

In this book the power levels used for microcooking are high, medium high, medium, medium low and low. These power levels are similar to an electric range; they correspond to the amount of energy being used to cook the food. The most frequently used are high, medium and medium low. You may run across a recipe that calls for a cooking percentage rather than a level. The chart below is designed as a general comparison of microwave cooking power levels.

Power Level	Power Percentage	Number Setting
High	100%	10
Medium high	70%	7
Medium	50%	5
Medium low	30%	3
Low	10%	1

CONVERTING RECIPES

Compare the recipe that you want to try with a similar one in a microwave cookbook, paying special attention to leavening, liquids and cooking time. Depending on the type of recipe being converted, it may be necessary to:

- Reduce moisture in casseroles.
- Reduce leavening by 1/2 to 3/4 in cakes and quick breads.
- Fill cake pans only half full of batter. Greased pans work best; elevate pan on inverted saucer during baking.
- Check food at 1/4 to 1/3 of the conventional cooking time.
- Season vegetables and meat during standing time as flavors are intensified and salt may cause toughness.

MICROWAVE LIMITATIONS

Microcooking has many advantages and can be used for many foods but it can't do everything. These are some of the foods which are better when cooked by conventional methods:

- Toast
- Puff pastry, cream puffs, popovers
- Eggs in the shell, souffles
- Angel food cakes
- Two-crust pies
- Crusty baked goods
- Turkey (over 12 pounds)
- Home canning
- Deep-fried foods

Symbols

Helpful cooking symbols are located throughout **Microwave Mastery**. Utilizing these symbols makes the art of microcooking easier.

Power Settings

For each microcooking direction there is a microwave oven symbol with the power setting listed in the oven window. These symbols are a reminder of the power your oven needs.

For example, while creating an entree, you may run across the direction:

Microcook on medium 3 minutes until cheese is melted.

The symbol reminds you to set your oven on **50%** for the 3-minute cooking period.

The Stirring Spoon

The stirring spoon symbol reminds you that stirring is needed for the particular food being cooked. Stirring makes the food cook more evenly. A stir command after the cooking command refers to the previous cooking process.

Rotate

Rotating dishes during cooking time helps the food to heat evenly. In some microwave ovens there are "hot spots" which overcook food in one area; rotating helps to prevent this. Rotation of food is used on foods that cannot be stirred, such as cakes.

Turn Over

Some foods cook faster on the bottom. To facilitate even cooking, turn large pieces of food such as baking potatoes, squash, meats and poultry over during cooking.

Arrangement

The ideal placement of foods to be microcooked is in a circle or dough-nut shape. Rearranging during cooking time is sometimes done to insure even heating.

Shape & Size

It is best to use round pans. Microwaves can get trapped in corners of a square pan and may cause dryness. Place thicker, less tender foods toward the outside of dishes because they will receive more microwave energy.

Standing Time

Foods continue to cook after they are removed from the microwave. This is called "standing time" and must be accounted for to prevent overcooking. The standing time depends on the amount and composition of the food which has been cooked. Standing time is extremely important in large dense food items like roasts.

Elevate

Raise food off the floor of the oven to assure doneness on the bottom of the food.

Pierce

Break the outer skin of foods, such as whole potatoes, squash or egg yolks to allow steam to escape.

Cover

Covering is used to prevent spattering and to hold moisture in, which helps food cook faster. The cover symbol reminds you to cover your food before placing it in the oven to be cooked. This is important because food spattered on the inside of your oven can increase cooking time as microwaves are attracted to the spatters.

If, for example, you run across a cover symbol and it reads:

Cover with vented plastic wrap.

You should cover the cooking utensil with plastic wrap and fold back a small opening on one corner of the dish. This process is necessary to let steam escape.

Several types of covering material are mentioned in this book: waxed paper, paper towels, plastic wrap, plastic bags, glass covers and foil. Each of these serves a specific purpose and you should not substitute one for another or it will make a difference in the final product.

Waxed Paper

Waxed paper is used primarily to prevent spattering and to keep the oven clean. It holds in some heat and moisture.

Paper Towels

Paper towels prevent spattering and absorb moisture and fat. They are used for covering or wrapping a sandwich to prevent a soggy product. White paper towels are recommended as colored towels contain ingredients that could discolor food. **DO NOT** use recycled paper towels as they may contain impurities and dyes.

Plastic Wrap

Plastic wrap holds in the most moisture. When used to cover fruits and vegetables, little or no water needs to be added because they can steam in their own juices. Plastic wrap may be used for covering other products that need to be steamed. It is very important to vent one side of the dish so that steam can escape during cooking. Fold back one edge to form a narrow vent. After standing time, carefully remove the plastic, away from yourself, to prevent a burn.

Plastic Cooking Bags

Plastic cooking bags may be used for less tender cuts of meat. Be sure to use plastic, not metal, twist ties. Tie loosely and make a slit in the top of bag to allow steam to escape.

Glass Cover

Glass covers hold in moisture, similar to plastic wrap, and may be used to cover casserole dishes.

Foil

Foil may be used in small amounts in some microwave ovens. Be sure to follow the manufacturer's directions for your oven. Small pieces of foil may be used to shield a part of some food to prevent overcooking. Examples are in the corners of a square baking dish, or the tips of turkey or other poultry wings and the ends of roasts. The foil must not touch the sides, top or bottom of the oven as this could cause arcing.

CLEANING

- Wipe oven cavity clean after each use. Pay special attention to the door seals and cavity. Do not use abrasives. Baking soda works well for cleaning.
- If there is an odor in the oven:

Place in a 1-cup glass measure:
    2 tablespoons lemon juice
Add . . .
    1/2 cup water
Microcook on high 2 minutes; leave in oven 3 minutes.
Remove measure; wipe oven.

MICROWAVE PROBE

Many microwave ovens today are equipped with a probe. This is a device that measures the temperature of foods and automatically stops the cooking when a desired temperature is reached. Be sure to follow manufacturer's directions for use and care.

GENERAL SAFETY

- •Keep the oven clean.
- •Do not operate an empty oven.
- •Fill containers only 1/2 to 2/3 full, leaving space for expansion of food. Microcooking may cause rapid release of steam.
- •In case of fire, unplug the oven and keep the oven door closed.
- •Be sure to prick all foods with tight skins, like potatoes and squash, to prevent them from bursting.
- •Remove metal twist ties from packages as they may cause arcing.
- •Some metal may be used in the microwave but only as directed in the use and care manual of your oven.
- •Avoid using foil-lined containers, fast food cartons with metal handles or foil plates more than 3/4" deep.
- •DO NOT use metal pots or pans as they cause arcing.
- •DO NOT use dishes with metal designs, rim rings and edging, fine china or lead crystal.
- •DO NOT place any object between the door and the oven seal.
- •DO NOT operate the oven with anything caught in the door.
- •It is best to have a microwave plugged into its own grounded outlet.
- •Avoid the use of an extension cord to connect microwave to outlet.
- •Remove lids from jars when heating in a microwave.
- •Be sure glassware is free of cracks because extreme heat may cause breakage.
- •Use extreme caution when heating baby formula or food; stir food or liquid to ensure even heating or a baby could be burned.
- •Watch small, curious children when opening the oven door as steam could burn them.
- •Some plastics such as Styrofoam cups could melt if left in the oven too long. Be sure any plastic containers are made for microwave use.
- •Avoid using colored or recycled paper towels.
- •Colored frozen food wrappers can leave an imprint on the oven surface. Place package on a plate to prevent ink transfer.

- Avoid using egg cartons as they may be soiled or have undesirable bacteria.
- Browning grills or dishes must be handled with pot holders to avoid burns. Other dishes may become hot from the heat of the food being cooked and need to be handled with potholders.
- Be careful not to overdry herbs or flowers as they could ignite.
- Do not pop corn in a brown paper bag, it could ignite.
- Do not soften nail polish or shoe polish or dry newspaper or other non-food items in a microwave oven.

B R O W N I N G

Foods heat so quickly in a microwave oven that there is normally insufficient time for browning (caramelization) to occur and some foods may look pale and undercooked even when cooked. Browners have a special metal that absorbs microwave energy and causes the area to get very hot.

There are three special pieces of microwave equipment which brown foods: a browning skillet, a browning grill and a browning dish. Some come with covers and they vary in diameter, between 10 and 12".

Be sure to follow the manufacturer's directions when using a browner; heating too long could damage the bottom of the oven.

Butter or margarine is sometimes used to prevent food from sticking to the surface of the browner.

- Meats will brown better if they are wiped dry.
- Turn food over at the first part of the cooking time.
- DO NOT cover a browning skillet if it did not come with a cover.
- DO NOT use abrasive cleaners.
- Avoid non-stick sprays; they will scorch.
- Always use pot holders as the browning skillet gets very hot.

HEALTHY DIET GUIDELINES

To prepare nutritious foods in a microwave, health-conscious cooks should be aware of the following dietary guidelines and hints. There are many similarities in the guidelines recommended for preventing heart disease, reducing the risk of certain cancers and preventing obesity.

- Include the basic four food groups in menu planning.
- Eat a variety of foods.
- Eat fiber-rich foods (see list, page 280).
- Lower your fat intake (see list, page 21).
- Lower your sugar intake (see list, page 21).
- Lower your sodium intake (see list, page 21).

Watch your weight

- Eat smaller portions.
- Do not stand or watch TV while eating.
- Use a smaller plate.
- Eat slowly.
- Never grocery shop when hungry.
- Be sure to exercise.
- Remember!   To lose one pound of body weight one must burn 3500 calories.

It is important to read labels to identify the ingredients in many food products. Commercial "fast foods" may contain hidden fat, sodium and sugar. Remember, many items are concealed; you must sometimes be a nutrition detective!

To become a label-watcher detective, look for the following names on food products:

Saturated Fat

- coconut oil
- palm oil
- palm kernel oil
- lard
- partially saturated and hydrogenated vegetable oil

Sugars

- dextrose
- sucrose
- sorbitol
- corn syrup
- honey
- mannitol
- fructose
- lactose

Sodium

- monosodium glutamate
- sodium sulfite
- brine
- sodium hydroxide
- sodium benzoate
- sodium propionate
- baking soda
- baking power
- sodium nitrite

F.D.A. Guidelines for labeling sodium & calories

- **Low-calorie** a food can contain no more than 40 calories serving.
- **Reduced-calorie** a food must be at least 1/3 lower in calories than comparable food.
- **Very low-sodium** a food must contain less than 35 milligrams/ serving.
- **Sodium-free** a food must contain less than 5 milligrams/serving.
- **Reduced sodium** a food must have a 75% or greater reduction in sodium than comparable food.
- **Unsalted** a food can have no salt added (this does not mean that the product is sodium-free).

From the Kitchen Counter of Carol Trench

Microwave Mastery is designed to be more than a cookbook; it is a toast to healthly lifestyles of the future. These recipes will guide you in creating meals that are nutritionally well balanced as well as fun to make. They take your microwave beyond food warming and teach you to use it as a major cooking appliance.

The recipes in **Microwave Mastery** will help educate the taste buds of children who are developing lifelong eating habits and adults who may need to change to healthier diets. Each recipe in this book has been evaluated for calories, fat, carbohydrates, protein and sodium content. This is, however, not a diet cookbook. Many recipes have been modified to reduce unhealthy amounts of calories, fat, sodium and cholesterol, but not all. Some recipes are family favorites and have not been altered.

The concepts in Microwave Mastery enable you to enhance the flavor of your meals while creating a healthier lifestyle. Many recipes are basic and easy, some are more advanced. As you experiment and try the many recipes in this book, you will eventually master the art of Microcooking.

APPETIZERS

Bean Dip

The calories for dips are based on 1 to 3 tablespoons per serving.
Serves 16. Microcook Time: 5 minutes.
Calories: 96. Fat: 6 g. Carbohydrates: 8 g. Protein: 4 g. Sodium: 161 mg.

- *1 (16-oz.) can refried beans*
- *3/4 cup cubed process cheese spread*
- *1/4 teaspoon garlic powder*
- *1 cup low-fat sour cream*
- *2 tablespoons instant minced onion*
- *1 (4-oz.) can chopped green chilies*
- *dash hot pepper sauce*

Combine in an 8-cup glass measure:
    1 (16-oz.) can refried beans
    3/4 cup cubed process cheese spread
    1/4 teaspoon garlic powder
Microcook on high 3 minutes until cheese is melted.
Stir in:
    1 cup low-fat sour cream
    2 tablespoons instant minced onion
    1 (4-oz.) can chopped green chilies
    dash hot pepper sauce
Microcook on high 2 minutes.

Beer Cheese Dip

Mini bread sticks make good dippers.
Serves 10. Microcook Time: 8 minutes.
Calories: 176. Fat: 15 g. Carbohydrates: 3 g. Protein: 7 g. Sodium: 491 mg.

- *1 (10-oz.) jar sharp cheese spread, softened*
- *1 (8-oz.) pkg. light cream cheese, softened*
- *1/4 cup beer*
- *6 drops hot pepper sauce*
- *1 teaspoon Dijon mustard*
- *2 strips bacon, cooked and crumbled**

Combine in a 1 1/2-quart casserole:
    1 (10-oz.) jar sharp cheese spread, softened
    1 (8-oz.) pkg. light cream cheese, softened
    1/4 cup beer
    6 drops hot pepper sauce
    1 teaspoon Dijon mustard
Microcook on medium 4 to 6 minutes.
Stir in:
    2 strips bacon, cooked and crumbled*
Serve with crackers.
*See bacon directions, on page 62.

Broccoli Dip

Great on baked potatoes.
Serves 16 as a dip. Microcook Time: 13 minutes.
Calories: 87. Fat: 6 g. Carbohydrates: 4 g. Protein: 4 g. Sodium: 304 mg.

Place in a 4-cup measure:
   1 (8-oz.) pkg. frozen chopped broccoli
Microcook on high 4 to 5 minutes.
Drain.
Place in an 8-cup glass measure:
   1/2 cup chopped celery
   3 tablespoons chopped onion
   2 tablespoons margarine
Microcook on high 2 minutes.
Add . . .
   1 (10 1/2-oz.) can low-sodium cream of
      chicken soup
   1 cup process cheese spread
   1/4 teaspoon hot pepper sauce
   1/2 teaspoon garlic powder
Microcook on high 3 to 4 minutes.
Stir twice.
Add cooked broccoli.
Microcook on high 2 minutes.
Serve with raw vegetables or on a baked potato.

[100%] [100%] [100%] [100%]

- *1 (8-oz.) pkg. frozen chopped broccoli*
- *1/2 cup chopped celery*
- *3 tablespoons chopped onion*
- *2 tablespoons margarine*
- *1 (10 1/2-oz.) can low-sodium cream of chicken soup*
- *1 cup process cheese spread*
- *1/4 teaspoon hot pepper sauce*
- *1/2 teaspoon garlic powder*

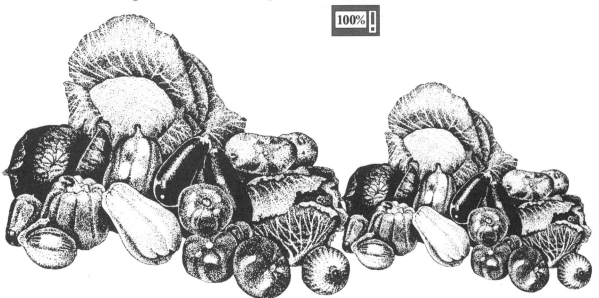

Con Queso Dip

Best with corn tortilla chips.
Serves 21. Microcook Time: 10 minutes.
Calories: 106. Fat: 8 g. Carbohydrates: 2 g. Protein: 7 g. Sodium: 137 mg.

- 1 (5-oz.) can chicken pieces
- 1/2 medium onion, chopped
- 1 clove garlic, minced
- 1 large tomato, diced
- 1 (4-oz.) can chopped green chilies
- 6 drops hot pepper sauce
- 1 lb. shredded Cheddar cheese
- 1 cup low-fat plain yogurt

Combine in an 8-cup glass measure:
    1 (5-oz.) can chicken pieces
    1/2 medium onion, chopped
    1 clove garlic, minced
Cover with vented plastic wrap.
Microcook on high 2 minutes, until tender.
Add . . .
    1 large tomato, diced
    1 (4-oz.) can chopped green chilies
    6 drops hot pepper sauce
Microcook on high 4 minutes.
Stir twice.
Add . . .
    1 lb. shredded Cheddar cheese
Microcook on medium 2 minutes or until cheese has melted.
Stir in:
    1 cup low-fat plain yogurt

Crab Dip

Seafood lovers love this one!
Serves 10. Microcook Time: 8 minutes.
Calories: 92. Fat: 8 g. Carbohydrates: 1 g. Protein: 4 g. Sodium: 197 mg.

- 1 (6 1/2-oz.) can crab meat, drained
- 1 clove garlic, minced
- 1 tablespoon chopped onion
- 1 teaspoon lemon juice
- 1 (8-oz.) pkg. light cream cheese
- 6 drops hot pepper sauce
- 1 tablespoon chopped parsley

Combine in a 2-quart casserole:
    1 (6 1/2-oz.) can crab meat, drained
    1 clove garlic, minced
    1 tablespoon chopped onion
    1 teaspoon lemon juice
Microcook on high 2 to 3 minutes.
Add . . .
    1 (8-oz.) pkg. light cream cheese
    6 drops hot pepper sauce
    1 tablespoon chopped parsley
Stir.
Microcook on medium 2 to 3 minutes.

Festive Chicken Dip

A favorite. Perfect for that special occasion.
Serves 25. Microcook Time: 20 minutes.
Calories: 65. Fat: 4 g. Carbohydrates: 3 g. Protein: 4 g. Sodium: 40 mg.

Combine in a 2-quart casserole:
    2 (5-oz.) cans chicken pieces
    1 (10 oz.) pkg. frozen chopped spinach,
      thawed and drained*
    1/4 cup chopped celery
    2 tablespoons chopped onion
    1 (4-oz.) can sliced mushrooms, drained
    1 (2 1/2-oz.) jar chopped pimiento
    1/2 teaspoon garlic powder
    1 (8-oz.) can sliced water chestnuts,
      drained
Cover with vented plastic wrap.

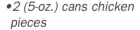

Microcook on high 3 minutes.
Remove plastic wrap.
Add . . .
    1 (8 oz.) pkg. light cream cheese
Stir.
Add . . .
    8 pitted ripe olives, sliced
Microcook on medium 8 to 10 minutes.

Stir in:
    3 tablespoons brandy or sherry
Top with:
    4 oz. cashew nuts
Serve as a hot appetizer with assorted crackers or
chips.
*1 pkg. frozen spinach can be defrosted on high in
package on plate for 5 to 7 minutes.

- 2 (5-oz.) cans chicken pieces
- 1 (10 oz.) pkg. frozen chopped spinach, thawed and drained*
- 1/4 cup chopped celery
- 2 tablespoons chopped onion
- 1 (4-oz.) can sliced mushrooms, drained
- 1 (2 1/2-oz.) jar chopped pimiento
- 1/2 teaspoon garlic powder
- 1 (8-oz.) can sliced water chestnuts, drained
- 1 (8 oz.) pkg. light cream cheese
- 8 pitted ripe olives, sliced
- 3 tablespoons brandy or sherry
- 4 oz. cashew nuts

Dip for Vegetables

Terrific with carrots, broccoli, cauliflower and zucchini; or as a topping for baked potatoes.
Serves 6. Microcook Time: 5 minutes.
Calories: 170. Fat: 16 g. Carbohydrates: 2 g. Protein: 6 g. Sodium: 441 mg.

- *1 (8-oz.) pkg. light cream cheese*
- *1 teaspoon instant minced onion*
- *1 tablespoon lemon juice*
- *2 tablespoons buttermilk salad dressing*
- *1 clove garlic, minced*
- *1/4 cup imitation bacon bits*

Combine in an 8-cup glass measure:
  1 (8-oz.) pkg. light cream cheese
  1 teaspoon instant minced onion
  1 tablespoon lemon juice
  2 tablespoons buttermilk salad dressing
  1 clove garlic, minced
Microcook on medium 45 seconds.
Add . . .
  1/4 cup imitation bacon bits
Stir.

Hot Chipped Beef Dip

Deliciously hearty.
Serves 10. Microcook Time: 8 minutes.
Calories: 94. Fat: 8 g. Carbohydrates: 2 g. Protein: 4 g. Sodium: 323 mg.

- *1 (8-oz.) pkg. light cream cheese*
- *1 (2-oz.) pkg. smoked beef slices*
- *1/2 cup low-fat yogurt*
- *2 tablespoons chopped green pepper*
- *1 teaspoon minced onion*
- *dash hot pepper sauce*

Place in a 4-cup glass measure:
  1 (8-oz.) pkg. light cream cheese
Microcook on medium 45 seconds.
Add . . .
  1 (2-oz.) pkg. smoked beef slices
  1/2 cup low-fat yogurt
  2 tablespoons chopped green pepper
  1 teaspoon minced onion
  dash hot pepper sauce
Stir.
Microcook on medium 3 to 4 minutes.

Hot Hamburger Dip

Another party favorite.
Serves 11. Microcook Time: 10 minutes.
Calories: 117. Fat: 7 g. Carbohydrates: 6 g. Protein: 9 g. Sodium: 229 mg.

Place in a microwave-safe colander over a 1 1/2-quart casserole:

    1 lb. lean ground beef, crumbled
    1/2 cup chopped onion.

Cover with waxed paper.
Microcook on high 4 to 5 minutes.
Drain fat.
Place meat in casserole.
Add . . .

    1/2 cup chili sauce
    1 tablespoon chili powder
    dash cumin
    1 (8-oz.) can refried beans

Microcook on high 2 minutes.
Stir.
Top with:

    1 cup shredded Cheddar cheese
    1 (2 1/2-oz.) can sliced olives

- *1 lb. lean ground beef, crumbled*
- *1/2 cup chopped onion*
- *1/2 cup chili sauce*
- *1 tablespoon chili powder*
- *dash cumin*
- *1 (8-oz.) can refried beans*
- *1 cup shredded Cheddar cheese*
- *1 (2 1/2-oz.) can sliced olives*

Italian Sausage Dip

Chef Doug Oaks, from St. Paul, introduced me to fennel as a seasoning.
Serves 16. Microcook Time: 15 minutes.
Calories: 58. Fat: 3 g. Carbohydrates: 2 g. Protein: 3 g. Sodium: 91 mg.

- 1/2 lb. Italian sausage
- 1 (8-oz.) carton low-fat sour cream
- 1 teaspoon sweet basil
- 1/2 teaspoon fennel
- 1 cup shredded Cheddar cheese
- 1 tomato, chopped
- 1/2 green pepper, chopped

Place in a microwave-safe colander over a 2-quart casserole:

    1/2 lb. Italian sausage

Cover with waxed paper.

Microcook on high 4 minutes.

Drain fat.

Spread the sausage in a layer on a 12x8x2" glass baking dish.

Combine in an 8-cup glass measure:

    1 (8-oz.) carton low-fat sour cream

    1 teaspoon sweet basil

    1/2 teaspoon fennel

Spread the mixture evenly over the meat.

Top with:

    1 cup shredded Cheddar cheese

    1 tomato, chopped

    1/2 green pepper, chopped

Microcook on medium 6 to 8 minutes.

Serve with corn chips.

Mexican Dip

Our Uncle Bob from California loves it.
Serves 18. Microcook Time: 10 minutes.
Calories: 78. Fat: 4 g. Carbohydrates: 8 g. Protein: 3 g. Sodium: 194 mg.

- 1 (16-oz.) can refried beans
- 1/2 cup low-fat sour cream
- 1/2 cup red salsa
- 1/4 cup chopped green onions
- 1 tomato, chopped
- 1/2 cup shredded Cheddar cheese

Combine in a 1-quart casserole:

    1 (16-oz.) can refried beans

    1/2 cup low-fat sour cream

    1/2 cup red salsa

    1/4 cup chopped green onions

Microcook on medium high 6 to 7 minutes.

Stir every 2 minutes.

Stir in:

    1 tomato, chopped

Add . . .

    1/2 cup shredded Cheddar cheese

Microcook on medium 2 minutes.

Nacho Dip

Another dip that's perfect with corn chips.
Serves 15. Microcook Time: 6 minutes.
Calories: 88. Fat: 4 g. Carbohydrates: 8 g. Protein: 4 g. Sodium: 355 mg.

Combine in an 8-cup glass measure:
   1 (11-oz.) can nacho cheese soup
   1 (11 1/2-oz.) can bean & bacon soup
   1 cup low-fat sour cream
   2 teaspoons imitation bacon bits
Microcook on high 6 minutes.
Stir twice.

- *1 (11-oz.) can nacho cheese soup*
- *1 (11 1/2-oz.) can bean & bacon soup*
- *1 cup low-fat sour cream*
- *2 teaspoons imitation bacon bits*

Shrimp Dip

Simply fantastic.
Serves 8. Microcook Time: 5 minutes.
Calories: 90. Fat: 5 g. Carbohydrates: 3 g. Protein: 8 g. Sodium: 178 mg.

Place in a 4-cup measure:
   1 (3-oz.) pkg. light cream cheese
Microcook on medium 20 seconds.
Stir once.
Add . . .
   1/2 cup low-fat sour cream
   1 (7 1/2-oz.) can shrimp, drained
   1 tablespoon horseradish sauce
   1 tablespoon lemon juice
   1 tablespoon chili sauce
Add to give desired consistency:
   few drops of water
Chill.

- *1 (3-oz.) pkg. light cream cheese*
- *1/2 cup low-fat sour cream*
- *1 (7 1/2-oz.) can shrimp, drained*
- *1 tablespoon horseradish sauce*
- *1 tablespoon lemon juice*
- *1 tablespoon chili sauce*
- *few drops of water*

Spinach Dip

Festive when served in hollowed Italian bread.
Serves 19. Microcook Time: 15 minutes.
Calories: 70. Fat: 5 g. Carbohydrates: 3 g. Protein: 3 g. Sodium: 214 mg.

- 2 (10-oz.) pkgs. frozen chopped spinach
- 1 (1.7 oz.) pkg. dry vegetable soup mix without noodles
- 1/2 cup water
- 1 (8-oz.) pkg. light cream cheese
- 1 cup low-fat sour cream
- dash hot pepper sauce

Defrost in carton on a glass plate:*
    2 (10-oz.) pkgs. frozen chopped spinach
Microcook on high 8 to 10 minutes.
Stand 4 minutes.
Drain well.
Place in a 4-cup glass measure:
    1 (1.7 oz.) pkg. dry vegetable soup mix without noodles
    1/2 cup water
Cover with plastic wrap.
Microcook on high 1 minute.
Place in a 8-cup glass measure:
    1 (8-oz.) pkg. light cream cheese
Microcook on medium 30 to 45 seconds.
Add to soup mix and spinach:
    1 cup low-fat sour cream
Add to cream cheese.
Stir in:
    dash hot pepper sauce

*paper-covered cartons only. If cartons are foil-covered, be sure to remove covering, as arcing may result.

Italian Artichokes

When you want something special, try this.
Serves 10. Microcook Time: 5 minutes.
Calories: 95. Fat: 9 g. Carbohydrates: 5 g. Protein: 1 g. Sodium: 342 mg.

- 1 (14-oz.) can artichoke hearts, drained
- 1 (5 3/4-oz.) can pitted ripe olives
- 1 pint fresh mushrooms (if large, cut in half)
- 1/2 (8-oz.) bottle Italian dressing

Combine in an 8-cup measure:
    1 (14-oz.) can artichoke hearts, drained
    1 (5 3/4-oz.) can pitted ripe olives
    1 pint fresh mushrooms (if large, cut in half)
Pour over mixture:
    1/2 (8-oz.) bottle Italian dressing
Stand 1 hour.
Stir.
Microcook on high 2 to 3 minutes until hot.
Serve immediately.
Hint: Low-calorie/low-sodium Italian dressings are available.

Swiss Almond Zucchini

Nothing but raves.
Serves 12. Microcook Time: 20 minutes.
Calories: 67. Fat: 4 g. Carbohydrates: 3 g. Protein: 4 g. Sodium: 199 mg.

Combine in an 8-cup glass measure:
    3 to 4 small zucchini, shredded
    1 clove garlic, chopped
    1 tablespoon chopped onion
    3/4 teaspoon basil
Cover with vented plastic wrap.
Microcook on high 3 minutes.
Add . . .
    1/2 cup crushed seasoned croutons
    3 eggs
    1/2 cup Swiss almond cheese food
    2 tablespoons grated Parmesan cheese
    6 drops hot pepper sauce
Stir.
Pour into a 9" microwave ring mold.
Microcook on medium high 10 to 12 minutes.
Stand 5 minutes.
Cut into bite-size pieces.

- 3 to 4 small zucchini, shredded
- 1 clove garlic, chopped
- 1 tablespoon chopped onion
- 3/4 teaspoon basil
- 1/2 cup crushed seasoned croutons
- 3 eggs
- 1/2 cup Swiss almond cheese food
- 2 tablespoons grated Parmesan cheese
- 6 drops hot pepper sauce

Cheese & Bacon Crackers

Grated Romano adds a special flavor.
Serves 40. Microcook Time: 10 minutes.
Calories: 35. Fat: 2 g. Carbohydrates: 1 g. Protein: 3 g. Sodium: 107 mg.

Combine in an 8-cup glass measure:
    1 (8-oz.) pkg. shredded Swiss cheese
    1 egg
    1 tablespoon brandy or white grape juice
    1/2 cup chopped onion
    1/2 cup imitation bacon bits
    1/2 teaspoon garlic powder
    fresh ground pepper
Mix well and **spread** on:
    whole grain crackers
Top with:
    1/4 cup grated Romano cheese
Microcook on high 1 to 2 minutes for 12 crackers.

- 1 (8-oz.) pkg. shredded Swiss cheese
- 1 egg
- 1 tablespoon brandy or white grape juice
- 1/2 cup chopped onion
- 1/2 cup imitation bacon bits
- 1/2 teaspoon garlic powder
- fresh ground pepper
- 1/4 cup grated Romano cheese
- whole grain crackers

J. D.'s Beef Jerky

Adapted from the National Livestock and Meat Board recipe.
Serves 48. Makes 24 slices. Microcook Time: 50 minutes. Stand 1 day.
Calories: 37. Fat: 3 g. Carbohydrates: 0 g. Protein: 2 g. Sodium: 72 mg.

- 1 1/2-lb. beef flank steak, fat removed
- 1 1/2 teaspoons salt
- 1/2 teaspoon garlic powder
- 1/4 teaspoon ground pepper

Cut into thin strips (1/8x3"):
    1 1/2-lb. beef flank steak, fat removed
Combine in a glass mixing bowl:
    1 1/2 teaspoons salt
    1/2 teaspoon garlic powder
    1/4 teaspoon ground pepper
Sprinkle over strips.
Place half of strips on microwave bacon rack.
Cover with waxed paper.
Microcook on medium low 21 minutes.

Turn over halfway through cooking.
Place drier strips in center.
Rotate rack.

Microcook on medium low 21 minutes, until dry.
Place strips on paper towel.
Repeat for remaining strips.
Stand 24 hours.
Store in a covered container.

Cajun Chicken Meatballs

Chicken with that great Cajun spice.
Serves 20. Microcook Time: 10 minutes.
Calories: 39. Fat: 2 g. Carbohydrates: 1 g. Protein: 5 g. Sodium: 30 mg.

- 1 whole chicken breast, skinned, cooked and ground
- 1/4 cup chopped onion
- 1/4 cup crushed croutons
- 2 eggs
- 2 teaspoons Cajun seasoning
- freshly ground pepper

Combine in an 8-cup glass measure:
    1 whole chicken breast, skinned, cooked and ground
    1/4 cup chopped onion
    1/4 cup crushed croutons
    2 eggs
    2 teaspoons Cajun seasoning
    freshly ground pepper
Mix well and **shape** into 15 to 20 balls.
Place in an 11x7x1 1/2 " glass dish.
Cover with waxed paper.

Microcook on high 6 to 7 minutes.
Turn and **rotate.**

Chinese Chicken Wings

I haven't met anyone who doesn't love these!
Serves 12. Microcook Time: 12 minutes. Marinate overnight.
Calories: 93. Fat: 2 g. Carbohydrates: 8 g. Protein: 9 g. Sodium: 628 mg.

Cut tips off:
    12 chicken wings
Cut wings at joint and **arrange** on a 9" round glass baking dish.
Combine in an 8-cup glass measure:
    1/2 cup white wine
    1/2 cup low-sodium soy sauce
    1/4 cup honey
    2 tablespoons pineapple juice
    1/2 teaspoon garlic powder
    1/2 teaspoon grated fresh gingerroot
Pour over wings and **refrigerate** overnight.
Cover with waxed paper.
Microcook on high 4 minutes.
Turn wings, **brush** with marinade sauce.
Microcook on high 2 to 3 minutes or until no longer pink.
Stand 5 minutes, **covered.**

- 12 chicken wings
- 1/2 cup white wine
- 1/2 cup low-sodium soy sauce
- 1/4 cup honey
- 2 tablespoons pineapple juice
- 1/2 teaspoon garlic powder
- 1/2 teaspoon grated fresh gingerroot

Drumette Chicken Wings

Party or open house? Try these.
Serves 12. Microcook Time: 2 1/4 hours.
Calories: 69. Fat: 2 g. Carbohydrates: 7 g. Protein: 6 g. Sodium: 249 mg.

- 1/4 cup teriyaki sauce
- 2 tablespoons honey
- 2 tablespoons apricot jam
- 2 tablespoons orange juice
- 2 tablespoons red wine vinegar
- 1/4 teaspoon grated fresh gingerroot
- 1/4 teaspoon garlic powder
- 1/4 teaspoon onion powder
- 1/4 teaspoon coconut curry seasoning, if desired
- 12 drumette chicken wings

Combine in a glass mixing bowl:
> 1/4 cup teriyaki sauce
> 2 tablespoons honey
> 2 tablespoons apricot jam
> 2 tablespoons orange juice
> 2 tablespoons red wine vinegar
> 1/4 teaspoon grated fresh gingerroot
> 1/4 teaspoon garlic powder
> 1/4 teaspoon onion powder
> 1/4 teaspoon coconut curry seasoning, if desired

Marinate for 2 hours over:
> 12 drumette chicken wings

Place wings in a 9" round glass dish, circular-fashion, with meaty portion to the outside.

Cover with waxed paper.

Microcook on high 5 to 7 minutes, until no longer pink.

Stand.

Hint: Drumettes or baby drums are purchased already trimmed of tips and middle sections.

French Cheese Spread

A lower-calorie version of an old favorite.
Serves 60. Microcook Time: 5 minutes. 3 days to ripen.
Calories: 32. Fat: 3 g. Carbohydrates: 0 g. Protein: 1 g. Sodium: 24 mg.

Combine in an 8-cup glass measure:
    2 (8-oz.) pkgs. light cream cheese
Microcook on medium 1 minute.
Stir.
Add . . .
    1 cup low-fat sour cream
    1/2 cup plain yogurt
    1 teaspoon garlic powder
    1 teaspoon onion powder
    1/2 teaspoon white pepper
    12 drops hot pepper sauce
    2 tablespoons freshly chopped parsley
Place in jar, **cover** and **ripen** in the refrigerator for
1 to 3 days.
Spread on toast rounds or crackers.

- *2 (8-oz.) pkgs. light cream cheese*
- *1 cup low-fat sour cream*
- *1/2 cup plain yogurt*
- *1 teaspoon garlic powder*
- *1 teaspoon onion powder*
- *1/2 teaspoon white pepper*
- *12 drops hot pepper sauce*
- *2 tablespoons freshly chopped parsley*

Tangy Cheese Spread

Try on fresh tomato slices for a great-tasting snack.
Serves 24. Microcook Time: 5 minutes.
Calories: 35. Fat: 3 g. Carbohydrates: 0 g. Protein: 1 g. Sodium: 61 mg.

Combine in an 8-cup glass measure:
    1 cup shredded Cheddar cheese
    1/2 cup light mayonnaise
    1/2 teaspoon horseradish sauce
    1/4 teaspoon dry mustard
    2 drops hot pepper sauce
Spread on:
    24 crackers
Place in a single layer on a 12" glass plate.
Microcook on high 30 seconds for 12 crackers.
Repeat.

- *1 cup shredded Cheddar cheese*
- *1/2 cup light mayonnaise*
- *1/2 teaspoon horseradish sauce*
- *1/4 teaspoon dry mustard*
- *2 drops hot pepper sauce*
- *24 crackers*

Mexican Corn Wedges

Everyone will beg for more!
Serves 12. Microcook Time: 15 minutes.
Calories: 105. Fat: 8 g. Carbohydrates: 3 g. Protein: 6 g. Sodium: 135 mg.

- 1 1/2 cups crushed corn chips
- 1 cup shredded Cheddar cheese
- 1 (4-oz.) can chopped green chilies
- 2 eggs

Combine in a 9" microwave ring mold:
  1 1/2 cups crushed corn chips
  1 cup shredded Cheddar cheese
  1 (4-oz.) can chopped green chilies
  2 eggs
Mix well.
Microcook on medium 10 minutes.
Stand 5 minutes before cutting into wedges.

Meatballs with Garden Dip

Good for "grazing."
Serves 18. Microcook Time: 20 minutes.
Calories: 74. Fat: 3 g. Carbohydrates: 2 g. Protein: 7 g. Sodium: 62 mg.

- 1 lb. lean ground beef
- 1/4 cup crushed seasoned croutons
- 1 egg
- 1 cup low-fat sour cream
- 2 tablespoons buttermilk salad dressing
- 1 tablespoon honey mustard
- 1 tablespoon chopped onion
- 1 tablespoon chopped green pepper
- 1 teaspoon grated carrot

Combine in an 8-cup glass measure:
  1 lb. lean ground beef
  1/4 cup crushed seasoned croutons
  1 egg
Mix well.
Shape into 18 small meatballs.
Arrange on bacon rack; **cover** with waxed paper.
Microcook on high 8 to 10 minutes.
Stand 5 minutes.

Combine in 2-cup microwave-safe serving dish:
  1 cup low-fat sour cream
  2 tablespoons buttermilk salad dressing
  1 tablespoon honey mustard
  1 tablespoon chopped onion
  1 tablespoon chopped green pepper
  1 teaspoon grated carrot
Microcook on high 1 to 2 minutes.

Italian Mushrooms

Try adding a few fennel seeds for that distinctive Italian flavor.
Serves 24. Microcook Time: 18 minutes.
Calories: 26. Fat: 1 g. Carbohydrates: 3 g. Protein: 1 g. Sodium: 45 mg.

Prepare and **remove** stems from:
24 large mushrooms
Place in a microwave-safe colander over a
1 1/2-quart casserole:
1/2 lb. hot Italian sausage
1/2 cup finely chopped onion
Cover with waxed paper.
Microcook on high 8 minutes.
Stir twice.
Drain fat.
Place meat mixture in casserole.
Add to meat mixture:
1/4 cup shredded mozzarella cheese
1/4 cup grated Romano cheese
3/4 teaspoon oregano
1/2 teaspoon garlic powder
1 (6-oz.) can tomato paste
Microcook on high 3 minutes.
Stir once.
Place half of the mushrooms in a circle on
microwave-safe serving plate.
Stuff with sausage mixture.
Top with more mozzarella.
Microcook on high 3 to 4 minutes.
Rotate once.
Hint: If mushroom size is not uniform, smaller
ones may cook in less time. You may also use
stems in a salad or vegetable plate.

- 24 large mushrooms
- 1/2 lb. hot Italian sausage
- 1/2 cup finely chopped
  onion
- 1/4 cup shredded
  mozzarella cheese
- 1/4 cup grated Romano
  cheese
- 3/4 teaspoon oregano
- 1/2 teaspoon garlic powder
- 1 (6-oz.) can tomato paste

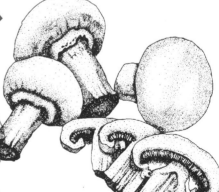

Cajun Nuts

For nuts with Pizazz!
Serves 8. Microcook Time: 10 minutes.
Calories: 218. Fat: 19 g. Carbohydrates: 7 g. Protein: 9 g. Sodium: 1 mg.

•*6 cloves garlic, pushed through a press or finely minced*
•*1 tablespoon olive oil*
•*2 cups unsalted peanuts*
•*1 tablespoon Cajun seasoning**

Preheat microwave browning skillet according to manufacturer's directions.
Combine . . .
>6 cloves garlic, pushed through a press or finely minced
>1 tablespoon olive oil

Add . . .
>2 cups unsalted peanuts

Stir.
Microcook on high 1 minute.
Add . . .
>1 tablespoon Cajun seasoning*

Microcook on high 1 minute.
Transfer to bowl.
Be careful as browner is very hot! Use pot holders.
Cool.
*Hint: You can make your own seasoning by mixing:
>1 teaspoon cumin
>1 teaspoon celery seed
>1 teaspoon garlic powder
>1/8 teaspoon cayenne (more if you like it hot)

Spicy Cocktail Olives & Onions

Olive lovers adore these.
Serves 10. Microcook Time: 5 minutes. Stand overnight.
Calories: 92. Fat: 10 g. Carbohydrates: 2 g. Protein: 0 g. Sodium: 135 mg.

Combine in a 4-cup measure:
    1/3 cup walnut oil
    2 tablespoons red wine vinegar
    2 cloves garlic, minced
    2 tablespoons lemon juice
    1 (6-oz.) jar cocktail onions, drained
Microcook on high 1 minute.
Add . . .
    1 (5 3/4-oz.) can pitted ripe olives, drained
Stand in refrigerator overnight.

- 1/3 cup walnut oil
- 2 tablespoons red wine vinegar
- 2 cloves garlic, minced
- 2 tablespoons lemon juice
- 1 (6-oz.) jar cocktail onions, drained
- 1 (5 3/4-oz.) can pitted ripe olives, drained

Chicken Dill Pâté

Try serving on whole grain crackers, for best flavor.
Serves 32. Microcook Time: 10 minutes.
Calories: 48. Fat: 4 g. Carbohydrates: 1 g. Protein: 4 g. Sodium: 29 mg.

Place on a microwave roasting rack:
    1 whole boned, skinless chicken breast
Cover with waxed paper.
Microcook on high 4 to 5 minutes.
Chop finely in food processor:
    1/2 cup walnuts
Add chicken to processor with:
    3-oz. light cream cheese
    1 clove garlic
Blend well.
Add . . .
    1/4 cup light mayonnaise
    1 tablespoon fresh dill or 1 1/2 teaspoons
      dill weed
    dash onion powder
Blend.
Hint: Turkey may be substituted for chicken
(use 1 cup). To lower calories; try yogurt in place
of cream cheese, substitute pecans for walnuts.

- 1 whole boned, skinless chicken breast
- 1/2 cup walnuts
- 3-oz. light cream cheese
- 1 clove garlic
- 1/4 cup light mayonnaise
- 1 tablespoon fresh dill or 1 1/2 teaspoons dill weed
- dash onion powder

Mushroom Pâté

A perfect Pâté for the calorie-conscious.
Serves 50. Microcook Time: 10 minutes. Refrigerate 2 hours.
Calories: 13. Fat: 0 g. Carbohydrates: 1 g. Protein: 2 g. Sodium: 8 mg.

- •1 pint fresh mushrooms, cleaned and halved
- •4 shallots, diced
- •1 clove garlic, minced
- •1 tablespoon low-sodium chicken bouillon granules
- •freshly ground nutmeg
- •2 tablespoons cognac
- •1 (14-oz.) carton dry curd cottage cheese
- •2 tablespoons lemon juice
- •1/2 (10-oz.) pkg. frozen spinach, thawed and drained
- •2 tablespoons fresh dill
- •1 tablespoon Dijon mustard
- •1/2 teaspoon fennel
- •6 drops hot pepper sauce

Place in a 2-quart casserole:
> 1 pint fresh mushrooms, cleaned and halved
> 4 shallots, diced
> 1 clove garlic, minced
> 1 tablespoon low-sodium chicken bouillon granules
> freshly ground nutmeg
> 2 tablespoons cognac

Cover with vented plastic wrap.
Microcook on high 4 to 5 minutes.
Place in a food processor:
> 1 (14-oz.) carton dry curd cottage cheese
> 2 tablespoons lemon juice

Pulse until smooth.
Add . . .
> 1/2 (10-oz.) pkg. frozen spinach, thawed and drained
> 2 tablespoons fresh dill
> 1 tablespoon Dijon mustard
> 1/2 teaspoon fennel
> 6 drops hot pepper sauce

Pulse.
Add mushroom mixture; **drain** most of liquid.
Pulse.
Refrigerate at least 2 hours.
Serve on celery ribs or whole grain crackers.

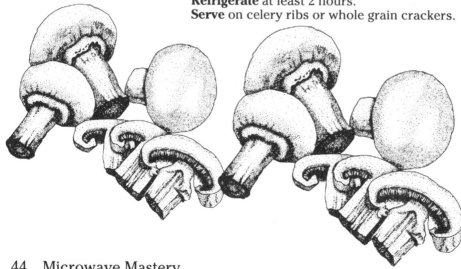

Spicy Swiss Spread

For some reason, this is a great favorite with men.
Serves 36. Microcook Time: 10 minutes.
Calories: 25. Fat: 2 g. Carbohydrates: 0 g. Protein: 1 g. Sodium: 46 mg.

Combine in an 8-cup glass measure:
    1 cup shredded Swiss cheese
    3 green onions, chopped
    1/3 cup light mayonnaise
    1/4 cup chopped green pepper
    1/4 cup chopped ripe olives
    1/4 cup chopped thuringer
    1/4 teaspoon garlic powder
Spread mixture on crackers or toast rounds.
Microcook on high 45 seconds to 1 minute for 12.
Repeat.

- *1 cup shredded Swiss cheese*
- *3 green onions, chopped*
- *1/3 cup light mayonnaise*
- *1/4 cup chopped green pepper*
- *1/4 cup chopped ripe olives*
- *1/4 cup chopped thuringer*
- *1/4 teaspoon garlic powder*

Tex-Mex

Friend John Ward thinks this is "hot" in more ways than one!
Serves 24. Microcook Time: 5 minutes.
Calories: 44. Fat: 3 g. Carbohydrates: 3 g. Protein: 2 g. Sodium: 77 mg.

Combine in an 8-cup glass measure:
    1 cup shredded Cheddar cheese
    1 (2 1/2-oz.) can chopped ripe olives, drained
    1 (4-oz.) can chopped green chilies
    2 tablespoons light mayonnaise
    1/4 teaspoon chili powder
    3 drops hot pepper sauce
    dash onion powder
    dash garlic powder
Arrange on a 12" glass plate:
    24 whole wheat crackers
Top each cracker with 1 teaspoon of mixture.
Microcook on high 1 minute until cheese starts to melt.

- *1 cup shredded Cheddar cheese*
- *1 (2 1/2-oz.) can chopped ripe olives, drained*
- *1 (4-oz.) can chopped green chilies*
- *2 tablespoons light mayonnaise*
- *1/4 teaspoon chili powder*
- *3 drops hot pepper sauce*
- *dash onion powder*
- *dash garlic powder*
- *24 whole wheat crackers*

Ira's Reubens

Named for a friend, Ira Bank, who fell in love with these.
Serves 12. Microcook Time: 5 minutes.
Calories: 53. Fat: 4 g. Carbohydrates: 4 g. Protein: 1 g. Sodium: 272 mg.

- *12 slices of cocktail rye or pumpernickel*
- *1/4 cup buttermilk salad dressing*
- *12 thin slices corned beef*
- *3/4 cup sauerkraut*
- *caraway seeds*
- *1/4 cup shredded Swiss cheese*

Place on each slice of cocktail rye or pumpernickel:
    1 teaspoon buttermilk salad dressing
    1 thin slice corned beef
    1 tablespoon sauerkraut
    caraway seeds
    1 teaspoon shredded Swiss cheese
Place open-face sandwiches on a 12" glass plate.
Microcook on high 1 to 2 minutes.

Water Chestnuts Wrapped in Bacon

The Oriental flavor makes these fab!
Serves 16. Microcook Time: 15 minutes.
Calories: 34. Fat: 2 g. Carbohydrates: 4 g. Protein: 1 g. Sodium: 226 mg.

- *8 slices bacon, halved*
- *1 (8-oz.) can whole water chestnuts*
- *1/4 cup teriyaki sauce*
- *1/2 teaspoon ground ginger*
- *1/2 teaspoon garlic powder*
- *1/4 teaspoon onion powder*

Place on a paper-towel-lined 12" glass plate:
    8 slices bacon, halved
Cover with paper towels.
Microcook on high 4 minutes.
Drain . . .
    1 (8-oz.) can whole water chestnuts
Wrap 1 slice of bacon around each water chestnut.
Place in a 9" glass baking dish.
Secure with a toothpick.
Combine in a 1-cup glass measure:
    1/4 cup teriyaki sauce
    1/2 teaspoon ground ginger
    1/2 teaspoon garlic powder
    1/4 teaspoon onion powder
Pour marinade over water chestnuts.
Refrigerate 2 hours or overnight.
Drain.
Arrange 8 water chestnuts in a circle.
Cover with paper towel.
Microcook on high 4 to 5 minutes until bacon is crisp.
Repeat.

Zucchini Mini Pizzas

A darling, low-calorie appetizer.
Serves 24. Microcook Time: 8 minutes.
Calories: 18. Fat: 1 g. Carbohydrates: 2 g. Protein: 1 g. Sodium: 28 mg.

Combine in an 8-cup glass measure:
    1 (6-oz.) can tomato paste
    1/2 cup shredded part skim mozzarella
      cheese
    1/4 cup grated Parmesan cheese
    1/2 teaspoon Italian seasoning
Cut into 12 slices:
    1 medium zucchini
Place zucchini slices in single layer in
11x7x1 1/2" glass baking dish.
Top each with cheese mixture.
Microcook on high 2 1/2 to 3 minutes.
Repeat with second zucchini.

- *1 (6-oz.) can tomato paste*
- *1/2 cup shredded part skim mozzarella cheese*
- *1/4 cup grated Parmesan cheese*
- *1/2 teaspoon Italian seasoning*
- *1 medium zucchini*

Zucchini Spread

A good snacking spread.
Serves 25. Microcook Time: 3 minutes.
Calories: 46. Fat: 2 g. Carbohydrates: 6 g. Protein: 2 g. Sodium: 66 mg.

Combine in an 8-cup glass measure:
    1/2 cup shredded Cheddar cheese
    1/2 cup grated zucchini
    3 tablespoons grated Parmesan cheese
    1/4 teaspoon instant minced onion
    1/4 teaspoon garlic powder
Spread on:
    50 small whole grain crackers
Place 25 crackers on a 12" glass plate.
Microcook on high 30 seconds.
Repeat.

- *1/2 cup shredded Cheddar cheese*
- *1/2 cup grated zucchini*
- *3 tablespoons grated Parmesan cheese*
- *1/4 teaspoon instant minced onion*
- *1/4 teaspoon garlic powder*
- *50 small whole grain crackers*

BREAD & BREAKFAST

Yeast Bread Hints

- When using yeast AVOID overcooking.
- Proofing bread works well (you need an oven with 10% power). **Place** 3 cups water in a 4-cup glass measure; bring to a boil. **Add** prepared dough in a bowl. **Microcook** at 10% for 5 minutes. **Stand** 10 to15 min. **Repeat** process until dough has doubled.
- Toppings may be added; cinnamon, wheat germ, oatmeal or seeds and you may use some whole grain flour in the dough to obtain color.
- After bread is cool, wrap in foil to prevent drying out.
- Microcooked bread is heavier and moist and should be used in 2 to 3 days.
- Toasting bread helps remove moisture.

Quick Bread Hints

- Ring-shaped pans work well; however, round, square and loaf pans may be used.
- Pans should be greased and coated with cinnamon/sugar for color.
- To obtain a brown color, add whole grain flour, wheat germ, brown sugar, molasses, chocolate or spices.
- Elevating helps the bottom of the bread cook better.

Banana Bread

Use very ripe bananas. This is the ultimate!
Serves 12. Microcook Time: 20 minutes.
Calories: 240. Fat: 9 g. Carbohydrates: 37 g. Protein: 3 g. Sodium: 159 mg.

- *1 cup sugar*
- *1/2 cup margarine*
- *2 eggs*
- *3 bananas, well mashed*
- *2 cups all-purpose flour*
- *1 teaspoon baking soda*
- *1 teaspoon vanilla*
- *1/4 teaspoon mace*

Cream together in a bowl:
  1 cup sugar
  1/2 cup margarine
Add . . .
  2 eggs
  3 bananas, well mashed
Add . . .
  2 cups all-purpose flour
  1 teaspoon baking soda
  1 teaspoon vanilla
  1/4 teaspoon mace
Mix well.
Pour into a greased glass 9x5x3" loaf pan that has been lined with waxed paper.
Elevate on inverted microwave-safe saucer.
Microcook on medium 8 to 9 minutes until no longer moist on top. 50%
Stand 10 minutes before removing from pan.

Wild Rice Bread

My friend Norm's favorite; this bread must be kept tightly wrapped and used within 3 days. Toast for best texture and flavor.
Serves 18. Microcook Time: 120 minutes.
Calories: 112. Fat: 2 g. Carbohydrates: 22 g. Protein: 3 g. Sodium: 136 mg.

Combine in an 8-cup glass measure:
> 1/3 cup washed wild rice
> 2 cups water

Cover with vented plastic wrap.
Microcook on high 6 minutes.
Stand 10 minutes.
Microcook on medium low 45 minutes.
Add . . .
> 2 tablespoons butter
> 1/4 cup brown sugar

Stand 10 to 15 minutes.
Check temperature; be sure it is not over 130 degrees.
Stir in:
> 2 cups whole wheat flour
> 1/2 cup oat bran cereal

Combine and **stir** into rice mixture:
> 1 pkg. rapid-rise dry yeast
> 3/4 cup all-purpose flour

Turn onto floured surface and **knead** until smooth and elastic, about 5 minutes.
Form a doughnut and place in a greased microwave-safe ring mold that has been sprinkled with:
> sesame seed

Cover with waxed paper.
Place in a 4-cup glass measure:
> 3 cups hot water

Microcook on high 6 minutes.
Place dough in oven.
Microcook on low for 5 minutes.
Stand 15 minutes.
Repeat until dough has doubled.
Remove water.
Place dough on a microwave-safe inverted saucer to elevate.
Microcook on medium 12 to 15 minutes.
Turn 3 times.
Stand 8 minutes and **invert** on cooling rack.

Ingredients:
- 1/3 cup washed wild rice
- 2 cups water
- 2 tablespoons butter
- 1/4 cup brown sugar
- 2 cups whole wheat flour
- sesame seed
- 1/2 cup oat bran cereal
- 1 pkg. rapid-rise dry yeast
- 3/4 cup all-purpose flour
- 3 cups hot water

Zucchini Bread

A good way to use your garden zucchini in the fall.
Serves 10. Microcook Time: 20 minutes.
Calories: 214. Fat: 12 g. Carbohydrates: 24 g. Protein: 3 g. Sodium: 78 mg.

- 1 3/4 cups shredded zucchini
- 3/4 cup all-purpose flour
- 1/4 cup whole wheat flour
- 1/2 teaspoon baking powder
- 1/2 teaspoon baking soda
- 1 teaspoon cinnamon
- 2 eggs
- 1/2 cup oil
- 2 tablespoons molasses
- 1/2 cup brown sugar
- 1 1/2 teaspoons vanilla
- 1 tablespoon wheat germ

Combine in a mixing bowl:
> 1 3/4 cups shredded zucchini
> 3/4 cup all-purpose flour
> 1/4 cup whole wheat flour
> 1/2 teaspoon baking powder
> 1/2 teaspoon baking soda
> 1 teaspoon cinnamon
> 2 eggs
> 1/2 cup oil
> 2 tablespoons molasses
> 1/2 cup brown sugar
> 1 1/2 teaspoons vanilla
> 1 tablespoon wheat germ

Beat for 2 minutes.
Pour into a greased glass 9x5x3" loaf pan that has been lined with waxed paper.
Top with:
> 1 tablespoon wheat germ

Elevate on inverted microwave-safe saucer.
Microcook on medium 8 minutes.
Rotate every 2 minutes.
Microcook on high 2 minutes.
Rotate every minute.
Stand 8 to 10 minutes before removing from pan.

Muffin Loaf

Toast this bread and try with Banana Jam (page 63).
Serves 8. Microcook Time: 1 hr.
Calories: 153. Fat: 1 g. Carbohydrates: 30 g. Protein: 5 g. Sodium: 295 mg.

Combine in an 8-cup glass measure:
    1 1/2 cups all-purpose flour
    1 pkg. rapid-rise dry yeast
    1 1/2 teaspoons sugar
    1 teaspoon salt
    1/8 teaspoon baking soda
Combine in a 2-cup glass measure:
    1 cup milk
    1/4 cup water
Microcook on high 1 to 2 minutes until very warm
125 to 130 degrees.
Add to dry ingredients.
Stir in:
    1 cup all-purpose flour
Pour into a greased 8 1/2x4 1/2" glass bread pan or
microwave-safe pan that has been dusted with
cornmeal.
Sprinkle cornmeal over top.
Rise until doubled in size.*
Place on an inverted microwave-safe saucer.
Microcook on medium 10 to 13 minutes.
Stand 5 minutes on counter top before removing
from pan.
*To make a warm, moist place for the dough to
rise:
Place in a 4-cup glass measure:
    3 cups water
Microcook on high 7 minutes.
Place bread pan in oven with water and close
door.
Microcook on medium 1 minute.
Stand 10 minutes.
Repeat until doubled.

> • 1 1/2 cups all-purpose flour
> • 1 pkg. rapid-rise dry yeast
> • 1 1/2 teaspoons sugar
> • 1 teaspoon salt
> • 1/8 teaspoon baking soda
> • 1 cup milk
> • 1/4 cup water
> • 1 cup all-purpose flour

Nectarine Bread

Health bread. Delicious bread.
Serves 12. Microcook Time: 20 minutes.
Calories: 195. Fat: 7 g. Carbohydrates: 32 g. Protein: 2 g. Sodium: 88 mg.

- *1 cup whole wheat flour*
- *3/4 cup sugar*
- *1/2 cup brown sugar*
- *1/2 teaspoon baking powder*
- *1/2 teaspoon baking soda*
- *dash salt*
- *2 eggs*
- *1/3 cup oil*
- *1 tablespoon lemon juice*
- *1 teaspoon grated lemon peel*
- *1/4 teaspoon nutmeg*
- *3 ripe nectarines, pitted and chopped*

Combine in a glass mixing bowl:
>1 cup whole wheat flour
>3/4 cup sugar
>1/2 cup brown sugar
>1/2 teaspoon baking powder
>1/2 teaspoon baking soda
>dash salt

Stir.
Add . . .
>2 eggs
>1/3 cup oil
>1 tablespoon lemon juice
>1 teaspoon grated lemon peel
>1/4 teaspoon nutmeg

Stir well.
Add . . .
>3 ripe nectarines, pitted and chopped

Pour into a greased 9" ring mold.
Elevate on an inverted microwave-safe saucer.
Microcook on medium 8 to 9 minutes.
Microcook on high 4 to 6 minutes.
Stand on countertop.

Strawberry Bread

Elegant and unique for brunch or breakfast.
Serves 8. Microcook Time: 15 minutes.
Calories: 379. Fat: 20 g. Carbohydrates: 49 g. Protein: 4 g. Sodium: 67 mg.

Combine in a bowl:
    1 1/3 cups all-purpose flour
    1 cup sugar
    1/2 teaspoon baking soda
    1 teaspoon cinnamon
    2 eggs
    2/3 cup oil
    1 (10-oz.) pkg. frozen strawberries, thawed
    1/2 banana, mashed
    1/2 teaspoon vanilla

Pour into a greased 9" microwave-safe tube pan.
Place on an inverted microwave-safe saucer.
Microcook on medium 7 to 8 minutes.
Rotate.

Microcook on high 3 to 5 minutes.

- 1 1/3 cups all-purpose flour
- 1 cup sugar
- 1/2 teaspoon baking soda
- 1 teaspoon cinnamon
- 2 eggs
- 2/3 cup oil
- 1 (10-oz.) pkg. frozen strawberries, thawed
- 1/2 banana, mashed
- 1/2 teaspoon vanilla

Veggie Breakfast Sandwich

Start your day off right with this.
Serves 4. Microcook Time: 8 minutes.
Calories: 139. Fat: 3 g. Carbohydrates: 19 g. Protein: 11 g. Sodium: 765 mg.

Combine in a 2-cup glass measure:
    2 tablespoons plain yogurt
    1 teaspoon Dijon mustard
Toast:
    4 slices whole grain bread, preferably low-
      calorie
Spread mixture on toast.
Top each with:
    sliced tomato
    alfalfa sprouts
    slice of low-fat cheese
    onion powder

Place 2 sandwiches on microwave plate.
Microcook on medium 2 to 3 minutes.
Rotate once.

- 2 tablespoons plain yogurt
- 1 teaspoon Dijon mustard
- 4 slices whole grain bread, preferably low-calorie
- sliced tomato
- alfalfa sprouts
- 4 slices low-fat cheese
- onion powder

Croissant Ham Sandwich

A popular lunch favorite.
Serves 1. Microcook Time: 10 minutes.
Calories: 257. Fat: 23 g. Carbohydrates: 20 g. Protein: 17 g. Sodium: 609 mg.

- •1 croissant
- •1 teaspoon honey mustard
- •1 teaspoon horseradish sauce
- •1 (1-oz.) slice cooked ham
- •1 slice Swiss cheese
- •1 slice tomato, cut in half
- •1 tablespoon sprouts

Preheat microwave browning skillet according to manufacturer's directions.
Slice in half:
    1 croissant
Spread one side with:
    1 teaspoon honey mustard
Spread the other side with:
    1 teaspoon horseradish sauce
Fold into quarters and place on croissant half:
    1 (1-oz.) slice cooked ham
Top with:
    1 slice Swiss cheese
    1 slice tomato, cut in half
    1 tablespoon sprouts
Place sandwich on browner.
Microcook on medium 10 to 15 seconds.
Stand 1 minute.

Turkey Variation

Turkey is low-fat.
Serves 1. Microcook Time: 10 minutes.
Calories: 344 Fat: 21 g. Carbohydrates: 20 g. Protein: 19 g. Sodium: 678 mg.

- •1 croissant
- •2 teaspoons Pepper Cream Dressing (page 97)
- •1 (1-oz.) slice of turkey
- •1 slice process cheese
- •1 slice tomato, cut in half
- •1 tablespoon sprouts

Follow directions above, except:
Spread croissant with:
    2 teaspoons Pepper Cream Dressing
     (page 97)
Add . . .
    1 (1-oz.) slice of turkey
    1 slice process cheese
    1 slice tomato, cut in half
    1 tablespoon sprouts

Bran Muffins

You may store the batter in the refrigerator and make muffins as you need them.
Serves 30. Microcook Time: 5 minutes for 6 muffins.
Calories: 127. Fat: 4 g. Carbohydrates: 21 g. Protein: 3 g. Sodium: 101 mg.

Combine in a mixing bowl:
    3 cups whole wheat flour
    1 1/2 cups bran cereal
    1/4 cup brown sugar
    2 teaspoons baking soda
    1 cup raisins
Combine in a 4-cup glass measure:
    2 eggs
    1/2 cup honey
    2 cups buttermilk
    1/2 cup oil
Pour liquid mixture on top of dry ingredients.
Stir until just mixed.
Hint: Do not beat.
Pour into a paper-lined microwave muffin pan or paper-lined glass custard cups; **fill** half full.
Microcook on high:
    1 muffin, 1/2 minute
    2 muffins, 1 3/4 minutes
    4 muffins, 2 minutes
    6 muffins, 2 1/2 minutes
Hint: Stir in a few sunflower nuts just before microcooking. Batter can be stored in the refrigerator up to 2 weeks in tightly covered container.

- 3 cups whole wheat flour
- 1 1/2 cups bran cereal
- 1/4 cup brown sugar
- 2 teaspoons baking soda
- 1 cup raisins
- 2 eggs
- 1/2 cup honey
- 2 cups buttermilk
- 1/2 cup oil

Whole Wheat Corn Muffins

Nice color and crunch; a good source of Folic Acid.
Serves 6. Microcook Time: 6 minutes.
Calories: 136. Fat: 4 g. Carbohydrates: 29.6 g. Protein: 3.2 g. Sodium: 1 mg.

- *2/3 cup all-purpose flour*
- *1/3 cup whole wheat flour*
- *1/4 cup cornmeal*
- *1 teaspoon baking soda*
- *1 teaspoon baking powder*
- *1/2 teaspoon cinnamon*
- *2/3 cup oil*
- *3 eggs*
- *1/2 cup brown sugar*
- *1 tablespoon corn syrup*
- *1 (16-oz.) can whole kernel corn, drained*
- *1/4 cup chopped sunflower nuts*

Combine in a 4-cup glass measure:
  2/3 cup all-purpose flour
  1/3 cup whole wheat flour
  1/4 cup cornmeal
  1 teaspoon baking soda
  1 teaspoon baking powder
  1/2 teaspoon cinnamon
Combine in an 8-cup glass measure:
  2/3 cup oil
  3 eggs
  1/2 cup brown sugar
  1 tablespoon corn syrup
  1 (16-oz.) can whole kernel corn, drained
  1/4 cup chopped sunflower nuts
Add liquid ingredients to dry ingredients
and **stir** until just moist.
Pour into 6 custard cups that have each been lined
with 2 cupcake liners.
Fill half full.
Microcook on high 2 1/2 minutes.
Rotate.

Fruit & Cereal

Great for athletes - supplies quick energy.
Serves 6. Microcook Time: 8 minutes.
Calories: 121. Fat: 2 g. Carbohydrates: 27 g. Protein: 2 g. Sodium: 81 mg.

Place in a 4-cup measure:
>2 apples, sliced
>2 bananas, sliced
>1/4 cup raisins
>1/4 cup cranberry juice
>dash cinnamon

Cover with vented plastic wrap.

Microcook on high 1 1/2 minutes.

Combine in an 8-cup glass measure:
>3/4 cup hot water
>1/3 cup quick-cooking rolled oats

Microcook on high 2 minutes.

Cool.

Combine fruits and oats.

Stir in:
>3/4 cup plain yogurt
>6 fresh strawberries, sliced

Hint: May be stored in refrigerator. Eat for breakfast or as a high-powered carbohydrate snack.

Hint: Breakfast cereals cook in a shorter time in the microwave. They can be prepared in the serving bowl, but must be stirred during cooking time. Dried fruits add color and taste.

- 2 apples, sliced
- 2 bananas, sliced
- 1/4 cup raisins
- 1/4 cup cranberry juice
- dash cinnamon
- 3/4 cup hot water
- 1/3 cup quick-cooking rolled oats
- 3/4 cup plain yogurt
- 6 fresh strawberries, sliced

Variation

A variation of the Fruit & Cereal recipe, for when you're really pressed for time.
Serves 6. Microcook Time: 8 minutes.
Calories: 131. Fat: 1 g. Carbohydrates: 35 g. Protein: 2 g. Sodium: 73 mg.

Prepare quick-cooking oatmeal with the following added:
>1 cooking apple, chopped
>3/4 cup golden raisins
>2 bananas, sliced
>1/4 cup orange juice
>1/4 teaspoon cinnamon

Store in refrigerator.

Serve hot or cold.

- 1 cooking apple, chopped
- 3/4 cup golden raisins
- 2 bananas, sliced
- 1/4 cup orange juice
- 1/4 teaspoon cinnamon

Quick-cooking Oatmeal

Great tasting source of fiber.
Serves 4. Microcook Time: 7 minutes.
Calories: 143. Fat: 2 g. Carbohydrates: 27 g. Protein: 5 g. Sodium: 521 mg.

- 3 cups hot water
- 1 1/3 cups quick-cooking rolled oats
- 1 tablespoon brown sugar, if desired

Combine in an 8-cup glass measure:
    3 cups hot water
    1 1/3 cups quick-cooking rolled oats
    1 tablespoon brown sugar, if desired
Microcook on high 2 1/2 to 3 minutes.
Stand 3 minutes.

Oat Bran Cereal

Recommended for heart watchers.
Serves 2. Microcook Time: 10 minutes.
Calories: 135 Fat: 21 g. Carbohydrates: 20 g. Protein: 19 g. Sodium: 678 mg.

- 2 cups water
- 2/3 cup oat bran cereal
- 2 tablespoons golden raisins

Combine in an 8-cup glass measure:
    2 cups water
    2/3 cup oat bran cereal
Microcook on high 4 minutes until cereal begins to thicken.
Stir in:
    2 tablespoons golden raisins

Farina Cereal

Good on a cold morning.
Serves 4. Microcook Time: 12 minutes.
Calories: 126. Fat: 0 g. Carbohydrates: 28 g. Protein: 2 g. Sodium: 267 mg.

- 3 cups hot water
- 2/3 cup farina cereal
- 1/4 cup brown sugar, if desired*

Combine in an 8-cup glass measure:
    3 cups hot water
    2/3 cup farina cereal
    1/4 cup brown sugar, if desired*
Microcook on high 7 to 8 minutes.
Stir after 3 minutes.
Stand 3 to 4 minutes.
*1/4 cup raisins may be substituted.

Egg Hints

- The egg yolk is high in fat and cooks more quickly than the white.
- The white will finish cooking during standing time.
- Prepare most eggs using low power.
- Scrambled eggs are cooked on high.
- Overcooking toughens the egg, and a rubbery texture is the result.
- Use minimum times for cooking eggs, they are easy to overcook.
- Hard-cooked eggs for casseroles and garnishes may be made by poaching the eggs and then slicing.
- Souffles do not work well in the microwave oven.
- Eggs in shells cannot be cooked in the microwave oven; they may explode.

Scrambled Eggs

Good for breakfast or anytime.
Serves 4. Microcook Time: 7 minutes.
Calories: 80. Fat: 6 g. Carbohydrates: 1 g. Protein: 6 g. Sodium: 60 mg.

Eggs should be soft, as they will become firm upon standing. Overcooking will toughen protein and produce a rubbery egg. Watch eggs closely.
Hint: Yolks and whites are mixed; therefore they can be cooked at 100% power.
Stand 1 to 2 minutes.

Eggs	Add Water	Power Setting	Microcook Time
1	1 Tbsp	High	3/4 to 1 minute
2	2 Tbsp	High	1 1/4 to 1 1/2 minutes
3	3 Tbsp	High	2 1/2 to 3 1/4 minutes
4	1/4 cup	High	3 1/2 to 4 1/4 minutes

Poached Eggs

For "just right" poached eggs.
Serves 1. Microcook Time: 3 minutes.
Calories: 80. Fat: 6 g. Carbohydrates: 1 g. Protein: 6 g. Sodium: 60 mg.

•*Eggs*

•1 egg is cooked in a 6-oz. microwave-safe custard cup.
•Heat water in 6-oz. microwave-safe custard cup to boiling before inserting egg.
•Use a toothpick to puncture the yolk before cooking whole eggs.
•Usually, making two or three holes will prevent bursting during the cooking time.
Cover with vented plastic wrap.
Stand 2 minutes after cooking.

Eggs	Add Water	Power Setting	Microcook Time
1	1/8 cup	Medium	40 to 45 seconds
2	1/4 cup	Medium	1 minute 35 seconds

Bacon

Bacon at its best.
Serves 1. Microcook Time: 1 minute per slice.
Calories: 36. Fat: 3 g. Carbohydrates: 0 g. Protein: 2 g. Sodium: 101 mg.

•*Bacon*

Place bacon slices on a microwave bacon rack or an 11x7x1 1/2" glass dish.
Hint: Baking dish should be lined with paper towels on the bottom.
Cover with paper towel.
Microcook on high 3/4 to 1 minute per slice.
Rotate.
Hint: Bacon may look slightly underdone when removed, but will continue to cook with standing time.

Eggs Benedict for 2

A vacation day breakfast.
Serves 2. Microcook Time: 4 minutes.
Calories: 283. Fat: 11 g. Carbohydrates: 32 g. Protein: 17 g. Sodium: 705 mg.

Place on a microwave-safe dish or bacon rack:
    2 slices Canadian bacon
Microcook on high 2 minutes.
Place bacon on:
    2 toasted whole grain English muffins
Place in each 6-oz. custard cup:
    2 tablespoons boiling water
    1 egg
Pierce the yolks three times with a toothpick or once with a fork.
Cover with vented plastic wrap.
Microcook at medium 1 1/2 minutes.
Stand 2 minutes.
Drain water.
Remove egg to top of bacon.
Serve with:
    Hollandaise Sauce (page 202).

- 2 slices Canadian bacon
- 2 toasted whole grain English muffins
- 4 tablespoons boiling water
- 2 eggs
- Hollandaise sauce (page 202)

Banana Jam

Wonderful with toasted Muffin Loaf (page 53).
Serves 3 cups. Microcook Time: 25 minutes.
Calories: 25. Fat: 0 g. Carbohydrates: 7 g. Protein: 0 g. Sodium: 0 mg.

Combine in an 8-cup glass measure:
    1 cup sugar
    1/2 teaspoon lime juice
    1/4 teaspoon cinnamon
Microcook on high 5 minutes.
Add . . .
    4 to 6 bananas, thinly sliced
Microcook at medium low 15 minutes.
Refrigerate when cool.
Hint: Use within 2 weeks.

1 cup sugar
1/2 teaspoon lime juice
1/4 teaspoon cinnamon
4 to 6 bananas, thinly sliced

Apple Pancakes

For when you really want to make someone feel special.
Serves 4. Microcook Time: 18 minutes.
Calories: 466. Fat: 52 g. Carbohydrates: 61 g. Protein: 3 g. Sodium: 766 mg.

- 1 tablespoon butter
- 3 apples, thinly sliced
- 1/2 cup sugar
- 1/4 teaspoon cinnamon
- 1 cup pancake mix
- 3/4 cup water
- 1 teaspoon vanilla
- 1 tablespoon sugar
- 1/2 teaspoon cinnamon

Place in a 9" round glass cake dish:
    1 tablespoon butter
Microcook on high 30 seconds until melted.
Add . . .
    3 apples, thinly sliced
    1/2 cup sugar
    1/4 teaspoon cinnamon
Cover.
Microcook on high 4 to 5 minutes.
Combine in a mixing bowl:
    1 cup pancake mix
    3/4 cup water
    1 teaspoon vanilla
Pour pancake mixture over cooked apples.
Top with:
    1 tablespoon sugar
    1/2 teaspoon cinnamon
Microcook on high 3 to 6 minutes.
Stand 3 to 5 minutes.
Hint: Serve with whipped cream.

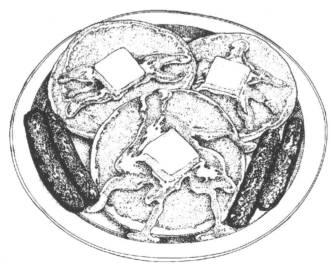

South of the Border

If you are in the mood for a delectably different breakfast . . .
Serves 6. Microcook Time: 15 minutes.
Calories: 336. Fat: 19 g. Carbohydrates: 33 g. Protein: 18 g. Sodium: 308 mg.

Crush . . .
 8 oz. corn chips
Place in 8x8x2" glass dish.
Sprinkle over chips:
 2 cups shredded farmer's cheese
 1 cup shredded Cheddar cheese
Spread over cheese:
 1 (4-oz.) can chopped green chilies
Combine . . .
 3 eggs
 1/3 cup evaporated skim milk
Pour over top.
Sprinkle top with:
 1/4 teaspoon onion flakes
 1/4 teaspoon garlic powder
 1/4 tablespoon cumin
 4 drops hot pepper sauce
Microcook on medium high 6 to 8 minutes.
Rotate twice.
Stand.
Cut into squares.

- 8 oz. corn chips
- 2 cups shredded farmer's cheese
- 1 cup shredded Cheddar cheese
- 1 (4-oz.) can chopped green chilies
- 3 eggs
- 1/3 cup evaporated skim milk
- 1/4 teaspoon onion flakes
- 1/4 teaspoon garlic powder
- 1/4 tablespoon cumin
- 4 drops hot pepper sauce

Variation

Top with:
 1 cup sour cream
 1 tomato, chopped
 1 (2 1/2-oz.) can chopped ripe olives,
  drained

Crustless Corn Quiche

Quiche works well in the microwave. Try topping with sliced ripe olives or chopped tomato.
Serves 6. Microcook Time: 20 minutes.
Calories: 300. Fat: 21 g. Carbohydrates: 14 g. Protein: 15 g. Sodium: 318 mg.

- 1 (4-oz.) can chopped green chilies
- 1 small onion, chopped
- 2 tablespoons butter
- 1 (10-oz.) pkg. frozen whole kernel corn
- 3 eggs, beaten
- 1 (5-oz.) can evaporated milk
- 2 cups shredded Cheddar cheese

Combine in a 4-cup glass measure:
    1 (4-oz.) can chopped green chilies
    1 small onion, chopped
    2 tablespoons butter
Microcook on high 2 minutes.
Add . . .
    1 (10-oz.) pkg. frozen whole kernel corn
Microcook on high 2 minutes.
Stir in:
    3 eggs, beaten
    1 (5-oz.) can evaporated milk
Spread over a 9" quiche dish:
    2 cups shredded Cheddar cheese*
Pour custard mixture over the cheese.
Microcook on medium high 12 to 16 minutes.
Rotate twice.
Stand 8 minutes.
*omit for fewer calories.

Blueberry Breakfast Treat

Requires a special 12" browning grill with cover.
Serves 8. Microcook Time: 20 minutes.
Calories: 240. Fat: 8 g. Carbohydrates: 43 g. Protein: 1 g. Sodium: 148 mg.

Prepare according to directions on envelope:
    1 (7-oz.) pkg. blueberry muffin mix
Add . . .
    1 tablespoon oil
Spread batter on nonstick microwave browning grill.
Top with:
    1 cup frozen blueberries
    1/2 cup brown sugar
    1/2 teaspoon cinnamon
Dot with:
    2 tablespoons butter
Cover.
Microcook on high 13 minutes.
Cool on pan 5 minutes.
Drizzle with frosting made of:
    3/4 cup powdered sugar
    1 teaspoon almond extract
Add for desired consistency:
    few drops of water

- *1 (7-oz.) pkg. blueberry muffin mix*
- *1 tablespoon oil*
- *1 cup frozen blueberries*
- *1/2 cup brown sugar*
- *1/2 teaspoon cinnamon*
- *2 tablespoons butter*
- *3/4 cup powdered sugar*
- *1 teaspoon almond extract*

Ham & Cheese Brunch

Elegant.
Serves 6. Microcook Time: 15 minutes.
Calories: 302. Fat: 15 g. Carbohydrates: 15 g. Protein: 15 g. Sodium: 120 mg.

- 1 (8-oz.) carton low-fat sour cream
- 1 tablespoon Dijon mustard
- 1 teaspoon instant onion
- 4 oz. ham, sliced and chopped
- 1 1/2 cups shredded Swiss cheese

Preheat microwave browning skillet according to manufacturer's directions.
Arrange 1 ready-to-cook pie crust on hot browner. Be careful, it will be very hot!!
Turn edge of crust up to fit the browner.
Microcook on high 3 1/2 to 4 minutes.
Combine in a 4-cup glass measure:
 1 (8-oz.) carton low-fat sour cream
 1 tablespoon Dijon mustard
 1 teaspoon instant onion
Spread over crust.
Top with:
 4 oz. ham, sliced and chopped
 1 1/2 cups shredded Swiss cheese
Microcook on medium 4 minutes.
Cover loosely with foil for 3 minutes.

French Toast

Adding vanilla gives a unique, old-time flavor.
Serves 1. Microcook Time: 10 minutes.
Calories: 178 Fat: 7 g. Carbohydrates: 17 g. Protein: 9 g. Sodium: 220 mg.

- 1 large egg
- 2 tablespoons milk
- dash of cinnamon or nutmeg
- 1/2 teaspoon vanilla
- 1 slice whole grain bread

Preheat microwave browning skillet according to manufacturer's directions.
Combine in an 8" glass cake dish:
 1 large egg
 2 tablespoons milk
 dash of cinnamon or nutmeg
 1/2 teaspoon vanilla
Place in mixture:
 1 slice whole grain bread
Turn over.
Place on hot browner. (Browner may be brushed with a few drops of oil, if desired.)
Microcook on high 1 1/2 minutes.
Turn with plastic spatula.
Microcook on high 1 1/2 minutes.

Blueberry Coffee Cake

Especially good when fresh blueberries are used!
Serves 6. Microcook Time: 20 minutes.
Calories: 512. Fat: 18 g. Carbohydrates: 86 g. Protein: 7 g. Sodium: 431 mg.

Cream together:
> 3/4 cup sugar
> 1/4 cup margarine

Add . . .
> 1 egg
> 1/2 cup milk
> 1/4 teaspoon vanilla

Sift together and add:
> 2 cups all-purpose flour
> 2 teaspoons baking powder
> 1/4 teaspoon salt
> 1/4 teaspoon cinnamon

Stir in . . .
> 2 cups fresh blueberries

Pour into a greased 9" round microwave-safe pan.

Top with mixture of:
> 1/4 cup butter, softened
> 1/2 cup brown sugar
> 1/4 cup all-purpose flour
> 3/4 teaspoon cinnamon

Place on an inverted microwave-safe saucer.
Microcook on medium 8 minutes.
Rotate twice.
Microcook on high 4 to 6 minutes.
Rotate 3 times.

- •3/4 cup sugar
- •1/4 cup margarine
- •1 egg
- •1/2 cup milk
- •1/4 teaspoon vanilla
- •2 cups all-purpose flour
- •2 teaspoons baking powder
- •1/4 teaspoon salt
- •1/4 teaspoon cinnamon
- •2 cups fresh blueberries
- •1/4 cup butter, softened
- •1/2 cup brown sugar
- •1/4 cup all-purpose flour
- •3/4 teaspoon cinnamon

Strawberry Butter Dip

A delightful spread for toast. Try with Strawberry Bread on page 55.
Serves 16. Microcook Time: 7 minutes.
Calories: 97. Fat: 6 g. Carbohydrates: 8 g. Protein: 1 g. Sodium: 87 mg.

•1 (8-oz.) pkg. light cream cheese
•1/4 cup butter
•1/2 cup powdered sugar
•8 whole strawberries*
•1/2 teaspoon almond extract

Place in a 4-cup measure:
  1 (8-oz.) pkg. light cream cheese
Microcook on medium 30 seconds.
Add . . .
  1/4 cup butter
Microcook on high 10 seconds.

Add . . .
  1/2 cup powdered sugar
Combine cheese mixture in food processor with:
  8 whole strawberries*
  1/2 teaspoon almond extract
Hint: This can also be used as a dip, or a cake filling or frosting or a toast spread.
*For pineapple dip, substitute 1/2 (8-oz.) can crushed pineapple, drained, and omit almond extract.

Fruit Compote

A delightful way to start the day.
Serves 8. Microcook Time: 15 minutes. Stand overnight.
Calories: 111. Fat: 1 g. Carbohydrates: 26 g. Protein: 1 g. Sodium: 5 mg.

•2 (10-oz.) pkgs. frozen raspberries
•2 cups seedless green grapes
•1 (8 1/2-oz.) can apricot halves, drained
•1 (11-oz.) can mandarin oranges, drained
•1 teaspoon grated orange peel
•juice from 1 lemon

Place in a 3-quart glass casserole:
  2 (10-oz.) pkgs. frozen raspberries
Microcook on medium low 7 to 8 minutes until berries are thawed.

Add . . .
  2 cups seedless green grapes
  1 (8 1/2-oz.) can apricot halves, drained
  1 (11-oz.) can mandarin oranges, drained
  1 teaspoon grated orange peel
  juice from 1 lemon
Microcook on high 5 to 7 minutes.

Chill overnight for a blending of flavors.

Cranberry Jelly

You'll love the beautiful color.
Serves 64. Microcook Time: 19 minutes.
Calories: 29. Fat: 0 g. Carbohydrates: 7 g. Protein: 0 g. Sodium: 0 mg.

Combine in an 8-cup glass measure:
  1 1/4 cups cranberry juice
  3/4 cup apple juice
  1 oz. powdered fruit pectin
Cover.
Microcook on high 5 minutes until mixture boils.
Stir once.
Add . . .
  2 cups sugar
Microcook on high 6 to 7 minutes, until mixture boils hard 1 minute.
Skim off foam.
Pour into hot sterilized glasses.
Seal.
Hint: To add orange flavor, heat small pieces of orange peel before pouring jelly into jars.

- *1 1/4 cups cranberry juice*
- *3/4 cup apple juice*
- *1 oz. powdered fruit pectin*
- *2 cups sugar*

Cranberry Jelly 2

Fabulous when served on Muffin Loaf (page 53).
Serves 56. Microcook Time: 25 minutes.
Calories: 21. Fat: 0 g. Carbohydrates: 6 g. Protein: 0 g. Sodium: 0 mg.

Combine in an 8-cup measure:
  1 1/2 cups cranberry juice cocktail*
  1 tablespoon lemon juice
  2 1/2 tablespoons liquid pectin
Microcook on high 5 to 6 minutes.
Stir in:
  1 1/3 cups sugar
Microcook on high 6 to 7 minutes.
Pour into hot sterilized glasses.
Seal.
Hint: Pour jelly into stemmed wine glasses for a unique gift.
*May use cranapple or cranberry juice.

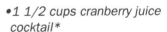

- *1 1/2 cups cranberry juice cocktail**
- *1 tablespoon lemon juice*
- *2 1/2 tablespoons liquid pectin*
- *1 1/3 cups sugar*

Cinnamon-Apple Breakfast Pizza

Requires a special 12" browning grill and cover.
Serves 8. Microcook Time: 20 minutes.
Calories: 312. Fat: 8 g. Carbohydrates: 61 g. Protein: 1 g. Sodium: 159 mg.

- 1 (7-oz.) pkg. apple cinnamon muffin mix
- 1 tablespoon oil
- 2 cooking apples, sliced
- 1 (14-oz.) can sliced peaches, drained
- 3/4 cup brown sugar
- 1/2 teaspoon cinnamon
- 2 tablespoons butter
- 3/4 cup powdered sugar
- 1 teaspoon vanilla

Prepare according to directions on envelope:
    1 (7-oz.) pkg. apple cinnamon muffin mix
Add . . .
    1 tablespoon oil
Spread batter on microwave browning grill.
Top with:
    2 cooking apples, sliced
    1 (14-oz.) can sliced peaches, drained
    3/4 cup brown sugar
    1/2 teaspoon cinnamon
Dot with:
    2 tablespoons butter
Cover.
Microcook on high 13 minutes.
Combine . . .
    3/4 cup powdered sugar
    1 teaspoon vanilla
Add a few drops of water to give pourable consistency.
Drizzle over pizza.
Stand until cool.

Mexican Coffee Mix

Serve with Capirotada (page 230) for a Mexican-style brunch.
Serves 30. Microcook Time: 15 minutes.
Calories: 41. Fat: 0 g. Carbohydrates: 8 g. Protein: 2 g. Sodium: 32 mg.

- 1 cup instant decaffeinated coffee crystals
- 1 1/2 cups instant nonfat dry milk
- 1/2 cup sugar
- 2 tablespoons cocoa
- 1/4 teaspoon cinnamon

Combine in blender:
    1 cup instant decaffeinated coffee crystals
    1 1/2 cups instant nonfat dry milk
    1/2 cup sugar
    2 tablespoons cocoa
    1/4 teaspoon cinnamon
Blend well.*
Hint: Use 2 tablespoons for a coffee mug filled with boiling water.
*May be topped with low-calorie dairy topping.

SOUPS

&

SALADS

Soup Hints

- Be sure to use a large container; **do not** fill over 1/2 full or boilovers may occur.
- A lower power level will help to avoid boilovers.
- Stir a mug of soup halfway through heating time to avoid a quick boilover.
- If using a probe, the temperature of soup should be 150 to 160 degrees.

Chicken Broccoli Soup

A great favorite of mine and a good source of fiber.
Serves 8. Microcook Time: 30 minutes.
Calories: 103. Fat: 3 g. Carbohydrates: 4 g. Protein: 15 g. Sodium: 225 mg.

- *1 lb. fresh broccoli, cut into small pieces (cut the stems very fine)*
- *1/2 onion, chopped*
- *1 cup chopped celery*
- *1/4 cup water*
- *2 (6 3/4-oz.) cans breast of chicken chunks*
- *1 (14 1/2-oz.) can low-sodium chicken broth*
- *1 teaspoon lemon juice*
- *1/2 teaspoon garlic powder*
- *2 tablespoons grated Parmesan cheese*

Combine in a 3-quart casserole:
    1 lb. fresh broccoli, cut into small pieces (cut the stems very fine)
    1/2 onion, chopped
    1 cup chopped celery
    1/4 cup water
Cover with vented plastic wrap.
Microcook on high 12 to 15 minutes.
Add . . .

    2 (6 3/4-oz.) cans breast of chicken chunks
    1 (14 1/2-oz.) can low-sodium chicken broth
    1 teaspoon lemon juice
    1/2 teaspoon garlic powder
Microcook on high 10 to 12 minutes.
Top each bowl with:
    2 tablespoons grated Parmesan cheese

Chili

Try topping with sour cream. Fabulous!
Serves 8. Microcook Time: 30 minutes.
Calories: 346. Fat: 16 g. Carbohydrates: 22 g. Protein: 25 g. Sodium: 223 mg.

Place in a 3-quart glass casserole:
    2 lbs. lean ground beef
    1 cup chopped onion
Cover loosely with plastic wrap.
Microcook on high 7 to 8 minutes.
Stir.
Pour off excess fat.
Add . . .
    2 (15-oz.) cans kidney beans, drained
    1 (8-oz.) can tomato sauce
    2 tablespoons chili powder
    1 bay leaf
    1/4 teaspoon garlic powder
    dash pepper
    dash hot pepper sauce
Cover loosely.
Microcook on high 15 to 20 minutes.
Stir.
Remove bay leaf and **serve.**

- *2 lbs. lean ground beef*
- *1 cup chopped onion*
- *2 (15-oz.) cans kidney beans, drained*
- *1 (8-oz.) can tomato sauce*
- *2 tablespoons chili powder*
- *1 bay leaf*
- *1/4 teaspoon garlic powder*
- *dash pepper*
- *dash hot pepper sauce*

Vegetarian Chili

I enjoyed vegetarian chili for the first time in a small restaurant in Chicago with my good friend, Mary Jo Bergland.

Serves 8. Microcook Time: 15 minutes.
Calories: 102. Fat: 1 g. Carbohydrates: 20 g. Protein: 5 g. Sodium: 43 mg.

- 1/2 cup chopped celery
- 1/2 cup sliced carrots
- 1/4 cup chopped zucchini
- 1/4 cup chopped green pepper
- 1/4 cup fresh parsley, chopped
- 1/2 onion, sliced
- 2 cloves garlic, sliced
- 2 tablespoons lemon juice
- 1 teaspoon grated lemon peel
- 4 whole tomatoes, chopped
- 1 (6-oz.) can low-sodium tomato paste
- 1 (15 1/2-oz.) can kidney beans
- 1 (4-oz.) can chopped chilies
- 1 cup water
- 1/4 teaspoon dry mustard
- 1 tablespoon chili powder
- 1/2 teaspoon coriander
- 1/4 teaspoon oregano
- 1/4 teaspoon cumin
- dash hot pepper sauce
- freshly ground pepper
- 1/4 cup plain low-fat yogurt

Combine in a 3-quart glass casserole:

    1/2 cup chopped celery
    1/2 cup sliced carrots
    1/4 cup chopped zucchini
    1/4 cup chopped green pepper
    1/4 cup fresh parsley, chopped
    1/2 onion, sliced
    2 cloves garlic, sliced
    2 tablespoons lemon juice
    1 teaspoon grated lemon peel

Cover with vented plastic wrap.
Microcook on high 8 minutes.
Add . . .

    4 whole tomatoes, chopped
    1 (6-oz.) can low-sodium tomato paste
    1 (15 1/2-oz.) can kidney beans
    1 (4-oz.) can chopped chilies
    1 cup water
    1/4 teaspoon dry mustard

Microcook on high 12 minutes.
Add . . .

    1 tablespoon chili powder
    1/2 teaspoon coriander
    1/4 teaspoon oregano
    1/4 teaspoon cumin
    dash hot pepper sauce
    freshly ground pepper

Stir.
Microcook on high 3 minutes.
Top each bowl with:

    1/4 cup plain low-fat yogurt

Richfield's Gourmet Chili

Richfield High School's homecoming favorite prepared by principal Dick Maas and students.
Serves 8. Microcook Time: 20 minutes.
Calories: 229. Fat: 5 g. Carbohydrates: 24 g. Protein: 19 g. Sodium: 277 mg.

Crumble into a 3-quart glass casserole:
    1 lb. lean ground beef
Microcook on high 5 to 6 minutes.
Drain fat.
Add . . .
    1 onion, chopped
    1 clove garlic, chopped
    1/2 green pepper, chopped
    2 tomatoes, chopped
Microcook on high 3 to 4 minutes.
Stir and **rotate** 3 times.
Add . . .
    2 (15-oz.) cans seasoned chili beans
    1/2 cup chili sauce
    1/2 cup water
    1 tablespoon chili powder
    1 (4-oz.) can mushroom bits and pieces
    1/4 teaspoon cumin
    dash pepper
    dash paprika
    dash coriander
    dash oregano
    dash hot pepper sauce
Microcook on high 8 to 10 minutes.
Stir every 2 minutes.

- 1 lb. lean ground beef
- 1 onion, chopped
- 1 clove garlic, chopped
- 1/2 green pepper, chopped
- 2 tomatoes, chopped
- 2 (15-oz.) cans seasoned chili beans
- 1/2 cup chili sauce
- 1/2 cup water
- 1 tablespoon chili powder
- 1 (4-oz.) can mushroom bits and pieces
- 1/4 teaspoon cumin
- dash pepper
- dash paprika
- dash coriander
- dash oregano
- dash hot pepper sauce

Hotter Chili Variation

Add . . .
    1 (4-oz.) can chopped green chiles
    sliced ripe olives
Top with:
    dollop of sour cream
    shredded Cheddar cheese

Minestrone

Teenagers really love it.
Serves 4. Microcook Time: 20 minutes.
Calories: 154. Fat: 8 g. Carbohydrates: 10 g. Protein: 12 g. Sodium: 609 mg.

- *2 slices bacon*
- *1/2 (10 3/4-oz.) can low-sodium chicken broth*
- *1/2 (5-oz.) can chunk chicken in water*
- *1/2 (8-oz.) can tomato sauce*
- *2 tablespoons frozen peas*
- *2 tablespoons frozen corn*
- *1/4 zucchini, chopped*
- *1 small carrot*
- *1/2 rib celery, chopped*
- *2 tablespoons macaroni*
- *1/2 teaspoon garlic powder*
- *1/2 teaspoon onion flakes*
- *1/4 teaspoon pepper*
- *1/4 teaspoon basil*
- *1/8 teaspoon oregano*
- *3/4 cup water*

Place on microwave-safe bacon rack:
>   2 slices bacon

Hint: Without a bacon rack, place bacon on paper-towel-lined microwave-safe plate.
Cover with a paper towel.
Microcook on high 2 minutes, until crisp.
Crumble.
Place bacon in an 8-cup glass measure:
Add . . .

>   1/2 (10 3/4-oz.) can low-sodium chicken broth
>   1/2 (5-oz.) can chunk chicken in water
>   1/2 (8-oz.) can tomato sauce
>   2 tablespoons frozen peas
>   2 tablespoons frozen corn
>   1/4 zucchini, chopped
>   1 small carrot
>   1/2 rib celery, chopped
>   2 tablespoons macaroni
>   1/2 teaspoon garlic powder
>   1/2 teaspoon onion flakes
>   1/4 teaspoon pepper
>   1/4 teaspoon basil
>   1/8 teaspoon oregano
>   3/4 cup water

Microcook on high 18 minutes.
Hint: Serve with grated Parmesan cheese. For a more chicken flavor add whole can of chicken broth and tomato sauce.

Oriental Soup

Wonderful and unusual flavor.
Serves 6. Microcook Time: 12 minutes.
Calories: 111. Fat: 2 g. Carbohydrates: 15 g. Protein: 9 g. Sodium: 772 mg.

Combine in a 3-quart glass casserole:
    1 (10 3/4-oz.) can low-sodium chicken
      broth
    1 (10 3/4-oz.) can chicken with rice soup
    1 (16-oz.) pkg. frozen Oriental vegetables
    1/2 cup hot water
    1/4 cup chopped celery leaves
    1 (4-oz.) can mushroom pieces
    2 teaspoons Oriental salt-free seasonings
    dash white pepper
Microcook on high 10 minutes.

- 1 (10 3/4-oz.) can low-sodium chicken broth
- 1 (10 3/4-oz.) can chicken with rice soup
- 1 (16-oz.) pkg. frozen Oriental vegetables
- 1/2 cup hot water
- 1/4 cup chopped celery leaves
- 1 (4-oz.) can mushroom pieces
- 2 teaspoons Oriental salt-free seasonings
- dash white pepper

Potato Soup

A nourishing, savory soup; not only for the Irish!
Serves 6. Microcook Time: 30 minutes.
Calories: 89. Fat: 2 g. Carbohydrates: 11 g. Protein: 6 g. Sodium: 504 mg.

Combine in a 3-quart glass casserole:
    3 potatoes, chopped
    1 small onion, chopped
    1 rib of celery with leaves, chopped
    1 tablespoon water
Cover with vented plastic wrap.
Microcook on high 10 to 12 minutes.
Hint: Test potatoes with a fork; add more time if needed.
Add . . .
    1 (14 1/2-oz.) can low-sodium chicken broth
    1/4 cup skim milk
    dash celery seed
Microcook on high 6 to 10 minutes.
Stir until melted:
    1/4 cup shredded American cheese
Hint: Top with bacon bits and Parmesan cheese.

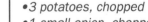

- 3 potatoes, chopped
- 1 small onion, chopped
- 1 rib of celery with leaves, chopped
- 1 tablespoon water
- 1 (14 1/2-oz.) can low-sodium chicken broth
- 1/4 cup skim milk
- dash celery seed
- 1/4 cup shredded American cheese

Pumpkin Soup

A rich, full-flavored soup. Fun for a Halloween party!
Serves 8. Microcook Time: 25 minutes.
Calories: 33. Fat: 0 g. Carbohydrates: 43 g. Protein: 2 g. Sodium: 322 mg.

- 1 small onion, chopped
- 1 carrot, chopped
- 1/2 rib celery, chopped
- 1/2 zucchini, chopped
- 1 tablespoon water
- 2 (14 1/2-oz.) cans low-sodium chicken broth
- 1 (15-oz.) can pumpkin
- 1/2 teaspoon lemon juice
- 1/4 teaspoon nutmeg

Place in a 3-quart glass casserole:
    1 small onion, chopped
    1 carrot, chopped
    1/2 rib celery, chopped
    1/2 zucchini, chopped
    1 tablespoon water
Cover with vented plastic wrap.
Microcook on high 8 to 10 minutes.
Stand 5 minutes.
Add and **stir:**
    2 (14 1/2-oz.) cans low-sodium chicken broth
    1 (15-oz.) can pumpkin
    1/2 teaspoon lemon juice
    1/4 teaspoon nutmeg
Microcook on high 4 to 5 minutes.
Stir twice.

Hearty Squash Soup

An autumn specialty when squash is plentiful.
Serves 8. Microcook Time: 30 minutes.
Calories: 156. Fat: 10 g. Carbohydrates: 7 g. Protein: 10 g. Sodium: 736 mg.

Cut in half:
> 1 acorn squash

Remove seeds.

Place squash in glass baking dish.

Cover with vented plastic wrap.

Microcook on high 8 to 12 minutes, depending on size of squash.

Hint: Remove from oven, wrap in foil during standing time.

Place in a 3-quart glass casserole:
> 1 Rome apple, chopped
> 1/2 onion, chopped
> 1 rib celery, chopped
> 2 cloves garlic, chopped

Cover with vented plastic wrap.

Microcook on high 4 minutes.

Add pulp from cooked squash.

Add . . .
> 1 (10 3/4-oz.) can low-sodium chicken broth
> 1 cup Swiss almond cold pack cheese food
> 8 drops hot pepper sauce
> dash cayenne

Stir well.

Microcook on medium 4 minutes.

Add . . .
> 1/2 cup half-and-half (12% cream)*

Stir.

Microcook on medium 2 minutes.

*For lower calories and fat, use skim milk.

- 1 acorn squash
- 1 Rome apple, chopped
- 1/2 onion, chopped
- 1 rib celery, chopped
- 2 cloves garlic, chopped
- 1 (10 3/4-oz.) can low-sodium chicken broth
- 1 cup Swiss almond cold pack cheese food
- 8 drops hot pepper sauce
- dash cayenne
- 1/2 cup half-and-half (12% cream)*

Fish Chowder

A coastal concept.
Serves 8. Microcook Time: 20 minutes.
Calories: 105. Fat: 0 g. Carbohydrates: 20 g. Protein: 6 g. Sodium: 809 mg.

- 1 small zucchini, sliced
- 1 carrot, sliced
- 1/2 green pepper, chopped
- 2 potatoes, sliced
- 4 fresh mushrooms, sliced
- 1/2 cup water
- 1 (6-oz.) jar chunky picante sauce
- 1/2 lb. fish (monk, white-fish), sliced thick
- 1 (6-oz.) can tomato paste
- 1/2 cup white grape juice

Place in a 3-quart glass casserole:
    1 small zucchini, sliced
    1 carrot, sliced
    1/2 green pepper, chopped
    2 potatoes, sliced
    4 fresh mushrooms, sliced
    1/2 cup water
    1 (6-oz.) jar chunky picante sauce
Cover with vented plastic wrap.
Microcook on high 10 minutes.
Add . . .
    1/2 lb. fish (monk, whitefish), sliced thick
Microcook on high 6 minutes.
Add . . .
    1 (6-oz.) can tomato paste
    1/2 cup white grape juice
Microcook on high 4 minutes.

100% !

100% !

Vichyssoise

A delectable first course for an elegant dinner.
Serves 4. Microcook Time: 15 minutes. Chill 1 hour.
Calories: 298. Fat: 16 g. Carbohydrates: 22 g. Protein: 16 g. Sodium: 1239 mg.

Place in a 3-quart glass casserole:
    1 onion, chopped
    2 tablespoons butter
Microcook on high 4 minutes.
Stir once.
Add . . .
    2 (10 3/4-oz.) cans low-sodium chicken
        broth
Microcook on high 8 minutes.
Stir once.
Mixture should be bubbly.
Add . . .
    2 cups instant potato flakes
Beat with whisk.
Add . . .
    1 cup half-and-half (12% cream)
Microcook on medium 1 minute.
Refrigerate at least 4 hours.
Serve.
Hint: Chopped chives, freshly ground pepper, a dash of nutmeg or minced parsley can be sprinkled on top.

- *1 onion, chopped*
- *2 tablespoons butter*
- *2 (10 3/4-oz.) cans low-sodium chicken broth*
- *2 cups instant potato flakes*
- *1 cup half-and-half (12% cream)*

Wild Rice Soup

From Minnesota, where wild rice grows naturally.
Serves 8. Microcook Time: 80 minutes.
Calories: 235. Fat: 17 g. Carbohydrates: 14 g. Protein: 7 g. Sodium: 626 mg.

- 1/4 cup wild rice
- 3/4 cup water
- 1/2 onion
- 1 carrot
- 1/2 green pepper
- 4 fresh mushrooms
- 1 clove garlic
- 1/2 rib celery
- 1/2 cup butter
- 1/2 cup all-purpose flour
- 1 (10-oz.) can low-sodium chicken broth
- 1/4 cup chopped cooked ham
- 1/4 cup finely chopped almonds
- 2 teaspoons freshly ground pepper
- 1/2 teaspoon curry powder
- 1/2 cup half-and-half (12% cream)

Wash wild rice thoroughly.
Place in an 8-cup glass measure:
>   1/4 cup wild rice
>   3/4 cup water

Microcook on high 5 minutes.
Cover with vented plastic wrap.
Microcook on medium low 45 minutes, until liquid is absorbed.
Grate in a blender:
>   1/2 onion
>   1 carrot
>   1/2 green pepper
>   4 fresh mushrooms
>   1 clove garlic
>   1/2 rib celery

Place in a 3-quart glass casserole:
>   1/2 cup butter

Microcook on high 2 minutes, or until melted.
Add . . .
>   1/2 cup all-purpose flour

Stir well.
Add . . .
>   vegetable mixture

Stir.
Add . . .
>   1 (10-oz.) can low-sodium chicken broth

Microcook on high 5 minutes.
Stir twice.
Add . . .
>   1/4 cup chopped cooked ham
>   1/4 cup finely chopped almonds
>   2 teaspoons freshly ground pepper
>   1/2 teaspoon curry powder

Microcook on high 8 to 10 minutes.
Add . . .
>   1/2 cup half-and-half (12% cream)

Microcook on medium 3 minutes.
Top each serving with 1 teaspoon sherry, if desired.

Croutons

Make your own; a tasty way to use leftover crusts and dry bread.
Serves 6. Microcook Time: 5 minutes.
Calories: 80. Fat: 5 g. Carbohydrates: 7 g. Protein: 2 g. Sodium: 122 mg.

Place in a 1-cup glass measure:
    2 tablespoons butter
Microcook on high 20 seconds.
Place in a microwave-safe baking dish:
    1 1/2 cups bread cubes
Pour butter over bread and **stir.**
Add . . .
    2 tablespoons grated Parmesan cheese
    1/2 teaspoon onion powder
    1/4 teaspoon garlic powder
Microcook on high 1 1/2 to 2 minutes.

- *2 tablespoons butter*
- *1 1/2 cups bread cubes*
- *2 tablespoons grated Parmesan cheese*
- *1/2 teaspoon onion powder*
- *1/4 teaspoon garlic powder*

Broccoli with Tomato/Yogurt Topping

Serve in place of salad or vegetable.
Serves 4. Microcook Time: 10 minutes.
Calories: 42. Fat: 0 g. Carbohydrates: 8 g. Protein: 4 g. Sodium: 29 mg.

Place in a microwave-safe steamer:
    2 stalks broccoli, cut into 1/2" pieces
    1 tablespoon water
Microcook on high 5 to 7 minutes.
Place in a 2-cup glass measure:
    1/2 cup nonfat plain yogurt
    1 Roma tomato, chopped
    1 teaspoon toasted dehydrated onion
    1/4 teaspoon lemon pepper
    1/4 teaspoon garlic powder
Stir and **pour** over broccoli.
Hint: Undercook broccoli and serve as a crunchy salad.

- *2 stalks broccoli, cut into 1/2" pieces*
- *1 tablespoon water*
- *1/2 cup nonfat plain yogurt*
- *1 Roma tomato, chopped*
- *1 teaspoon toasted dehydrated onion*
- *1/4 teaspoon lemon pepper*
- *1/4 teaspoon garlic powder*

Bean Salad for Company

Good enough for company, and rich in protein and fiber, to boot!
Serves 12. Microcook Time: 10 minutes.
Calories: 260. Fat: 12 g. Carbohydrates: 28 g. Protein: 8 g. Sodium: 415 mg.

- *2 carrots, sliced*
- *1 (9-oz.) pkg. frozen green beans*
- *1 (10-oz.) pkg. frozen lima beans*
- *1 (15 1/2-oz.) can kidney beans*
- *1 (15-oz.) can garbanzo beans*
- *1 (8-oz.) can sliced water chestnuts, drained*
- *1 sweet onion, sliced*
- *1 green pepper, sliced*
- *2 cloves garlic, sliced*
- *2 tablespoons fresh basil, minced*
- *8 oz. Italian salad dressing*

Place in a microwave-safe steamer:
    2 carrots, sliced
    1 (9-oz.) pkg. frozen green beans
    1 (10-oz.) pkg. frozen lima beans
Microcook on high 7 minutes.
Layer in a large salad bowl:
    1 (15 1/2-oz.) can kidney beans
    1 (15-oz.) can garbanzo beans
    1 (8-oz.) can sliced water chestnuts, drained
    1 sweet onion, sliced
    1 green pepper, sliced
    2 cloves garlic, sliced
    2 tablespoons fresh basil, minced
Add cooked carrots, green and lima beans.
Pour over top:
    8 oz. Italian salad dressing
Stir.
Refrigerate overnight.
Hint: This salad keeps well for several days. Beans are high in protein and fiber.; they are fat and cholesterol free. Use beans as a replacement for meat in spaghetti, casseroles or in salads.

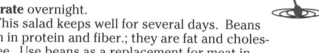

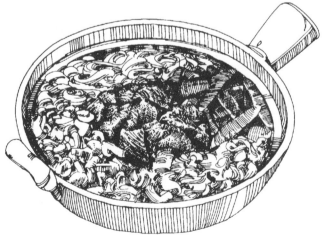

El Paso Salad

Only the best from Texas.
Serves 8. Microcook Time: 15 minutes.
Calories: 267. Fat: 16 g. Carbohydrates: 18 g. Protein: 15 g. Sodium: 185 mg.

Cut into 4 pieces:
    1 whole boned, skinless chicken breast
Place in a 9" round microwave baking dish.
Cover with waxed paper.
Microcook on high 5 to 6 minutes until juice runs clear.

Set aside.
Combine in a salad bowl:
    1/4 cup olive oil
    1/4 cup lime juice
    1 clove garlic, minced
    1 teaspoon chili powder
Stir.
Add . . .
    cooked chicken, cut into bite-size pieces
    1 red pepper, sliced
    6 green onions, sliced
    1 tomato, chopped
    1 green pepper, chopped
    1 tablespoon minced cilantro

Chill.
Add . . .
    2 cups cooked brown rice
    2 avocados, cut into bite-size pieces
Stir and **serve.**

- 1 whole boned, skinless chicken breast
- 1/4 cup olive oil
- 1/4 cup lime juice
- 1 clove garlic, minced
- 1 teaspoon chili powder
- 1 red pepper, sliced
- 6 green onions, sliced
- 1 tomato, chopped
- 1 green pepper, chopped
- 1 tablespoon minced cilantro
- 2 cups cooked brown rice
- 2 avocados, cut into bite-size pieces

Taco Salad

Every kid's favorite salad!
Serves 8. Microcook Time: 30 minutes.
Calories: 433. Fat: 20 g. Carbohydrates: 42 g. Protein: 20 g. Sodium: 920 mg.

- 1 lb. ground beef, crumbled
- 1 onion, chopped
- 1/2 green pepper, chopped
- 1 (15-oz.) can seasoned chili beans
- 1 (8-oz.) can tomato sauce
- 1 (8-oz.) jar taco sauce
- 1/2 cup chili sauce
- 1/4 teaspoon cumin
- 1 (10-oz.) pkg. tortilla chips
- 1 cup shredded Cheddar cheese
- 4 cups shredded lettuce
- 1 large tomato, chopped

Place in a microwave-safe colander over a 2-quart casserole:

> 1 lb. ground beef, crumbled

Cover with waxed paper.
Microcook on high 5 to 6 minutes.
Drain fat.
Place meat in casserole.
Add . . .

> 1 onion, chopped
> 1/2 green pepper, chopped
> 1 (15-oz.) can seasoned chili beans

Cover with waxed paper.
Microcook on high 4 minutes.
Combine in an 8-cup glass measure:

> 1 (8-oz.) can tomato sauce
> 1 (8-oz.) jar taco sauce
> 1/2 cup chili sauce
> 1/4 teaspoon cumin

Microcook on high 8 minutes.
Layer meat mixture in a large salad bowl with:

> 1 (10-oz.) pkg. tortilla chips
> 1 cup shredded Cheddar cheese
> 4 cups shredded lettuce
> 1 large tomato, chopped

Pour tomato sauce over and **toss.**

Pasta Salad

Summer or Winter, a never-fail winner!
Serves 20. Microcook Time: 35 minutes.
Calories: 210. Fat: 9 g. Carbohydrates: 23 g. Protein: 10 g. Sodium: 76 mg.

Place on a meat roasting rack and dish:
    1 whole boned chicken breast
Cover with waxed paper.
Microcook on high 7 to 10 minutes, depending on size.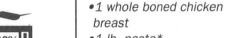
Hint: Cook until juices run clear.
Cool.
Remove skin.
Cut into bite-size pieces.
Cook 1 lb. pasta.*
Drain.
Microcook on high 3 to 4 minutes:
    1 (10-oz.) pkg. frozen peas
Combine chicken pasta and peas with:
    1 (15-oz.) can garbanzo beans
    1 (2 1/2-oz.) can sliced black olives,
        drained
    1 (4-oz.) jar chopped pimiento
    1 green pepper, chopped
    1/2 cup chopped fresh parsley
Combine and **pour** over mixture:
    1/2 cup oil (olive gives good flavor)
    3 tablespoons red wine vinegar
    2 tablespoons Dijon mustard
    1/2 teaspoon curry powder
    1 clove garlic, minced
    freshly ground pepper
Refrigerate.
Hint: May be served the next day. Radiatore and Rotini pastas work well.
*May be cooked in microwave. See directions, page 186.

- 1 whole boned chicken breast
- 1 lb. pasta*
- 1 (15-oz.) can garbanzo beans
- 1 (10-oz.) pkg. frozen peas
- 1 (2 1/2-oz.) can sliced black olives, drained
- 1 (4-oz.) jar chopped pimiento
- 1 green pepper, chopped
- 1/2 cup chopped fresh parsley
- 1/2 cup oil (olive gives good flavor)
- 3 tablespoons red wine vinegar
- 2 tablespoons Dijon mustard
- 1/2 teaspoon curry powder
- 1 clove garlic, minced
- freshly ground pepper

Popcorn Salad

Not only for popcorn lovers, this salad is different.
Serves 16. Microcook Time: 15 minutes.
Calories: 147. Fat: 11 g. Carbohydrates: 8 g. Protein: 4 g. Sodium: 324 mg.

- 6 to 8 cups popped corn
- 1 (8-oz.) can sliced water chestnuts, drained
- 1/2 red or green pepper, chopped
- 1 rib celery, sliced
- 2 green onions, sliced
- 1 cup shredded Cheddar cheese
- 1 cup light mayonnaise
- 1/2 cup low-calorie sour cream
- 3 slices cooked bacon, chopped*

Microcook popcorn using a microwave popper according to manufacturer's directions.*
Hint: Never make popcorn in a brown paper bag.

Combine in a large bowl just before serving:

6 to 8 cups popped corn
1 (8-oz.) can sliced water chestnuts, drained
1/2 red or green pepper, chopped
1 rib celery, sliced
2 green onions, sliced
1 cup shredded Cheddar cheese
1 cup light mayonnaise
1/2 cup low-calorie sour cream
3 slices cooked bacon, chopped**

*See Popcorn Hints, page 255.
**See directions for cooking bacon, page 62.

Tabbouli Salad

A healthy treat.
Serves 8. Microcook Time: 70 minutes.
Calories: 210. Fat: 10 g. Carbohydrates: 24 g. Protein: 6 g. Sodium: 405 mg.

Place in an 8-cup glass measure:
    2 cups water
Microcook on high 6 minutes, until it boils.
Add . . .
    1 cup cracked wheat bulgur
Stand, covered, 1 hour.
Drain excess liquid.
Add . . .
    1/4 cup olive oil
    1/4 cup fresh lemon juice
    1 tablespoon garlic vinegar
    6 green onions, sliced
    1 large tomato, chopped
    1/2 cup chopped celery
    1 zucchini, sliced
    1/2 cup shredded Cheddar cheese
    1/4 cup chopped fresh parsley
    freshly ground pepper
Stir.
Chill before serving.

- *2 cups water*
- *1 cup cracked wheat bulgur*
- *1/4 cup olive oil*
- *1/4 cup fresh lemon juice*
- *1 tablespoon garlic vinegar*
- *6 green onions, sliced*
- *1 large tomato, chopped*
- *1/2 cup chopped celery*
- *1 zucchini, sliced*
- *1/2 cup shredded Cheddar cheese*
- *1/4 cup chopped fresh parsley*
- *freshly ground pepper*

Japanese Salad

Try it with sushi!
Serves 6. Microcook Time: 10 minutes.
Calories: 29. Fat: 1 g. Carbohydrates: 4 g. Protein: 2 g. Sodium: 253 mg.

- 1/2 lb. fresh spinach
- 1 cup bean sprouts
- 2 tablespoons white vinegar
- 1 1/2 tablespoons low-sodium soy sauce
- 1 tablespoon toasted sesame seed
- 1 teaspoon sugar

Place in a 2-quart casserole:
    1/2 lb. fresh spinach
    1 cup bean sprouts
Cover.
Microcook on high 2 minutes.
Stir twice.
Combine and pour over spinach:
    2 tablespoons white vinegar
    1 1/2 tablespoons low-sodium soy sauce
    1 tablespoon toasted sesame seed
    1 teaspoon sugar

Creamy Wild Rice Salad

A mouth-watering way to use Thanksgiving leftovers.
Serves 8. Prep Time: 10 minutes.
Calories: 241. Fat: 5 g. Carbohydrates: 26 g. Protein: 22 g. Sodium: 123 mg.

- 3 cups chopped cooked turkey
- 3 cups cooked wild rice
- 2 ribs celery, sliced
- 1 (8-oz.) can sliced water chestnuts, drained
- 3/4 cup nonfat plain yogurt
- 1/4 cup light mayonnaise
- 1 teaspoon lemon juice

Combine in a 3-quart casserole:
    3 cups chopped cooked turkey
    3 cups cooked wild rice
    2 ribs celery, sliced
    1 (8-oz.) can sliced water chestnuts, drained
Place in a 2-cup glass measure:
    3/4 cup non fat plain yogurt
    1/4 cup light mayonnaise
    1 teaspoon lemon juice
Pour over turkey-rice mixture and **stir.**
Hint: 1/2 cup chopped mixed red and green peppers adds nice color.

Wild Rice Salad - Oriental

Created for Dr. James Grimmer and Sue McKnight from Richfield High School.
Serves 8. Prep Time: 10 minutes.
Calories: 330. Fat: 16 g. Carbohydrates: 26 g. Protein: 22 g. Sodium: 391 mg.

Combine in a 3-quart casserole:
    3 cups chopped cooked turkey
    3 cups cooked wild rice
    2 ribs celery, sliced
    1(8-oz.) can sliced water chestnuts,
      drained
Place in a 2-cup glass measure:
    1/3 cup herb-flavored rice vinegar
    2 tablespoons light soy sauce
    1/2 cup safflower oil
    1 tablespoon Oriental salt-free seasoning
Pour over turkey-rice mixture.
Hint: May top with cashew nuts.

- *3 cups chopped cooked turkey*
- *3 cups cooked wild rice*
- *2 ribs celery, sliced*
- *1 (8-oz.) can sliced water chestnuts, drained*
- *1/3 cup herb-flavored rice vinegar*
- *2 tablespoons light soy sauce*
- *1/2 cup safflower oil*
- *1 tablespoon Oriental salt-free seasoning*

Wild Rice Salad/Paris Style

One of my specialties. Absolutely fabulous!
Serves 8. Prep Time: 10 minutes.
Calories: 385. Fat: 23 g. Carbohydrates: 25 g. Protein: 21 g. Sodium: 58 mg.

Combine in a 3-quart casserole:
    3 cups chopped cooked turkey
    3 cups cooked wild rice
    2 ribs celery, sliced
    1 (8-oz.) can sliced water chestnuts,
      drained
Combine in a 2-cup glass measure:
    1/3 cup rosemary, thyme and marjoram
      flavored vinegar
    2/3 cup olive oil
    1 teaspoon Herbes de Provence
    freshly ground pepper
Pour over turkey-rice mixture.

- *3 cups chopped cooked turkey*
- *3 cups cooked wild rice*
- *2 ribs celery, sliced*
- *1 (8-oz.) can sliced water chestnuts, drained*
- *1/3 cup rosemary, thyme, marjoram-flavored vinegar*
- *2/3 cup olive oil*
- *1 teaspoon Herbes de Provence*
- *freshly ground pepper*

Buttermilk Dressing

A staple dressing that's always popular.
Serves 16. Prep Time: 10 minutes.
Calories: 6. Fat: 0 g. Carbohydrates: 1 g. Protein: 1 g. Sodium: 22 mg.

- 1 cup buttermilk
- 1 clove garlic, minced
- 2 teaspoons minced onion
- 1/2 teaspoon low -salt Dijon mustard
- 1/2 teaspoon dill weed
- a few drops hot pepper sauce

Combine in a 2-cup glass measure:
    1 cup buttermilk
    1 clove garlic, minced
    2 teaspoons minced onion
    1/2 teaspoon low-salt Dijon mustard
    1/2 teaspoon dill weed
    a few drops hot pepper sauce
Hint: Flavors will gain authority upon standing.

Dill Weed Dressing

A wonderful oil & vinegar dressing made even better with the addition of dill weed.
Serves 16. Prep Time: 10 minutes.
Calories: 33. Fat: 3 g. Carbohydrates: 1 g. Protein: 0 g. Sodium: 1 mg.

- 1/2 cup raspberry vinegar
- 1/4 cup safflower oil
- 1/4 cup dehydrated tomatoes
- 1 tablespoon dill weed
- 1/4 teaspoon onion powder
- 1/4 teaspoon garlic powder
- 1/4 teaspoon dry mustard

Combine in a 4-cup glass measure:
    1/2 cup raspberry vinegar
    1/4 cup safflower oil
    1/4 cup dehydrated tomatoes
    1 tablespoon dill weed
    1/4 teaspoon onion powder
    1/4 teaspoon garlic powder
    1/4 teaspoon dry mustard
Hint: This dressing must stand for at least 1 hour for the tomatoes to "bloom."

Pepper Cream Dressing

A tasty, creamy dressing.
Serves 28. Prep Time: 10 minutes.
Calories: 36. Fat: 3 g. Carbohydrates: 1 g. Protein: 1 g. Sodium: 67 mg.

Combine in a 2-cup glass measure:
    1 cup light mayonnaise
    1/2 cup light sour cream
    2 cloves garlic, chopped
    1/4 cup grated Parmesan cheese
    1 teaspoon freshly ground black pepper

- *1 cup light mayonnaise*
- *1/2 cup light sour cream*
- *2 cloves garlic, chopped*
- *1/4 cup grated Parmesan cheese*
- *1 teaspoon freshly ground black pepper*

Salt-free Salad Seasoning

Prepare ahead of time and store to use when needed.
Serves 11. Prep Time: 10 minutes.
Calories: 4. Fat: 0 g. Carbohydrates: 1 g. Protein: 0 g. Sodium: 1 mg.

Combine . . .
    2 teaspoons paprika
    1 teaspoon dry mustard
    1/2 teaspoon garlic powder
    1/2 teaspoon onion powder
    1/2 teaspoon dill weed
    1/2 teaspoon celery seed
    1/2 teaspoon marjoram
Place in blender and mix well.
Hint: Store in a shaker-top jar in a cool, dry place.
You may want to double or triple this recipe.

- *2 teaspoons paprika*
- *1 teaspoon dry mustard*
- *1/2 teaspoon garlic powder*
- *1/2 teaspoon onion powder*
- *1/2 teaspoon dill weed*
- *1/2 teaspoon celery seed*
- *1/2 teaspoon marjoram*

Sprinkle on Top Seasoning

To add a little extra zest!
Serves 32. Prep Time: 10 minutes.
Calories: 5. Fat: 0 g. Carbohydrates: 1 g. Protein: 0 g. Sodium: 1 mg.

- *2 tablespoons dill weed*
- *1 tablespoon thyme*
- *1 tablespoon sesame seed*
- *1 1/2 teaspoons garlic powder*
- *1 1/2 teaspoons onion powder*
- *1 teaspoon paprika*

Combine . . .
2 tablespoons dill weed
1 tablespoon thyme
1 tablespoon sesame seed
1 1/2 teaspoons garlic powder
1 1/2 teaspoons onion powder
1 teaspoon paprika
Hint: Store in a cool, dry place.

Sweet & Sour Dressing

A German favorite; try with potatoes for salad.
Serves 8. Microcook Time: 10 minutes.
Calories: 70.5. Fat: 6 g. Carbohydrates: 3.5 g. Protein: 1.5 g. Sodium: 76 mg.

- *1/4 cup cold water*
- *2 teaspoons cornstarch*
- *1/2 cup water*
- *2 tablespoons red wine or cider vinegar*
- *2 tablespoons vegetable oil*
- *1 tablespoon honey*
- *1 teaspoon lemon juice*
- *1 teaspoon dry mustard*
- *2 slices cooked bacon, chopped*

Place in 2-cup glass measure:
1/4 cup cold water
2 teaspoons cornstarch
Stir until dissolved
Add . . .
1/2 cup water
Microcook on high 2 minutes.
Stir twice.
Add . . .
2 tablespoons red wine or cider vinegar
2 tablespoons vegetable oil
1 tablespoon honey
1 teaspoon lemon juice
1 teaspoon dry mustard
Microcook on high 30 seconds.
Add . . .
2 slices cooked bacon, chopped

V
E
G
G
I
E
S

Vegetable Hints

- Microcooking vegetables is one of the best cooking methods for retaining vitamins and minerals, color, texture and flavor.
- Most vegetables are microcooked at 100% power.
- Covering dishes will help speed the cooking process.
- Small amounts of water may be added to prevent dryness.
- Large pieces are placed on the outside of cooking plate or dish.
- Whole vegetables need to be turned over and rotated during cooking time.
- Use a fork to pierce heavy-skinned vegetables so they don't burst during cooking.
- Avoid overcooking; remember that food continues to cook during standing time. Overcooked vegetables are dry or rubbery.
- Chopped vegetables are microcooked 2 to 3 minutes per cup on high power.
- Corn on the cob, potatoes and squash should be placed on a rack.
- Frozen vegetables may be cooked in their original carton (if it is paper). Put on a plate or paper plate to prevent color transfer to the bottom of the oven. Foil cartons may cause arcing; remove contents before microcooking.
- It is possible to stir-fry vegetables if you use a browning dish. Preheat the dish according to manufacturer's directions, add 1 to 2 tablespoons oil and microcook on high 4 to 6 minutes for 1 cup of fresh vegetables.

Asparagus

Delectable and so low-cal!
Serves 4. Microcook Time: 10 minutes.
Calories: 28. Fat: 1 g. Carbohydrates: 4 g. Protein: 2 g. Sodium: 46 mg.

Place in an 11x7x1 1/2" glass baking dish:
    1 lb. fresh asparagus
    2 tablespoons lemon juice
Hint: Place washed and trimmed asparagus with stem ends toward the outside of dish.
Cover with vented plastic wrap.
Microcook on medium high 3 to 4 minutes.
Spread over asparagus:
    2 teaspoons Dijon mustard
    1 tablespoon grated Parmesan cheese
Cover.
Stand 2 to 3 minutes.

- *1 lb. fresh asparagus*
- *2 tablespoons lemon juice*
- *2 teaspoons Dijon mustard*
- *1 tablespoon grated Parmesan cheese*

Green Bean Casserole

Water chestnuts add crunch.
Serves 8. Microcook Time: 15 minutes.
Calories: 138. Fat: 6 g. Carbohydrates: 1 g. Protein: 5 g. Sodium: 212 mg.

Combine in a 2-quart casserole:
    2 (10 oz.) pkgs. frozen cut green beans, thawed
    1 (10 1/2-oz.) can low-sodium cream of mushroom soup
    1 (8-oz.) can sliced water chestnuts, drained
    1 teaspoon instant minced onion
Top with:
    1/4 cup crushed seasoned croutons
    1/4 cup chopped cashews, if desired
Microcook on high 8 to 10 minutes.
Hint: To thaw 10-oz. pkg. of green beans, **microcook** on high 5 to 6 minutes.

- *2 (10 oz.) pkgs. frozen cut green beans, thawed*
- *1 (10 1/2-oz.) can low-sodium cream of mushroom soup*
- *1 (8-oz.) can sliced water chestnuts, drained*
- *1 teaspoon instant minced onion*
- *1/4 cup crushed seasoned croutons*
- *1/4 cup chopped cashews, if desired (adds calories)*

Broccoli with Cheese

A great side dish to accompany entrée.
Serves 4. Microcook Time: 8 minutes.
Calories: 121. Fat: 9 g. Carbohydrates: 4 g. Protein: 8 g. Sodium: 389 mg.

- 1 (10-oz.) pkg. frozen chopped broccoli, thawed
- 1/2 cup cubed process cheese
- 2 drops hot pepper sauce

Combine in a 1 1/2-quart casserole:
> 1 (10-oz.) pkg. frozen chopped broccoli, thawed
> 1/2 cup cubed process cheese
> 2 drops hot pepper sauce

Cover with vented plastic wrap.
Microcook on high 2 to 3 minutes.
Stand 5 minutes.

Broccoli Ring

Chopped pimiento adds nice color.
Serves 8. Microcook Time: 17 minutes.
Calories: 151. Fat: 8 g. Carbohydrates: 10 g. Protein: 10 g. Sodium: 190 mg.

- 1 tablespoon margarine
- 1 clove garlic
- 1/2 cup chopped onion
- 2 (10-oz.) pkgs. chopped broccoli, thawed and drained
- 1 cup shredded Swiss cheese
- 1 cup seasoned croutons
- 1/2 cup skim milk
- 3 eggs
- 2 tablespoons grated Parmesan cheese

Combine in an 8-cup glass measure:
> 1 tablespoon margarine
> 1 clove garlic
> 1/2 cup chopped onion

Microcook on high 2 minutes.
Add . . .
> 2 (10-oz.) pkgs. chopped broccoli, thawed and drained
> 1 cup shredded Swiss cheese
> 1 cup seasoned croutons
> 1/2 cup skim milk
> 3 eggs
> 2 tablespoons grated Parmesan cheese

Stir.
Pour into a greased 9" microwave ring mold.
Microcook on medium high 12 to 15 minutes.
Rotate.
Stir.
Hint: Chopped pimiento adds nice color.

German Cabbage

Tantalizingly sweet & sour.
Serves 4. Microcook Time: 20 minutes.
Calories: 74. Fat: 0 g. Carbohydrates: 18 g. Protein: 1 g. Sodium: 14 mg.

Place in a 2-quart casserole:
   1 lb. chopped red cabbage
   1 apple, peeled and sliced
   1/4 cup red wine vinegar
   1/4 teaspoon caraway seed, if desired
   2 tablespoons honey
Cover with vented plastic wrap.
Microcook on high 15 to 18 minutes.
Stand 5 minutes.

- *1 lb. chopped red cabbage*
- *1 apple, peeled and sliced*
- *1/4 cup red wine vinegar*
- *1/4 teaspoon caraway seed, if desired*
- *2 tablespoons honey*

Honey Orange Carrots

Not only pretty, but lots of Vitamin A & C.
Serves 6. Microcook Time: 10 minutes.
Calories: 46. Fat: 0 g. Carbohydrates: 11 g. Protein: 1 g. Sodium: 24 mg.

Combine in a 2-quart casserole:
   4 carrots, peeled and sliced into circles
   1/4 cup orange juice
   1/2 teaspoon grated orange peel
   2 tablespoons honey
   dash mace
Cover with vented plastic wrap.
Microcook on high 4 to 6 minutes.
Stand uncovered 5 minutes.

- *4 carrots, peeled and sliced into circles*
- *1/4 cup orange juice*
- *1/2 teaspoon grated orange peel*
- *2 tablespoons honey*
- *dash mace*

Cajun Cauliflower

Mild cauliflower gets hot!.
Serves 8. Microcook Time: 15 minutes.
Calories: 73. Fat: 5 g. Carbohydrates: 4 g. Protein: 5 g. Sodium: 95 mg.

- 1 whole head cauliflower
- 1/4 cup water
- 1 cup shredded Cajun Cheddar cheese*
- 6 drops hot pepper sauce, if desired
- 1/2 teaspoon garlic powder
- 1/2 teaspoon onion powder

Trim outer leaves and **cut** base of:
> 1 whole head cauliflower

Wash well.
Place in microwave steamer with 1/4 cup water.
Microcook on high 7 to 10 minutes depending upon size.
Pour water off.
Add . . .
> 1 cup shredded Cajun Cheddar cheese*
> 6 drops hot pepper sauce, if desired
> 1/2 teaspoon garlic powder
> 1/2 teaspoon onion powder

Cover.
Microcook on high 2 minutes.
Stand 3 minutes.
*****Hint:** Use Cheddar cheese or hot pepper cheese.

Cauliflower Casserole

Curry makes the difference.
Serves 8. Microcook Time: 15 minutes.
Calories: 128. Fat: 8 g. Carbohydrates: 8 g. Protein: 7 g. Sodium: 405 mg.

- 1 head cauliflower, cut into flowerettes
- 1/4 cup water
- 1 (10 3/4-oz.) can low-sodium cream of chicken soup
- 1 cup process cheese spread
- 1 tablespoon Dijon mustard
- 1 teaspoon curry powder
- 1/2 teaspoon onion powder

Place in a microwave steamer:
> 1 head cauliflower, cut into flowerettes
> 1/4 cup water

Microcook on high 5 to 7 minutes.
Drain.
Add . . .
> 1 (10 3/4-oz.) can low-sodium cream of chicken soup
> 1 cup process cheese spread
> 1 tablespoon Dijon mustard
> 1 teaspoon curry powder
> 1/2 teaspoon onion powder

Cover.
Microcook on high 4 to 5 minutes.

Oriental Celery

Celery like you've never had it.
Serves 8. Microcook Time: 15 minutes.
Calories: 110. Fat: 6 g. Carbohydrates: 12 g. Protein: 4 g. Sodium: 270 mg.

Place in a 2-quart casserole:
  4 cups sliced celery
Add . . .
  2 tablespoons water
Add . . .
  1 (8-oz.) can sliced water chestnuts,
    drained
  1 (10 3/4-oz.) can low-sodium cream of
    chicken soup
  1/4 cup chopped almonds
  1 (2 1/2-oz.) can chopped pimiento
Cover with vented plastic wrap.
Microcook on high 7 minutes.
Top with:
  1/4 cup crushed seasoned croutons
Cover with vented plastic wrap.
Microcook on high 4 minutes.

- *4 cups sliced celery*
- *2 tablespoons water*
- *1 (8-oz.) can sliced water chestnuts, drained*
- *1 (10 3/4-oz.) can low-sodium cream of chicken soup*
- *1/4 cup chopped almonds*
- *1 (2 1/2-oz.) can chopped pimiento*
- *1/4 cup crushed seasoned croutons*

Corn Casserole

Simply mouth-watering.
Serves 8. Microcook Time: 15 minutes.
Calories: 353. Fat: 19 g. Carbohydrates: 38 g. Protein: 10 g. Sodium: 635 mg.

Place in a 2-quart glass casserole:
  2 tablespoons margarine
  1/2 cup chopped onion
  1/2 cup chopped green pepper
Microcook on high 2 minutes.
Add . . .
  1 (15-oz.) can chili without beans
  1 (15-oz.) can chili beans
  1 (17-oz.) can whole kernel corn, drained
  1 (2 1/2-oz.) can sliced ripe olives
  1 (6-oz.) pkg. corn chips
Mix well.
Microcook on high 8 to 10 minutes.

- *2 tablespoons margarine*
- *1/2 cup chopped onion*
- *1/2 cup chopped green pepper*
- *1 (15-oz.) can chili without beans*
- *1 (15-oz.) can chili beans*
- *1 (17-oz.) can whole kernel corn, drained*
- *1 (2 1/2-oz.) can sliced ripe olives*
- *1 (6-oz.) pkg. corn chips*

Corn & Pepper Ring Casserole

Tastes as appetizing as it looks.
Serves 8. Microcook Time: 15 minutes.
Calories: 116. Fat: 6 g. Carbohydrates: 10 g. Protein: 7 g. Sodium: 154 mg.

- *2 cups frozen whole kernel corn*
- *1/4 cup chopped green pepper*
- *1/4 cup chopped onion*
- *3 eggs, beaten*
- *1 (4-oz.) can chopped green chilies*
- *1/2 cup cubed process cheese*
- *1/4 cup grated Parmesan cheese*
- *1/2 cup skim milk*
- *few drops hot pepper sauce, if desired*
- *salt-free vegetable seasoning*

Place in a 4-cup glass measure:

    2 cups frozen whole kernel corn
    1/4 cup chopped green pepper
    1/4 cup chopped onion

Microcook on high 4 minutes.
Stir once.
Place mixture in a 9" microwave ring mold.
Add . . .

    3 eggs, beaten
    1 (4-oz.) can chopped green chilies
    1/2 cup cubed process cheese
    1/4 cup grated Parmesan cheese
    1/2 cup skim milk
    few drops hot pepper sauce, if desired
    salt-free vegetable seasoning

Stir to combine ingredients.
Microcook on high 4 to 5 minutes.
Rearrange ingredients twice.
Stand 2 to 3 minutes.

Stir-Fry Corn

Stoplight colors.
Serves 4. Microcook Time: 12 minutes.
Calories: 182. Fat: 8 g. Carbohydrates: 27 g. Protein: 5 g. Sodium: 63 mg.

Preheat a microwave browning dish according to manufacturer's directions.
Add . . .
>2 tablespoons butter
>1 (10-oz.) pkg. frozen whole kernel corn
>1/2 cup chopped green pepper

Cover.
Microcook on high 5 to 8 minutes.
Stir twice.
Season with:
>1/4 teaspoon garlic powder
>1/4 teaspoon onion powder
>dash pepper
>chopped red pimiento

- *2 tablespoons butter*
- *1 (10-oz.) pkg. frozen whole kernel corn*
- *1/2 cup chopped green pepper*
- *1/4 teaspoon garlic powder*
- *1/4 teaspoon onion powder*
- *dash pepper*
- *chopped red pimiento (adds nice color)*

Corn on the Cob

If you've never tried corn cooked in the husk, try it now!
Serves 1. Microcook Time: 5 minutes.
Calories: 169. Fat: 3 g. Carbohydrates: 31 g. Protein: 5 g. Sodium: 0 mg.

Hint: Corn may be cooked in the husk.
Allow 3 to 4 minutes per ear.
Microcook on an elevated rack on high 5 minutes.
Hint: Corn may also be husked and wrapped in plastic wrap.
Hint: You may add butter and pepper before wrapping. Larger, more mature corn may require more cooking time.
Hint: Corn cooked in plastic wrap requires about 1 minute less cooking time than corn cooked in husks.

- *1 ear of corn*

Corn Pudding

A cozy, old Iowa recipe.
Serves 8. Microcook Time: 26 minutes.
Calories: 143. Fat: 3 g. Carbohydrates: 25 g. Protein: 5 g. Sodium: 329 mg.

- 1/4 cup milk
- 2 tablespoons cornstarch
- 2 (16 1/2-oz.) cans creamed corn
- 3 eggs, beaten
- 1/4 teaspoon mace
- freshly ground pepper
- dash salt

Place in a 1 1/2-quart greased casserole:
> 1/4 cup milk
> 2 tablespoons cornstarch

Stir until cornstarch is dissolved.
Add ...
> 2 (16 1/2-oz.) cans creamed corn
> 3 eggs, beaten
> 1/4 teaspoon mace
> freshly ground pepper
> dash salt

Microcook on high 15 minutes.
Stir and **rotate** every 2 to 3 minutes.
Stand 5 to 8 minutes.

Okra

A wonderful Cajun-style dish.
Serves 6. Microcook Time: 15 minutes.
Calories: 26. Fat: 0 g. Carbohydrates: 6 g. Protein: 2 g. Sodium: 5 mg.

- 8 oz. frozen okra
- 3 Roma tomatoes
- 1 (4-oz.) can green chilies
- 1/2 teaspoon onion powder
- 1/2 teaspoon garlic powder
- 1/2 teaspoon Cajun seasoning (page 160)

Place in an 8-cup glass measure:
> 8 oz. frozen okra
> 3 Roma tomatoes
> 1 (4-oz.) can green chilies
> 1/2 teaspoon onion powder
> 1/2 teaspoon garlic powder
> 1/2 teaspoon Cajun seasoning (page 160)

Cover with vented plastic wrap.
Microcook on high 8 minutes.
Hint: Rinse okra in hot water before microcooking.

Stuffed Onion

Not just for onion lovers.
Serves 2. Microcook Time: 18 minutes.
Calories: 169. Fat: 4 g. Carbohydrates: 23 g. Protein: 4 g. Sodium: 486 mg.

Slice crosswise into 3 layers:
    1 large sweet onion
Combine in a 4-cup glass measure:
    1 cup crushed seasoned croutons
    1/4 cup low-sodium chicken broth
    1 tablespoon butter, melted
Place large piece of plastic wrap on bottom of a 1-quart casserole.
Place bottom slice of onion on plastic wrap.
Layer onion slices and stuffing.
Gather plastic wrap at top.
Twist top.
Microcook on high 6 minutes.
Stand 10 minutes.
Hint: Onion should be tender when pierced with fork.

- *1 large sweet onion*
- *1 cup crushed seasoned croutons*
- *1/4 cup low-sodium chicken broth*
- *1 tablespoon butter, melted*

100% !

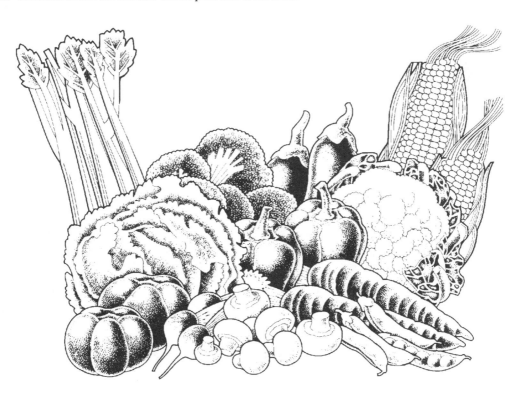

Twice-Cooked Potato Boats

This recipe has everything. Delicious!
Serves 3. Microcook Time: 25 minutes.
Calories: 413. Fat: 24 g. Carbohydrates: 38 g. Protein: 13 g. Sodium: 415 mg.

- *3 baking potatoes*
- *2/3 cup sour cream*
- *2 tablespoons minced onion*
- *1/4 cup milk*
- *2 tablespoons margarine*
- *1/2 cup diced cooked ham*
- *1/4 cup shredded Cheddar cheese*

Microcook on high 12 to 16 minutes:
　　3 baking potatoes, pierced
Hint: Place potatoes in a spoke formation from center on paper towel or elevated on a rack.
Rotate once.
Wrap in foil.
Stand 5 minutes.
Cut potatoes in half, lengthwise.
Scoop out pulp and mash.
Beat in:
　　2/3 cup sour cream
　　2 tablespoons minced onion
　　1/4 cup milk
　　2 tablespoons margarine
　　1/2 cup diced cooked ham
　　1/4 cup shredded Cheddar cheese
Fill shells.
Microcook on high 3 to 4 minutes.

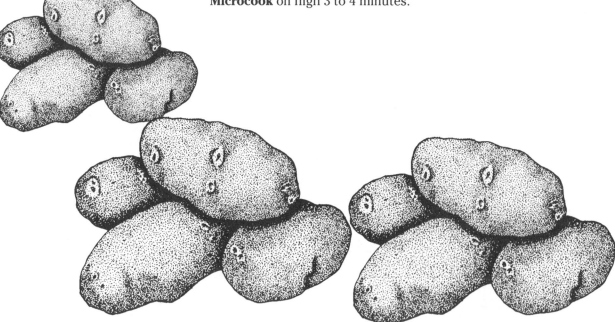

Taco Potatoes

Another dish that kids love to devour!
Serves 2. Microcook Time: 25 minutes.
Calories: 703. Fat: 31 g. Carbohydrates: 74 g. Protein: 37 g. Sodium: 2060 mg.

Scrub:
    2 baking potatoes
Pierce.
Place on elevated rack.
Microcook on high 8 to 12 minutes
(depending on size and variety of potato).
Remove from oven.
Wrap in foil or towel.
Stand 5 to 6 minutes.

- *2 baking potatoes*
- *1/2 lb. ground beef*
- *1/2 small onion, chopped*
- *1 cup taco sauce*
- *1/4 cup shredded Cheddar cheese*
- *1/4 cup sour cream*
- *1 tomato, chopped*
- *1 cup chopped lettuce*

Sauce

Combine in a 4-cup glass measure:
    1/2 lb. ground beef
    1/2 small onion, chopped
Cover with waxed paper.
Microcook on high 4 to 5 minutes.
Stir once.
Drain fat.
Add . . .
    1 cup taco sauce
Stir.
Cut potatoes open.
Fill with meat sauce and:
    1/4 cup shredded Cheddar cheese
    1/4 cup sour cream
    1 tomato, chopped
    1 cup chopped lettuce

Skinners

If you have the munchies – try skinners.
Serves 4. Microcook Time: 18 minutes.
Calories: 224. Fat: 10 g. Carbohydrates: 20 g. Protein: 17 g. Sodium: 1000 mg.

- 2 baking potatoes
- 2 tablespoons melted butter
- 1/2 cup imitation bacon bits
- 1/4 cup shredded Cheddar cheese
- 1/4 cup grated Parmesan cheese
- 1/4 cup chopped green pepper

Microcook on high 6 to 10 minutes:
    2 baking potatoes, pierced
Stand 6 minutes in foil.
Cut potatoes in half.
Scoop out part of center.*
Slice potatoes lengthwise.
Brush on potatoes:
    2 tablespoons melted butter
Place in glass baking dish.
Top with:
    1/2 cup imitation bacon bits
    1/4 cup shredded Cheddar cheese
    1/4 cup grated Parmesan cheese
    1/4 cup chopped green pepper
Microcook on high 1 to 2 minutes until cheese melts.
Hint: Serve with sour cream.
*Hint: Potato pulp may be used to make soup.

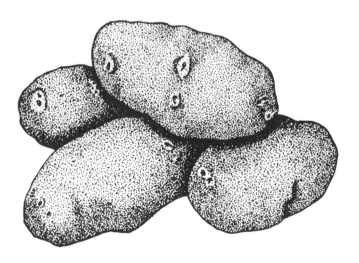

Company Potatoes

Try serving as a side dish with Ham, page 151.
Serves 6. Microcook Time: 26 minutes.
Calories: 174. Fat: 7.5 g. Carbohydrates: 14 g. Protein: 11 g. Sodium: 190 mg.

Place in a 2-quart casserole:
> 3 large potatoes, shredded
> 1/4 cup water

Cover with vented plastic wrap.
Microcook on high 8 to 10 minutes.
Rotate once.
Add . . .
> 1/2 cup cottage cheese
> 1 cup low-fat sour cream*
> 2 tablespoons minced onion

Stir.
Cover.
Microcook on medium 8 to 9 minutes.
Add . . .
> 1/2 cup shredded Cheddar cheese
> 1/4 cup grated Parmesan cheese
> 1 teaspoon ground pepper
> 8 drops hot pepper sauce

Cover.
Microcook on medium for 2 minutes.
Stand 5 minutes.
> *Substitute low-fat plain yogurt for fewer calories.

- 3 large potatoes, shredded
- 1/4 cup water
- 1/2 cup cottage cheese
- 1 cup low-fat sour cream*
- 2 tablespoons minced onion
- 1/2 cup shredded Cheddar cheese
- 1/4 cup grated Parmesan cheese
- 1 teaspoon ground pepper
- 8 drops hot pepper sauce

Cheesy Potatoes

Great with any meat, or try alone.
Serves 2. Microcook Time: 15 minutes.
Calories: 433. Fat: 28 g. Carbohydrates: 37 g. Protein: 10 g. Sodium: 459 mg.

- 1/4 cup margarine
- 1/3 cup crushed seasoned croutons
- 1/4 cup grated Parmesan cheese
- 1 1/4 teaspoons onion powder
- 1 teaspoon garlic powder
- 3 tablespoons flour
- 2 medium potatoes, peeled and cubed

Place in a 2-cup glass measure:
>   1/4 cup margarine

Microcook on high 30 seconds.

Combine and **put** in a plastic bag:
>   1/3 cup crushed seasoned croutons
>   1/4 cup grated Parmesan cheese
>   1 1/4 teaspoons onion powder
>   1 teaspoon garlic powder

Coat:
>   2 medium potatoes, peeled and cubed

with:
>   3 tablespoons flour

Dip potatoes in butter and then shake in bag of crushed croutons.

Arrange on microwave-safe plate.

Cover with waxed paper.

Microcook on high 10 to 12 minutes.

Rotate.

Stir twice.

Spinach Ring

Colorful main dish or accompaniment.
Serves 4. Microcook Time: 20 minutes.
Calories: 182. Fat: 11 g. Carbohydrates: 12 g. Protein: 9 g. Sodium: 388 mg.

Place in a 4-cup glass measure:
- 1 1/2 tablespoons butter
- 8 fresh mushrooms, sliced

Microcook on high 2 minutes.

Stir in:
- 1 (10-oz.) pkg. chopped spinach, thawed and drained
- 2 eggs
- 1/2 (10 3/4-oz.) can low-sodium cream of celery soup
- 1/2 cup seasoned croutons
- 1/4 teaspoon lemon juice
- 2 tablespoons grated Parmesan cheese
- dash pepper

Place in a 9" greased microwave ring mold.

Microcook on high 6 minutes.

Rotate twice.

Stir.

Microcook on high 6 minutes, or until knife inserted comes out clean.

Stand 5 minutes.

- •1 1/2 tablespoons butter
- •8 fresh mushrooms, sliced
- •1 (10-oz.) pkg. chopped spinach, thawed and drained
- •2 eggs
- •1/2 (10 3/4-oz.) can low-sodium cream of celery soup
- •1/2 cup seasoned croutons
- •1/4 teaspoon lemon juice
- •2 tablespoons grated Parmesan cheese
- •dash pepper

Creamy Spinach Casserole

Artichoke hearts are the surprise ingredient.
Serves 8. Microcook Time: 20 minutes.
Calories: 193. Fat: 14 g. Carbohydrates: 14 g. Protein: 8 g. Sodium: 293 mg.

- 2 (10-oz.) pkgs. chopped spinach
- 1/4 cup butter
- 1 (8-oz.) pkg. light cream cheese
- 1 (8-oz.) can water chestnuts, drained and chopped
- 6 drops hot pepper sauce
- dash nutmeg
- 1 (14-oz.) can sliced artichoke hearts, drained
- 1/4 cup grated Parmesan cheese
- 1/2 cup seasoned croutons

Place in an 8-cup glass measure:

    2 (10-oz.) pkgs. chopped spinach

Microcook on high 6 minutes until defrosted.

Drain well.

Add . . .

    1/4 cup butter

    1 (8-oz.) pkg. light cream cheese

Microcook on medium 2 minutes.

Stir until combined.

Add . . .

    1 (8-oz.) can water chestnuts, drained and chopped

    6 drops hot pepper sauce

    dash nutmeg

Place in an 11x7x1 1/2" glass pan:

    1 (14-oz.) can sliced artichoke hearts, drained

Pour spinach mixture over top.

Sprinkle over the top:

    1/4 cup grated Parmesan cheese

    1/2 cup seasoned croutons

Microcook on medium 12 minutes.

Butternut Squash

Very tasty.
Serves 4. Microcook Time: 15 minutes.
Calories: 169. Fat: 6 g. Carbohydrates: 28 g. Protein: 2 g. Sodium: 65 mg.

Cut in half lengthwise:
  1 butternut squash
Remove seeds.
Place squash, cut side down, in an 11x7x1 1/2"
glass baking dish.
Cover with vented plastic wrap.
Microcook on high 8 to 10 minutes.
Test with fork; time will depend on size of squash.
Rotate.
Add to the hollowed sections of squash:
  2 tablespoons butter
  1/4 cup brown sugar
  dash cinnamon
Cover.
Stand 3 to 4 minutes.

> •1 butternut squash
> •2 tablespoons butter
> •1/4 cup brown sugar
> •dash cinnamon

Swiss Squash Casserole

A casserole you'll be proud to serve.
Serves 6. Microcook Time: 26 minutes.
Calories: 184. Fat: 11 g. Carbohydrates: 14 g. Protein: 9 g. Sodium: 597 mg.

- 1 small butternut squash or acorn squash
- 2 cooking apples, thinly sliced
- 1 medium onion, minced
- 1 rib celery, minced
- 1 clove garlic, minced
- 2 tablespoons low-sodium chicken bouillon granules
- 2 tablespoons water
- 1 cup Swiss cold pack cheese food
- 1/2 teaspoon nutmeg
- freshly ground pepper

Cut in half and remove seeds:

    1 small butternut squash or acorn squash

Place on microwave rack and dish.
Cover with vented plastic wrap.
Microcook on high 12 minutes until squash is soft.

Place in a 2-quart glass casserole:

    2 cooking apples, thinly sliced
    1 medium onion, minced
    1 rib celery, minced
    1 clove garlic, minced
    2 tablespoons low-sodium chicken bouillon granules
    2 tablespoons water

Cover with vented plastic wrap.
Microcook on high 6 to 8 minutes.
Remove pulp from cooked squash and **add** to vegetable mixture.
Stir.
Add . . .

    1 cup Swiss cold pack cheese food
    1/2 teaspoon nutmeg
    freshly ground pepper

Microcook on medium 4 to 6 minutes.

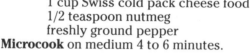

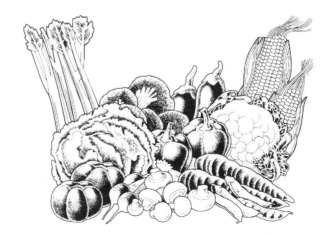

Mexican Zucchini

Try serving with plain yogurt or sour cream.
Serves 4. Microcook Time: 10 minutes.
Calories: 19. Fat: 0 g. Carbohydrates: 5 g. Protein: 1 g. Sodium: 5 mg.

Place in a 2-quart glass casserole:
    3 medium zucchini, sliced into 1/8" circles
Cover with vented plastic wrap.
Microcook on high 3 minutes.
Add . . .
    1 whole tomato, chopped
    1 (4-oz.) can chopped chilies, drained
    1 tablespoon instant onion
    1/2 teaspoon cumin
    dash hot pepper sauce
Cover with vented plastic wrap.
Microcook on high 3 to 4 minutes.
May be served with plain yogurt or
sour cream as a topping.

- *3 medium zucchini, sliced into 1/8" circles*
- *1 whole tomato, chopped*
- *1 (4-oz.) can chopped chilies, drained*
- *1 tablespoon instant onion*
- *1/2 teaspoon cumin*
- *dash hot pepper sauce*

Acorn Squash

A mouth-watering complement to any meal.
Serves 4. Microcook Time: 25 minutes.
Calories: 107. Fat: 3 g. Carbohydrates: 20 g. Protein: 1 g. Sodium: 42 mg.

Cut in half lengthwise:
    1 acorn squash
Remove seeds.
Place both halves in a 7x11x1 1/2" glass baking
dish.
Cover with vented plastic wrap.
Microcook on high 8 to 10 minutes.
Rotate 3 times.
Test with fork; time depends on size of squash.
If not done, add 4 to 6 minutes .
Combine in a 2-cup glass measure:
    1/4 cup brown sugar
    1 tablespoon margarine
    1 tablespoon pineapple-apricot jam
Microcook on high 3 minutes.
Pour into squash cavity.

- *1 acorn squash*
- *1/4 cup brown sugar*
- *1 tablespoon margarine*
- *1 tablespoon pineapple-apricot jam*

Spaghetti Squash

Unique! Serve as a main dish.
Serves 8. Microcook Time: 30 minutes.
Calories: 183. Fat: 9 g. Carbohydrates: 19 g. Protein: 8 g. Sodium: 351 mg.

- 1 spaghetti squash
- 1 cup chopped celery
- 1 small onion, chopped
- 1 tablespoon margarine
- 3 tablespoons flour
- 3/4 cup skim milk
- 3/4 cup cubed process cheese
- 1/4 cup grated Parmesan cheese
- 1/2 teaspoon dry mustard
- dash freshly ground pepper

Pierce several times with fork:
> 1 spaghetti squash

Place in a glass baking dish on a microwave-safe rack .

Microcook on high approximately 15 minutes depending upon size of squash.

Rotate 5 times.

Turn.
Check shell to be sure it is easy to pierce with fork.
If not, **microcook** 2 to 3 minutes on high.
Stand 2 to 3 minutes.
Split lengthwise and remove seeds.
Toss out of shell with fork into serving dish.
Combine in an 8-cup glass measure:
> 1 cup chopped celery
> 1 small onion, chopped
> 1 tablespoon margarine

Cover with waxed paper.

Microcook on high 2 minutes.
Stir.
Add . . .
> 3 tablespoons flour

Stir.
Add . . .
> 3/4 cup skim milk

Cover with waxed paper.

Microcook on high 3 to 4 minutes.
Stir.
Add . . .
> 3/4 cup cubed process cheese
> 1/4 cup grated Parmesan cheese
> 1/2 teaspoon dry mustard
> dash freshly ground pepper

Stir until cheese melts.
Pour sauce over spaghetti squash which has been tossed out of shell with a fork onto a plate.*
Hint: For lower calories and fat, use 1 cup plain yogurt with the celery-onion mixture and top with freshly ground pepper.
*May be topped with spaghetti sauce, grated Parmesan cheese and parsley.

Zucchini Lasagna

Use zucchini to replace pasta.
Serves 4. Microcook Time: 15 minutes.
Calories: 239. Fat: 15 g. Carbohydrates: 11 g. Protein: 17 g. Sodium: 508 mg.

Combine in a mixing bowl:
    1 (8-oz.) can tomato sauce
    1 onion, chopped
    1 clove garlic, minced
    1/4 teaspoon oregano
    dash hot pepper sauce
Combine in another bowl:
    1 cup ricotta or 2% cottage cheese
    1/2 cup shredded mozzarella cheese
    1 tablespoon parsley flakes
    1/4 cup grated Parmesan cheese
Slice lengthwise:
    3 (10" long) zucchini
Arrange strips in an 11x7x1 1/2" glass baking dish.
Cover with waxed paper.
Microcook on high 6 to 8 minutes.
Drain.
Layer 1/2 of the strips in bottom of dish.
Spread cheese mixture over zucchini.
Add . . .
    1 tomato, sliced
Top with:
    remaining zucchini
Pour sauce over top.
Sprinkle with:
    1/4 cup grated Romano cheese
Cover with waxed paper.
Microcook on medium 10 to 14 minutes.
Stand.
Hint: Italian tomatoes hold their shape because they are smaller. Use 2.

- 1 (8-oz.) can tomato sauce
- 1 onion, chopped
- 1 clove garlic, minced
- 1/4 teaspoon oregano
- dash hot pepper sauce
- 1 cup ricotta or 2% cottage cheese
- 1/2 cup shredded mozzarella cheese
- 1 tablespoon parsley flakes
- 1/4 cup grated Parmesan cheese
- 3 (10" long) zucchini
- 1 tomato, sliced
- 1/4 cup grated Romano cheese

Carol's Italian Vegetables

Veggies at their best.
Serves 8. Microcook Time: 10 minutes.
Calories: 128. Fat: 11 g. Carbohydrates: 7 g. Protein: 3 g. Sodium: 67 mg.

- *2 carrots, sliced*
- *2 zucchini, sliced*
- *1 summer squash, sliced*
- *6 large mushrooms, halved*
- *1 tomato, sliced*
- *1/2 green pepper, sliced*
- *1 leek, sliced*
- *1/3 cup olive oil*
- *1/3 cup garlic vinegar*
- *1 tablespoon Dijon mustard*
- *1 teaspoon Italian seasoning*
- *freshly ground pepper*
- *1/3 cup freshly grated Parmesan cheese*

Place on a 12" glass plate:
> 2 carrots, sliced
> 2 zucchini, sliced
> 1 summer squash, sliced
> 6 large mushrooms, halved
> 1 tomato, sliced
> 1/2 green pepper, sliced
> 1 leek, sliced

Place larger and more dense pieces, like carrots, on the outside edge.

Combine in a 1-cup glass measure:
> 1/3 cup olive oil
> 1/3 cup garlic vinegar
> 1 tablespoon Dijon mustard
> 1 teaspoon Italian seasoning
> freshly ground pepper

Pour over vegetables.
Cover with vented plastic wrap.
Microcook on high 4 to 6 minutes, depending on amount of vegetables. They should still be crisp when removed from oven.

Top with:
> 1/3 cup freshly grated Parmesan cheese

Microcook on high 45 seconds.
Stand 3 minutes.

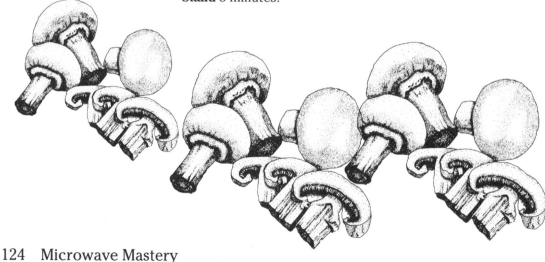

Ratatouille

A French favorite.
Serves 8. Microcook Time: 15 minutes.
Calories: 87. Fat: 8 g. Carbohydrates: 5 g. Protein: 1 g. Sodium: 5 mg.

Combine in a 3-quart microwave-safe casserole:
    1 medium eggplant, peeled and cubed
    2 zucchini, sliced
    2 tomatoes, peeled and chopped
    sliced green pepper
    chopped onion
    1/4 cup olive oil
    2 large cloves garlic, minced
    1/4 teaspoon basil
Cover with vented plastic wrap.
Microcook on high 9 to 10 minutes.

- *1 medium eggplant, peeled and cubed*
- *2 zucchini, sliced*
- *2 tomatoes, peeled and chopped*
- *sliced green pepper*
- *chopped onion*
- *1/4 cup olive oil*
- *2 large cloves garlic, minced*
- *1/4 teaspoon basil*

Cheesy Squash

A dish to be savored! Try serving with pot roast.
Serves 8. Microcook Time: 30 minutes.
Calories: 188. Fat: 10 g. Carbohydrates: 16 g. Protein: 10 g. Sodium: 239 mg.

Place in a 2-quart casserole:
    1/4 cup chopped onion
    2 tablespoons margarine
Microcook on high 1 1/2 minutes.
Stir in:
    4 cups cooked, mashed squash*
    4 eggs
    1 cup grated Parmesan cheese
    1/8 teaspoon nutmeg
    dash hot pepper sauce
Pour into greased 9" microwave ring mold.
Microcook on high 13 to 18 minutes.
Rotate every 3 minutes.
Stand 8 minutes; invert onto serving dish.
*buttercup or butternut varieties work well.

- *1/4 cup chopped onion*
- *2 tablespoons margarine*
- *4 cups cooked, mashed squash**
- *4 eggs*
- *1 cup grated Parmesan cheese*
- *1/8 teaspoon nutmeg*
- *dash hot pepper sauce*

Red Yellow Green Casserole

This will turn your dinner table into a colorful scene.
Serves 8. Microcook Time: 10 minutes.
Calories: 34 Fat: 0 g. Carbohydrates: 0 g. Protein: 1 g. Sodium: 1 mg.

- *1 (10-oz.) pkg. frozen whole kernel corn*
- *1 zucchini, sliced*
- *1 tomato, sliced*
- *1 onion, sliced*
- *juice of 1 lemon*
- *1 1/2 teaspoons salt-free seasoning*
- *1/2 teaspoon lemon pepper*
- *1/2 teaspoon dry mustard*

Place in a 3-quart glass casserole:
    1 (10-oz.) pkg. frozen whole kernel corn
    1 zucchini, sliced
    1 tomato, sliced
    1 onion, sliced
    juice of 1 lemon
    1 1/2 teaspoons salt-free seasoning
    1/2 teaspoon lemon pepper
    1/2 teaspoon dry mustard
Cover with vented plastic wrap.
Microcook on high 10 to 12 minutes.

Potpourri of Summer Vegetables

A great dieter's plate.
Serves 6. Microcook Time: 20 minutes.
Calories: 54. Fat: 1 g. Carbohydrates: 9 g. Protein: 4 g. Sodium: 40 mg.

- *4 patty pan squash, sliced*
- *2 yellow summer squash, sliced*
- *1 zucchini, sliced*
- *1 medium green pepper, chopped*
- *3 Roma tomatoes, sliced*
- *1 onion, chopped*
- *6 large mushrooms*
- *6 asparagus spears, cut into 1" pieces*
- *1/4 cup freshly grated Romano or Parmesan cheese*

Place on a 12" glass plate:
    4 patty pan squash, sliced
    2 yellow summer squash, sliced
    1 zucchini, sliced
    1 medium green pepper, chopped
    3 Roma tomatoes, sliced
    1 onion, chopped
    6 large mushrooms
    6 asparagus spears, cut into 1" pieces
Cover with vented plastic wrap.
Microcook on high 8 to 12 minutes.
Add . . .
    1/4 cup freshly grated Romano or Parmesan cheese
Re-cover.
Stand 5 minutes.

Italian Vegetables

Surprise your guests; serve as a side dish with anything.
Serves 8. Microcook Time: 15 minutes.
Calories: 109. Fat: 9 g. Carbohydrates: 8 g. Protein: 2 g. Sodium: 332 mg.

Arrange on glass pie plate or 12" plate:
    2 cups cauliflower flowerettes
    2 cups broccoli flowerettes
    2 carrots, sliced
    1 red or green pepper, sliced
Hint: Cauliflower on outside ring, then broccoli, carrots and peppers in center.
Pour over vegetables:
    1/2 cup Italian dressing
Cover with vented plastic wrap.
Microcook on high 6 to 10 minutes.
Rotate dish twice.
Hint: Garnish with 10 pitted ripe olives, sliced.

- *2 cups cauliflower flowerettes*
- *2 cups broccoli flowerettes*
- *2 carrots, sliced*
- *1 red or green pepper sliced*
- *1/2 cup Italian dressing*

Jazzed Up Veggies

The topping is the secret.
Serves 4. Microcook Time: 20 minutes.
Calories: 86. Fat: 3 g. Carbohydrates: 14 g. Protein: 6 g. Sodium: 191 mg.

Place on the outer edge of a 9" round microwave-safe plate:
    1 stalk broccoli, sliced into 1/4" pieces
Place in a circular pattern:
    2 carrots peeled and sliced into rounds
Place in the center of the plate:
    1/4 cup low-calorie Italian dressing.*
Cover with vented plastic wrap.
Microcook on high 7 to 8 minutes.
Rotate twice.
Top with:
    3/4 cup plain yogurt
    1 tablespoon lemon juice
    1 teaspoon toasted onion flakes
    4 drops hot pepper sauce
    2 tablespoons grated Parmesan cheese, if desired
*Low-sodium and low-fat dressing is available.

- *1 stalk broccoli, sliced into 1/4" pieces*
- *2 carrots, peeled and sliced into rounds*
- *1/4 cup low-calorie Italian dressing**
- *3/4 cup plain yogurt*
- *1 tablespoon lemon juice*
- *1 teaspoon toasted onion flakes*
- *4 drops hot pepper sauce*
- *2 tablespoons grated Parmesan cheese, if desired*

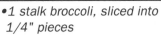

Vegetables - Putting the Bite on Cancer

Artichoke

Vitamin A & Potassium.
Serves 1. Microcook Time: 15 minutes.
Calories: 30. Fat: 0 g. Carbohydrates: 12 g. Protein: 3 g. Sodium: 35 mg.

•1 medium artichoke
•3 tablespoons water

Place in a 4-cup glass measure:
      1 medium artichoke, stem end up
      3 tablespoons water
Cover with vented plastic wrap.
Microcook on high 6 to 8 minutes.
Stand 5 minutes.
Hint: Add 1 teaspoon of water in plastic wrap.
Place flower end in center and pull ends to the top; twist ends. Microcook in custard cup.

Asparagus

Vitamin A, fiber, Folic Acid.
Serves 1. Microcook Time: 12 minutes.
Calories: 12. Fat: 0 g. Carbohydrates: 2 g. Protein: 1 g. Sodium: 1 mg.

•4 asparagus spears, cut into thirds

Place in a 4-cup glass measure:
      4 asparagus spears, cut into thirds
Cover with vented plastic wrap.
Microcook on high 5 1/2 minutes.
Stand 5 minutes.

Beets

Folic Acid.
Serves 2. Microcook Time: 15 minutes.
Calories: 27. Fat: 0 g. Carbohydrates: 6 g. Protein: 1 g. Sodium: 36 mg.

•3 beets (8 oz.)
•1/2 cup water

Place in a 4-cup glass measure:
      3 beets (8 oz.)
      1/2 cup water
Cover with vented plastic wrap.
Microcook on high 10 minutes.
Stand 5 minutes.

Broccoli

Vitamin C & Folic Acid.
Serves 2. Microcook Time: 11 minutes.
Calories: 20. Fat: 0 g. Carbohydrates: 4 g. Protein: 3 g. Sodium: 8 mg.

Place in a 4-cup glass measure:
    1 stalk broccoli, sliced into 1/2" pieces
    1 tablespoon water
Cover with vented plastic wrap.
Microcook on high 5 to 6 minutes.
Stir once.
Stand 5 minutes.

- *1 stalk broccoli, sliced into 1/2" pieces*
- *1 tablespoon water*

Brussels Sprouts

Vitamin C.
Serves 2. Microcook Time: 11 minutes.
Calories: 30. Fat: 0 g. Carbohydrates: 5 g. Protein: 4 g. Sodium: 8 mg.

Place in a 4-cup glass measure:
    1 cup Brussels sprouts
Cover with vented plastic wrap.
Microcook on high 5 minutes.
Stir once.
Stand 5 minutes.

- *1 cup Brussels sprouts*

Cabbage

Vitamin C.
Serves 4. Microcook Time: 17 minutes.
Calories: 19. Fat: 0 g. Carbohydrates: 4 g. Protein: 1 g. Sodium: 13 mg.

Cut into 8 wedges:
    1 small head cabbage
    2 tablespoons water
Cover with vented plastic wrap.
Microcook on high 10 minutes.
Stand 5 minutes.

- *1 small head cabbage*
- *2 tablespoons water*

Carrots

Vitamin A.
Serves 2. Microcook Time: 9 minutes.
Calories: 16. Fat: 0 g. Carbohydrates: 8 g. Protein: 0 g. Sodium: 20 mg.

•*1/2 lb. carrots* •*1 teaspoon water*

Slice into 1/4" circles:
    1/2 lb. carrots
Place carrots in a 4-cup glass measure with:
    1 teaspoon water
Cover with vented plastic wrap.
Microcook on high 3 to 4 minutes.
Stir once.
Stand 5 minutes.

Cauliflower

Vitamin C.
Serves 2. Microcook Time: 24 minutes.
Calories: 15. Fat: 0 g. Carbohydrates: 3 g. Protein: 2 g. Sodium: 10 mg.

•*1/2 head cauliflower*   *flowerettes (8 oz.)* •*2 tablespoons water*

Place in an 8-cup glass measure:
    1/2 head cauliflower flowerettes (8 oz.)
    2 tablespoons water
Cover with vented plastic wrap.
Microcook on high 8 minutes.
Stir once.
Stand 5 minutes.

Corn on the Cob

Vitamin A.
Serves 2. Microcook Time: 15 minutes.
Calories: 169. Fat: 3 g. Carbohydrates: 31 g. Protein: 5 g. Sodium: 0 mg.

Place on a microwave-safe rack:
    2 ears corn, not husked
Microcook on high 7 to 8 minutes.
Turn and **rotate** once.
Stand 5 minutes.

•*2 ears corn, not husked*

Green Beans

Vitamin A & C.
Serves 2. Microcook Time: 14 minutes.
Calories: 31. Fat: 0 g. Carbohydrates: 7 g. Protein: 2 g. Sodium: 5 mg.

Place in a 4-cup glass measure:
    8 oz. green beans
    1/4 cup low-sodium vegetable juice
Cover with vented plastic wrap.
Microcook on high 8 minutes.
Stir once.
Stand 5 minutes.

•*8 oz. green beans*
•*1/4 cup low-sodium vegetable juice*

Mushrooms

Potassium.
Serves 2. Microcook Time: 6 minutes.
Calories: 32. Fat: 0 g. Carbohydrates: 5 g. Protein: 3 g. Sodium: 17 mg.

Place in a 4-cup glass measure:
    4 oz. fresh mushrooms, cut in half
Cover with vented plastic wrap.
Microcook on high 2 minutes.
Stir once.
Stand 2 minutes.

•*4 oz. fresh mushrooms, cut in half*

Parsnips

Potassium.
Serves 2. Microcook Time: 12 minutes.
Calories: 66. Fat: 0 g. Carbohydrates: 15 g. Protein: 2 g. Sodium: 8 mg.

•*1 medium parsnip, cut in circles* •*2 tablespoons water*

Place in a 4-cup glass measure:
    1 medium parsnip, cut in circles
    2 tablespoons water
Cover with vented plastic wrap.
Microcook on high 8 minutes.
Stir once.
Stand 3 minutes.

Peas

Vitamin A.
Serves 4. Microcook Time: 12 minutes.
Calories: 62. Fat: 0 g. Carbohydrates: 10 g. Protein: 5 g. Sodium: 102 mg.

•*1 lb. peas, shelled* •*1 teaspoon water*

Place in a 4-cup glass measure:
    1 lb. peas, shelled
    1 teaspoon water
Cover with vented plastic wrap.
Microcook on high 5 to 6 minutes.
Stir once.
Stand 5 minutes.

Bell Peppers

Vitamin C.
Serves 2. Microcook Time: 7 minutes.
Calories: 18. Fat: 0 g. Carbohydrates: 3.8 g. Protein: 1 g. Sodium: 9 mg.

Place in a 4-cup glass measure:
    1 bell pepper, sliced
Cover with vented plastic wrap.
Microcook on high 4 minutes.
Stir once.
Stand 2 minutes.

•1 bell pepper, sliced

Potatoes

Vitamin C, fiber & Potassium
Serves 1. Microcook Time: 15 minutes.
Calories: 76. Fat: 0 g. Carbohydrates: 17 g. Protein: 2 g. Sodium: 3 mg.

Pierce with fork:
    1 baking potato
Place on a microwave-safe rack.
Microcook on high 4 to 6 minutes.
Turn and **Rotate** once.
Cover with aluminum foil or terry towel.
Stand 6 minutes.

•1 baking potato

Spinach

Vitamin A & C.
Serves 4. Microcook Time: 5 minutes.
Calories: 21. Fat: .5 g. Carbohydrates: 3.2 g. Protein: 2.7 g. Sodium: 45 mg.

Place in an 8-cup glass measure:
    8 oz. fresh spinach
Cover with vented plastic wrap.
Microcook on high 2 minutes.
Stand 2 minutes.

•8 oz. fresh spinach

Acorn Squash

Vitamin A.
Serves 2. Microcook Time: 15 minutes.
Calories: 48. Fat: .4 g. Carbohydrates: 11.5 g. Protein: 1 g. Sodium: 1 mg.

•*1 (10-oz.) acorn squash*

Pierce with a fork :
     1 (10-oz.) acorn squash
Place on a microwave-safe rack.
Microcook on high 8 to 10 minutes.
Turn and **rotate** once.
Wrap in foil.
Stand 5 minutes.

Tomatoes

Vitamin A & C.
Serves 4. Microcook Time: 7 minutes.
Calories: 26. Fat: .2 g. Carbohydrates: 5.5 g. Protein: 1.3 g. Sodium: 4 mg.

•*2 medium tomatoes,*   *quartered*

Place in a 4-cup glass measure:
     2 medium tomatoes, quartered
Cover with vented plastic wrap.
Microcook on high 2 1/2 minutes.
Stand 5 minutes.

Turnips

Vitamin C.
Serves 2. Microcook Time: 15 minutes.
Calories: 20. Fat: 0 g. Carbohydrates: 4 g. Protein: 1 g. Sodium: 25 mg.

Place in a 4-cup glass measure:
    2 turnips, sliced
Cover with vented plastic wrap.
Microcook on high 7 minutes.
Stir once.
Stand 5 minutes.

•*2 turnips, sliced*

Rutabagas

Vitamin A.
Serves 6. Microcook Time: 25 minutes.
Calories: 20. Fat: 0 g. Carbohydrates: 5 g. Protein: 1 g. Sodium: 3 mg.

Place in a 4-cup glass measure:
    1 (12-oz.) rutabaga, sliced
    1/4 cup water
Cover with vented plastic wrap.
Microcook on high 20 minutes.
Stir.
Stand 5 minutes.

•*1 (12-oz.) rutabaga, sliced*
•*1/4 cup water*

Yams

Vitamin A.
Serves 6. Microcook Time: 14 minutes.
Calories: 125. Fat: 0 g. Carbohydrates: 27 g. Protein: 3 g. Sodium: 12 mg.

Pierce with a fork :
    2 (13-oz.) yams
Place on a microwave-safe rack.
Microcook on high 6 minutes.
Turn and **rotate**.
Wrap in foil.
Stand 6 minutes.

•*2 (13-oz.) yams*

ENTREES

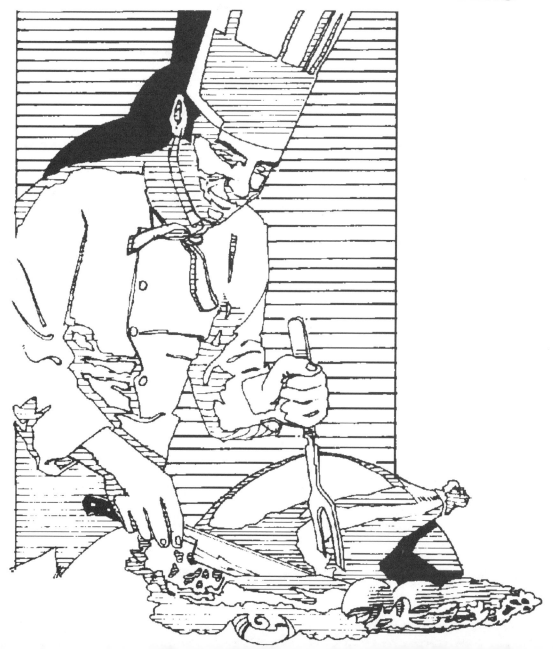

Meat Hints

Beef Cuts That Microcook Well

Steaks
- Tenderloin
- Lean Beef, Cubed
- Top Round
- Top Sirloin
- Flank

Roasts
- Beef Tip
- Beef Eye Round
- Top Round
- Rump
- Top Loin
- Rib Eye

Roast Hints

- Shop for meat cuts that are tender and boneless. They should be compact and uniform in shape, weighing 2 1/2 to 3 lbs.
- Meats cooked in the microwave do not brown. If cooked for short periods of time they will need a browning agent or sauce to look more appealing.
- A browning dish will add color.
- Remove excess fat from meats to help in even cooking. Microwaves are attracted to fat and will overcook that area.
- Place roast on rack in dish.
- Do not add liquid.
- Place waxed paper over top.
- Use medium low power 30%.
- Turn roast during cooking.
- Rotate meat during cooking.
- Irregularly shaped edges may overcook; shield with a small amount of foil.
- Use a microwave thermometer or sensor probe to check temperature: 140 degrees-rare, 160 degrees-medium, 170 degrees-well done.
- When meat is 5 to 10 degrees from being done, remove from oven and tent with foil; allow 10 minutes standing time.
- Sauces will add color and keep meat moist.
- Plastic cooking bags are good for less tender cuts of meat.

Marinades for Less Tender Cuts of Meat

Less tender cuts of meat like Pot Roast and Brisket work well when a marinade is used. These three are excellent as overnight marinades:

Oriental
- 1/2 cup light soy sauce
- 1/4 cup lime or orange juice
- 2 slices fresh gingerroot
- 1/4 teaspoon crushed red pepper
- 1 clove garlic, sliced

Italian
- 1 (8-oz. can) tomato puree
- 1/2 onion, chopped
- 2 cloves garlic, chopped
- 1/4 teaspoon oregano
- 1/4 teaspoon basil

Wine
- 1 1/2 cups red wine
- 1/4 cup oil
- 3 cloves garlic, sliced
- freshly ground pepper

Browning Agents for Meat

- Meats microcooked will not brown if cooked for short periods of time.
- A browning skillet may be used.
- The use of browning agents will make meats look more appetizing. For example:

• Light Soy Sauce	• Worcestershire Sauce (low-sodium)
• Teriyaki Sauce	• Taco Seasoning
• Barbecue Sauce	• Jams
• Margarine & Paprika	• Jelly
• Gravy Mix	• Preserves

Barbecued Beef

A dish that will be devoured with gusto.
Serves 10. Microcook Time: 3 hrs. Marinate 12 hours.
Calories: 451. Fat: 36 g. Carbohydrates: 6g. Protein: 27 g. Sodium: 262 mg.

- *3 to 3 1/2-lb. beef brisket*
- *3/4 cup red wine or cider vinegar*
- *3/4 cup catsup*
- *1/2 cup oil*
- *2 tablespoons smoke flavoring*
- *2 cups chopped onion*
- *1 teaspoon Dijon mustard*
- *1 teaspoon (low-sodium) Worcestershire sauce*
- *2 drops hot pepper sauce*
- *dash ground black pepper*

Marinate a 3 to 3 1/2-lb. beef brisket overnight in:
    3/4 cup red wine or cider vinegar
    3/4 cup catsup
    1/2 cup oil
    2 tablespoons smoke flavoring
    2 cups chopped onion
    1 teaspoon Dijon mustard
    1 teaspoon low-sodium Worcestershire sauce
    2 drops hot pepper sauce
    dash ground black pepper

Place meat in flour-coated microwave plastic cooking bag; use enclosed plastic strip to fasten loosely.
Cut slits for vents.
Put in a 10" round glass baking dish.
Microcook on medium low 2 1/2 hours.
Turn over once halfway through cooking time.
Rotate several times during cooking.
Stand 10 minutes before cutting.
Serve hot or cold.

Hamburger Patties

The All-American meal.
Serves 1 to 4. Microcook Time: 5 minutes.
Calories: 240. Fat: 17 g. Carbohydrates: 0 g. Protein: 20 g. Sodium: 50 mg.

Hint: Use 4 oz. of ground beef for an average-size serving. Shape the ground beef into a patty and press indentation in the center with your thumb. This will help the patty cook more evenly, especially in the center.

•*Ground beef*

One Patty

Place on a microwave-safe dish:
     1 (4-oz.) hamburger patty
Cover with waxed paper.
Microcook on high 1 minute, 15 seconds.
Turn and **rotate** after 1 minute.
Stand 2 minutes.

Two Patties

Place on a microwave-safe dish:
     2 (4-oz.) hamburger patties
Cover with waxed paper.
Microcook on high 2 minutes, 30 seconds.
Turn and **rotate** after 1 minute.
Stand 2 minutes.

Four Patties

Place on a microwave-safe dish:
     4 (4-oz.) patties
Cover with waxed paper.
Microcook on high 3 minutes, 30 seconds.
Turn and **rotate** after 2 minutes.
Stand 2 minutes.

Hint: To make your own browning mix for burgers:
Combine . . .
     2 teaspoons salt
     2 teaspoons flour
     1 teaspoon paprika
     1/4 teaspoon pepper
Also try adding your favorite flavor; garlic, onion, dry mustard or chili powder.

Flank Steak Provence

I adapted this succulent recipe from one that was served to me in Toulouse, France.
Serves 4. Microcook Time: 10 minutes.
Calories: 388. Fat: 27 g. Carbohydrates: 6 g. Protein: 21 g. Sodium: 71 mg.

- •1 lb. flank steak
- •juice of 1 lemon
- •2 teaspoons Herbes de Provence
- •1/4 teaspoon garlic powder
- •1/4 teaspoon onion powder
- •2 zucchini, sliced length-wise
- •2 carrots, sliced lengthwise
- •3/4 cup white wine
- •1/4 cup low-sodium chicken bouillon granules

Pound with a mallet until 1/3" thick:
      1 lb. flank steak
Place meat in a 12x8x2" glass casserole.
Pour over meat:
      juice of 1 lemon
Add . . .
      2 teaspoons Herbes de Provence*
      1/4 teaspoon garlic powder
      1/4 teaspoon onion powder
Cover with plastic wrap.
Stand 2 hours or overnight.
Place meat in a 10" skillet and allow meat to brown on a conventional range on one side only, about 5 minutes.
Transfer back to glass casserole.
Top meat with
      2 zucchini, sliced lengthwise
      2 carrots, sliced lengthwise
      3/4 cup white wine
      1/4 cup low-sodium chicken bouillon granules
Cover with vented plastic wrap.
Microcook on medium 20 to 23 minutes.
Stand 10 minutes.
Slice meat across the grain in 1/8" slices.
*Already mixed. Contains thyme, marjoram, rosemary, basil, fennel and sage.

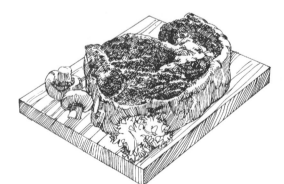

Pot Roast

We always had Pot Roast for Sunday dinner when I was a girl.
Serves 1/3 lb./person. Microcook Time: Approx. 45 minutes/lb.
Calories: 400. Fat: 28 g. Carbohydrates: 0 g. Protein: 38 g. Sodium: 67 mg.

Season surface of:
    2 to 3-lb. beef chuck, blade, arm or shoulder roast

With:
    1 tablespoon instant low-sodium beef bouillon granules

Place in plastic cooking bag:
    1 teaspoon flour
    1 teaspoon freshly ground pepper
    1/2 teaspoon paprika

Shake.

Add meat and **place** in an 11x7x1 1/2" glass baking dish.

Add . . .
    1/4 cup water

Close bag with strip enclosed in cooking bags.
Leave opening loose for venting.
Microcook on medium low.

Boneless chuck, 37 minutes per lb.
Arm, 27 to 33 minutes per lb.
Blade-in Blade, 23 to 29 minutes per lb.
Boneless Blade, 32 to 39 minutes per lb.
Boneless Shoulder, 41 to 48 minutes per lb.
Turn and **rotate** 3 times.
Stand 10 to 15 minutes.

- *2 to 3-lb. beef chuck, blade, arm or shoulder roast*
- *1 tablespoon instant low-sodium beef bouillon granules*
- *1 teaspoon flour*
- *1 teaspoon freshly ground pepper*
- *1/2 teaspoon paprika*
- *1/4 cup water*

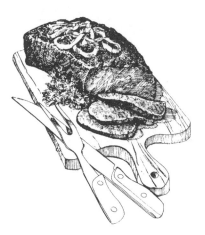

Chili Casserole

Great to serve after the game.
Serves 6. Microcook Time: 15 minutes.
Calories: 478. Fat: 26 g. Carbohydrates: 53 g. Protein: 13 g. Sodium: 1106 mg.

- *2 tablespoons margarine*
- *1/2 cup chopped onion*
- *1/2 cup chopped green pepper*
- *1 (15-oz.) can chili without beans*
- *1 (15-oz.) can chili beans in gravy*
- *1 (17-oz.) can whole kernel corn*
- *1 (2 1/2-oz.) can sliced ripe olives, drained*
- *1 (6-oz.) pkg. corn chips, crushed*

Combine in a 3-quart microwave casserole:
    2 tablespoons margarine
    1/2 cup chopped onion
    1/2 cup chopped green pepper
Microcook on high 2 to 3 minutes.
Add . . .
    1 (15-oz.) can chili without beans
    1 (15-oz.) can chili beans in gravy
    1 (17-oz.) can whole kernel corn
    1 (2 1/2-oz.) can sliced ripe olives, drained
    1 (6-oz.) pkg. corn chips, crushed
Mix well.
Cover with waxed paper.
Microcook on high 8 to 10 minutes.

Falafel Protein Ring

A great meat stretcher.
Serves 6. Microcook Time: 26 minutes.
Calories: 287. Fat: 7 g. Carbohydrates: 3 1g. Protein: 24 g. Sodium: 933 mg.

Combine in a 4-cup glass measure:
    1 (6-oz.) box falafel vegetable-burger mix
    3 tablespoons water
Stand 10 to 15 minutes.
Add . . .
    1/2 lb. lean ground beef
    1 egg
    2 cloves garlic
    1/2 onion, minced
    1/2 cup water
Stir.
Place in a 9" microwave ring mold.
Tip: If you do not have a ring mold, make your own.
Place an inverted 6-oz. custard cup in the center of an 8" round glass cake dish.
Pour mixture into ring.
Cover with waxed paper.
Microcook on high 6 to 7 minutes.
Stand 3 to 4 minutes.

> - *1 (6-oz.) box falafel vegetable-burger mix*
> - *3 tablespoons water*
> - *1/2 lb. lean ground beef*
> - *1 egg*
> - *2 cloves garlic*
> - *1/2 onion, minced*
> - *1/2 cup water*

Meat Loaf Ring

Serve with cooked peas in the center for a colorful dish.
Serves 6. Microcook Time: 15 minutes.
Calories: 271. Fat: 16 g. Carbohydrates: 10 g. Protein: 20 g. Sodium: 417 mg.

- *1 1/2 lbs. lean ground beef*
- *1/2 cup chopped onion*
- *1/2 cup chili sauce**
- *1/4 cup quick-cooking rolled oats*
- *1 egg*
- *1/2 teaspoon garlic powder*
- *1/2 teaspoon sodium-free seasoning mix*
- *1/2 teaspoon nutmeg*

Combine in a mixing bowl:
  1 1/2 lbs. lean ground beef
  1/2 cup chopped onion
  1/2 cup chili sauce*
  1/4 cup quick-cooking rolled oats
  1 egg
  1/2 teaspoon garlic powder
  1/2 teaspoon sodium-free seasoning mix
  1/2 teaspoon nutmeg
Mix well.
Press into a 9" round glass baking dish.
Hint: Make a small 2" hole in the center for even cooking, or place an inverted 6-oz. custard cup in the center.
Cover with waxed paper.
Microcook on high 9 to 10 minutes for a firm ring or
Microcook on medium 12 to 14 minutes for a juicy ring.
Stand 10 minutes.
*Use tomato puree to lower sodium content.

Sloppy Joes

I haven't met a kid yet who didn't love this one.
Serves 6. Microcook Time: 15 minutes.
Calories: 221. Fat: 8 g. Carbohydrates: 16 g. Protein: 21 g. Sodium: 671 mg.

Place in a microwave-safe colander over a 2-quart casserole:
  1 lb. lean ground beef
  1 onion, chopped
Cover with waxed paper.
Microcook on high 4 to 6 minutes.
Drain fat.
Place meat mixture in the 2-quart casserole.
Add . . .
  1 (10 3/4-oz.) can chicken gumbo soup
  3/4 cup light catsup
  1 teaspoon low-sodium Worcestershire
    sauce
  dash pepper
Microcook on high 3 1/2 to 5 minutes.
Stir twice.
Serve on hamburger buns.

- 1 lb. lean ground beef
- 1 onion, chopped
- 1 (10 3/4-oz.) can chicken gumbo soup
- 3/4 cup light catsup
- 1 teaspoon low-sodium Worcestershire sauce
- dash pepper

Stuffed Peppers

One of my family's favorites.
Serves 4. Microcook Time: 20 minutes.
Calories: 327. Fat: 16 g. Carbohydrates: 26 g. Protein: 22 g. Sodium: 383 mg.

Combine in a mixing bowl:
  1 lb. lean ground beef
  1/2 small onion, chopped
  1 tomato, chopped
  1 cup cooked rice
  2 tablespoons chili sauce
  1 teaspoon chili powder
Place mixture in:
  4 green peppers, cleaned, with stems and
    seeds removed
Place on microwave-safe roasting rack and dish.
Cover with waxed paper.
Microcook on high for 13 to 17 minutes until meat
is no longer pink.

- 1 lb. lean ground beef
- 1/2 small onion, chopped
- 1 tomato, chopped
- 1 cup cooked rice
- 2 tablespoons chili sauce
- 1 teaspoon chili powder
- 4 green peppers, cleaned, with stems and seeds removed

Creamy Beef Stroganoff

Beef Stroganoff at its best.
Serves 6. Microcook Time: 20 minutes.
Calories: 280. Fat: 13 g. Carbohydrates: 15 g. Protein: 22 g. Sodium: 480 mg.

- 1 lb. very lean ground beef
- 1/2 cup chopped onion
- 1 clove garlic, minced
- 1 (8-oz.) can mushrooms, drained
- 1 (10 3/4-oz.) can low-sodium cream of celery soup
- 3 tablespoons flour
- 1/4 teaspoon pepper
- 2 tablespoons sherry
- 1 cup light sour cream

Place in a microwave-safe plastic colander over a 2-quart glass casserole:

　　　1 lb. very lean ground beef

Cover with waxed paper.
Microcook on high 4 to 5 minutes.
Drain fat.
Place meat in the 2-quart glass casserole.
Add:

　　　1/2 cup chopped onion
　　　1 clove garlic, minced
　　　1 (8-oz.) can mushrooms, drained
　　　1 (10 3/4-oz.) can low-sodium cream of celery
　　　　soup
　　　3 tablespoons flour
　　　1/4 teaspoon pepper
　　　2 tablespoons sherry

Stir well.
Cover.
Microcook on high 10 to 13 minutes.
Stir.
Add . . .

　　　1 cup light sour cream
Serve over cooked rice or noodles.

Oriental Meatballs

An exciting way to dress up ground beef.
Serves 6. Microcook Time: 20 minutes.
Calories: 196. Fat: 12 g. Carbohydrates: 4 g. Protein: 15 g. Sodium: 71 mg.

Combine in a glass mixing bowl:
    1 lb. lean ground beef
    1/4 cup bread crumbs
    2 tablespoons chopped onion
    2 tablespoons sherry , if desired
    1/2 teaspoon ginger
    1/2 teaspoon garlic powder
    1 egg

- *1 lb. lean ground beef*
- *1/4 cup bread crumbs*
- *2 tablespoons chopped onion*
- *2 tablespoons sherry , if desired*
- *1/2 teaspoon ginger*
- *1/2 teaspoon garlic powder*
- *1 egg*

Mix ingredients well and **form** into 16 to 20 balls.
Place in an 11x7x1 1/2" glass baking dish.
Cover with waxed paper.
Microcook on high 10 to 14 minutes.
Rearrange and **turn**.
Rotate dish.
Serve with Oriental Sweet & Sour Sauce, page 203.

Cabbage Rolls

A tangy German favorite.
Serves 4. Microcook Time: Approx. 45 minutes/lb.
Calories: 177. Fat: 7 g. Carbohydrates: 18 g. Protein: 11 g. Sodium: 474 mg.

- 4 cabbage leaves
- 2 tablespoons water
- 1/2 lb. lean ground beef
- 3/4 cup cooked rice

- 1 tablespoon chopped onion
- 1 teaspoon horseradish
- 1 teaspoon garlic powder
- 1 (8-oz.) can low-sodium tomato sauce or juice
- 4 drops hot pepper sauce

Place in a 7x11x1 1/2" glass baking dish:
    4 cabbage leaves
    2 tablespoons water
Cover with vented plastic wrap.
Microcook on high 4 to 5 minutes.
Drain water.
Combine in a 4-cup glass measure:
    1/2 lb. lean ground beef
    3/4 cup cooked rice
    1 tablespoon chopped onion
    1 teaspoon horseradish
    1 teaspoon garlic powder
Place mixture in cabbage leaves and **roll**.
Fasten with a toothpick.
Return to baking dish.
Combine:
    1 (8-oz.) can low-sodium tomato sauce or
      juice
    4 drops hot pepper sauce
Pour over rolls.
Cover with vented plastic wrap.
Microcook on high 7 to 9 minutes.
Remove toothpicks.

Pork Hints

- When cooking pork it is important that the meat cooks evenly and thoroughly.
- Plastic cooking bags are very helpful because steam produced cooks the meat more evenly.
- Vented plastic wrap may be use instead of cooking bags.
- Pork should be cooked to 170 degrees.

Pork Cuts That Microcook well

Pork Type	Microcook Time	Power
• Bacon	3/4 to 1 minute per slice	High
• Loin Chops	20 minutes per lb.	Medium low
• Boneless Roasts	22 minutes per lb.	Medium low
• Fully Cooked Ham	10 to 15 minutes per lb.	Medium
• Ham Slices	25 to 35 minutes/2" thick slice	Medium

Ham

Serve with Cheesy Potatoes, page 116.
Serves 6. Microcook Time: 25 minutes.
Calories: 430. Fat: 22 g. Carbohydrates: 28 g. Protein: 30 g. Sodium: 1340 mg.

Cover the cut surface with plastic wrap and **shield** with foil any edges of:

    3-lb. ham

Microcook on medium 10 to 15 minutes per lb. for a 3-lb. ham.

Hint: Microcook on a microwave-safe meat rack and dish.

Canned hams require more time.

Turn ham halfway through cooking time.

Rotate dish several times.

Brush with sauce, if desired:

    3/4 cup apricot jam
    1/2 cup cassis syrup*

Stand 10 minutes.

*If cassis is not available, try raspberry.

- 3-lb. ham
- 3/4 cup apricot jam
- 1/2 cup cassis syrup*

Stuffed Pork Chops

Wonderful with cranberry-apple sauce. Try it!
Serves 4. Microcook Time: 60 minutes.
Calories: 584. Fat: 44 g. Carbohydrates: 21 g. Protein: 28 g. Sodium: 663 mg.

- *4 pork chops 1" thick (8 oz. each)*
- *1/2 cup crushed croutons*
- *1/4 cup chopped onion*
- *1/4 cup chopped celery*
- *1/2 teaspoon sage*
- *1/4 teaspoon pepper*
- *1/2 cup catsup*
- *2 tablespoons brown sugar*
- *2 teaspoons Dijon mustard*

Cut a 2 to 3" pocket in:
    4 pork chops 1" thick (8 oz. each)
Combine in an 8-cup measure:
    1/2 cup crushed croutons
    1/4 cup chopped onion
    1/4 cup chopped celery
    1/2 teaspoon sage
    1/4 teaspoon pepper
Fill chops with stuffing.
Arrange chops in a 12x8x2" microwave-safe dish, with thickest sides out and tails at center.
Combine in a 2-cup glass measure:
    1/2 cup catsup
    2 tablespoons brown sugar
    2 teaspoons Dijon mustard
Pour half of sauce over chops.
Cover with vented plastic wrap.
Microcook on medium low 36 to 38 minutes. (170 degrees)
Turn and **rotate** chops after 15 minutes.
Stand 5 minutes.

Jenny's Pork Chops

Serve with Jenny's Pork Chop Stuffing (page 153).
Serves 2/lb. Microcook Time: 25 minutes.
Calories: 284. Fat: 23 g. Carbohydrates: 0 g. Protein: 19 g. Sodium: 54 mg.

- *pork chops 3/4 to 1" thick (5 to 7 oz. each)*

Place on a microwave cooking rack and dish:
    pork chops 3/4 to 1" thick (5 to 7 oz. each)
Cover with vented plastic wrap.
Microcook at medium low:
20 minutes per lb. for 1 lb.
18 minutes per lb. for 2 lbs.
Turn and **rotate** halfway through cooking.

Scalloped Potatoes & Ham

Makes a great combo with Stir-Fry Corn (page 109).
Serves 6. Microcook Time: 25 minutes.
Calories: 248. Fat: 11 g. Carbohydrates: 25 g. Protein: 12 g. Sodium: 41 mg.

Place in a 4-cup glass measure:
    3 tablespoons margarine
Microcook on high 30 seconds.
Add . . .
    3 tablespoons flour
Stir.
Add . . .
    1 cup skim milk
Stir.
Microcook on high 2 1/2 to 3 minutes.
Set aside.
Place in a 2-quart casserole:
    4 red potatoes, sliced
    1/4 cup chopped celery leaves
    1 onion, sliced
    6 to 8 oz. cooked sliced ham, cut into 2"
       strips
    1 teaspoon celery seed
Pour cream sauce over potato mixture.
Cover with vented plastic wrap.
Microcook on high 12 to 16 minutes.
Rotate 4 times.

- 3 tablespoons margarine
- 3 tablespoons flour
- 1 cup skim milk
- 4 red potatoes, sliced
- 1/4 cup chopped celery leaves
- 1 onion, sliced
- 6 to 8 oz. cooked sliced ham, cut into 2" strips
- 1 teaspoon celery seed

Jenny's Pork Chop Stuffing

Daughter-in-law Jenny begs for this stuffing whenever I serve pork chops.
Serves 4. Microcook Time: 10 minutes.
Calories: 253. Fat: 7 g. Carbohydrates: 44 g. Protein: 7 g. Sodium: 592 mg.

Combine in a 1-quart casserole:
    1 (10 3/4-oz.) can low-sodium cream of
       celery soup
    2 Rome apples, peeled and chopped
    1 onion, chopped
    1 1/2 cups seasoned croutons
    2 tablespoons honey
Cover with vented plastic wrap.
Microcook on high 6 to 7 minutes.

- 1 (10 3/4-oz.) can low-sodium cream of celery soup
- 2 Rome apples, peeled and chopped
- 1 onion, chopped
- 1 1/2 cups seasoned croutons
- 2 tablespoons honey

Boneless Pork Loin

Try dressing this up with cinnamon apple slices.
Serves 8. Microcook Time: 2 hrs.
Calories: 414. Fat: 32 g. Carbohydrates: 0 g. Protein: 28 g. Sodium: 67 mg.

•*4 to 5-lb. roast*

Hint: Look for an even-shaped roast.
Place in a flour-coated plastic cooking bag.
Secure bag with plastic tie.
Place fat side down on a microwave meat roasting rack and dish:

       4 to 5-lb. roast

Microcook on medium low 22 minutes per lb.
Turn and **rotate** roast halfway through cooking time.
Check internal temperature in several places. A temperature of 170 degrees must be reached to assure pork is fully cooked.
Remove from oven; **cover** tightly with foil.
Stand 10 minutes.
Hint: Try with Jenny's Pork Chop Stuffing, page 153.

1 Chop Lamb Chop

Topping gives lamb a delectable flavor.
Serves 1. Microcook Time: 25 minutes.
Calories: 381. Fat: 26 g. Carbohydrates: 16 g. Protein: 20 g. Sodium: 64 mg.

•*1 lamb chop 1" thick*
•*2 tablespoons plain yogurt*
•*1 tablespoon brown sugar*
•*1/4 teaspoon rosemary*
•*dash garlic powder*
•*1 slice onion*

Place on a microwave-safe meat roasting rack and dish:

       1 lamb chop 1" thick

Combine and **spread** over chop:

       2 tablespoons plain yogurt
       1 tablespoon brown sugar
       1/4 teaspoon rosemary
       dash garlic powder

Place on top:

       1 slice onion

Cover with waxed paper.
Microcook on medium high 9 to 12 minutes.
Stand 5 minutes.

Mandarin Lamb Chops

Citrus flavors add pizazz!
Serves 4. Microcook Time: 30 minutes.
Calories: 515. Fat: 25 g. Carbohydrates: 55 g. Protein: 19 g. Sodium: 58 mg.

Arrange in microwave-safe 8" square dish with thickest side towards outside of dish:

    4 lamb chops, 1 1/4" thick

Cover with waxed paper.
Microcook on medium 10 minutes.
Drain off fat.
Turn chops over.
Arrange over chops:

    1 (11-oz.) can mandarin oranges

Combine in a 4-cup glass measure:

    1/4 cup brown sugar
    1/4 cup orange marmalade
    1/4 cup apricot preserves
    2 tablespoons lemon juice

Pour mixture over chops.
Re-cover with waxed paper.
Microcook on medium 8 to 10 minutes, until tender.

- 4 lamb chops, 1 1/4" thick
- 1 (11-oz.) can mandarin oranges
- 1/4 cup brown sugar
- 1/4 cup orange marmalade
- 1/4 cup apricot preserves
- 2 tablespoons lemon juice
- 1 tablespoon cornstarch

Leg of Lamb with Cranberry Sauce

This is so festive! Try it for a holiday.
Serves 12. Microcook Time: 2 hrs.
Calories: 208. Fat: 7 g. Carbohydrates: 8 g. Protein: 26 g. Sodium: 66 mg.

- *3 to 4-lb. boneless leg of lamb*
- *1 cup jellied cranberry-raspberry sauce*
- *1/4 cup dry white wine*
- *1/4 cup orange juice*
- *1 teaspoon mace*

Place on a microwave meat roasting rack and dish, fat side down:

    3 to 4-lb. boneless leg of lamb

Combine in an 8-cup glass measure:

    1 cup jellied cranberry-raspberry sauce
    1/4 cup dry white wine
    1/4 cup orange juice
    1 teaspoon mace

Cover with waxed paper.
Microcook on high 2 1/2 to 3 minutes.
Brush sauce over lamb.
Cover lamb with waxed paper.
Microcook on medium low:
14 to 17 minutes/lb. rare.
18 to 21 minutes/lb. medium.
22 to 26 minutes/lb. well done.
Baste during cooking.
Rotate dish 1/4.
Turn fat side up halfway through cooking.
Shield any edges that are overcooking with foil.
Check internal temperature for completion of cooking.
Remove 5 degrees before desired doneness.
Rare = 140 degrees.
Medium = 160 degrees.
Well done = 170 degrees.
Stand 10 minutes.

Fish Hints

Fillet & Steak

- Fish requires a short cooking time; overcooking will make fish tough and dry.
- Poaching in a liquid is an ideal way to cook, as this method adjusts well to microcooking.
- Fat fish (salmon, tuna and mackerel) may be cooked without sauce.
- Lean fish (cod, sole, red snapper and perch) may be cooked with a sauce; cover tightly during cooking time. Average serving of fillet is 4 to 6 oz.
- Fish is done when flesh is opaque, firm and flakes easily with a fork.
- Fillets are boneless, lengthwise slices; fish steaks are cross-cut slices.
- When microcooking, place the thickest portion toward the outside of the dish.
- Try to overlap thinner pieces for more even cooking.
- **Cover** with vented plastic wrap for poaching.
- **Defrost** 1-lb. fillet, **microcook** on medium low for 4 to 6 minutes, **turn** once.
- **Microcook** 1-lb. fillet on high 4 to 5 minutes.
- **Microcook** 1-lb. fillet in sauce, on high 5 to 8 minutes.
- **Stand** 3 to 5 minutes.

Whole Fish

- Prick the skin of whole fish to avoid a buildup of pressure.
- Use a vented plastic cover and make sure there is a small vent on one side to allow steam to escape.
- Microcook 1 1/2-lb. whole fish on high 5 to 9 minutes.

Breaded Fish

- Place on a rack to maintain texture; do not cover.

Shell Fish

- Defrost 5 to 6 minutes/lb. on high.
- Microcook in a baking dish; cover with vented plastic wrap.
- Microcook on high 3 to 5 minutes/lb.
- Lobster (6 to 8-oz.), microcook on high 3 to 5 minutes.

Cod Amandine

Almonds add crunch and flavor.
Serves 4. Microcook Time: 10 minutes.
Calories: 206. Fat: 12 g. Carbohydrates: 1 g. Protein: 22 g. Sodium: 149 mg.

- 2 tablespoons butter
- 2 tablespoon lemon juice
- 1 teaspoon low-sodium Worcestershire sauce
- freshly ground pepper
- 1 lb. cod fillets
- toasted slivered almonds

Place in a 9" round microwave-safe baking dish:
    2 tablespoons butter
Microcook on high 30 seconds.
Stir in:
    2 tablespoon lemon juice
    1 teaspoon low-sodium Worcestershire sauce
    freshly ground pepper
Add . . .
    1 lb. cod fillets
Cover with vented plastic wrap.
Microcook on high 3 minutes.
Rotate.
Microcook on high 2 to 3 minutes until fish flakes easily with a fork.
Stand 3 minutes.
Top with:
    toasted slivered almonds

Tomato-Basil Halibut

Try growing your own basil.
Serves 2. Microcook Time: 10 minutes.
Calories: 211. Fat: 7 g. Carbohydrates: 9 g. Protein: 28 g. Sodium: 218 mg.

- 1 small onion, chopped
- 1 rib of celery, sliced
- 2 Roma tomatoes, sliced
- 6 mushrooms, sliced
- 1/4 green pepper, chopped
- juice of 1/2 lemon
- 2 fresh basil leaves, chopped
- 1 (8-oz.) halibut

Combine in an 8-cup glass measure:
    1 small onion, chopped
    1 rib of celery, sliced
    2 Roma tomatoes, sliced
    6 mushrooms, sliced
    1/4 green pepper, chopped
    juice of 1/2 lemon
    2 fresh basil leaves, chopped
Cover with vented plastic wrap.
Microcook on high 3 minutes.
Place in an 11x7x1 1/2" glass casserole:
    1 (8-oz.) halibut
Pour vegetable mixture over fish.
Cover with vented plastic wrap.
Microcook on high 3 to 4 minutes.

Halibut with Apple/Ginger Sauce

Wonderful flavor.
Serves 2. Microcook Time: 10 minutes.
Calories: 283 Fat: 7 g. Carbohydrates: 20 g. Protein: 26 g. Sodium: 205 mg.

Combine in an 8-cup glass measure:
    1 Rome apple, chopped
    1 apricot, chopped
    1 onion
    1/2 cup red wine
    1 clove garlic, chopped
    1/2 teaspoon grated fresh gingerroot
Cover with vented plastic wrap.
Microcook on high 4 minutes.
Place in an 11x7x1 1/2" glass casserole:
    8-oz. halibut
Pour apple mixture over fish.
Cover with vented plastic.
Microcook on high 3 to 4 minutes.
Stand 2 to 3 minutes.

- *1 Rome apple, chopped*
- *1 apricot, chopped*
- *1 onion*
- *1/2 cup red wine*
- *1 clove garlic, chopped*
- *1/2 teaspoon grated fresh gingerroot*
- *8-oz. halibut*

Orange Roughy

Lime and grape juices add a subtle flavor.
Serves 4. Microcook Time: 10 minutes.
Calories: 74. Fat: 1 g. Carbohydrates: 2 g. Protein: 14 g. Sodium: 111 mg.

Place in a 9" round glass baking dish:
    2 orange roughy fillets (1 lb.)
    1 tablespoon dill weed
    2 tablespoons lime juice
    2 tablespoons white grape juice
    1 teaspoon parsley
    dash paprika
Cover with waxed paper.
Microcook on high 4 to 5 minutes, until opaque.
Turn over.
Stand 3 minutes.
Serve with dill juice and/or lemon juice, if desired.
Hint: Slices of orange, lemon, lime and fresh
parsley make a nice garnish.

- *2 orange roughy fillets (1 lb.)*
- *1 tablespoon dill weed*
- *2 tablespoons lime juice*
- *2 tablespoons white grape juice*
- *1 teaspoon parsley*
- *dash paprika*

Cajun Fish

Hot and delicious.
Serves 2. Microcook Time: 5 minutes.
Calories: 70. Fat: 1 g. Carbohydrates: 2 g. Protein: 13 g. Sodium: 235 mg.

•1 (8-oz.) orange roughy fillet
•2 teaspoons Cajun seasoning*

Preheat microwave browning skillet according to manufacturer's directions.
Coat:
      1 (8-oz.) orange roughy fillet
with:
      2 teaspoons Cajun seasoning*
Place on hot browner.
Microcook on high 2 to 3 minutes.
Turn once halfway through cooking time.
Stand 2 minutes on browner.
Hint: Fish should flake with a fork.
Hint: You may want to add a few drops of red pepper sauce for a hotter flavor.
* Cajun seasoning may be purchased, or see recipe below.

Carol's Cajun Seasoning

Seasoning for any Cajun dishes.

•1/2 teaspoon cayenne
  pepper
•1/2 teaspoon white pepper
•1 teaspoon garlic powder
•1/4 teaspoon onion powder
•1/4 teaspoon paprika
•1/4 teaspoon thyme
•dash salt, optional

Combine . . .
    1/2 teaspoon cayenne pepper
    1/2 teaspoon white pepper
    1 teaspoon garlic powder
    1/4 teaspoon onion powder
    1/4 teaspoon paprika
    1/4 teaspoon thyme
    dash salt, optional

Poached Salmon

Poaching adds an intriguing flavor.
Serves 4. Microcook Time: 15 minutes.
Calories: 228. Fat: 7 g. Carbohydrates: 3 g. Protein: 27 g. Sodium: 119 mg.

Place in a 7x11x1 1/2" glass baking dish:
    1 cup white wine
    1/2 lemon, sliced
    freshly ground pepper
Microcook on high 3 to 4 minutes until boiling.

Add . . .
    1(1-lb.) salmon fillet
Cover with vented plastic wrap.
Microcook on high 3 1/2 to 6 minutes.

Rotate once.
Stand 3 minutes.
Hint: Fish should flake easily with a fork.

- 1 cup white wine
- 1/2 lemon, sliced
- freshly ground pepper
- 1 (1-lb.) salmon fillet

Salmon Steaks

Try serving with Potpourri of Summer Vegetables (page 126).
Serves 4. Microcook Time: 10 minutes.
Calories: 433. Fat: 27 g. Carbohydrates: 3 g. Protein: 43 g. Sodium: 189 mg.

Combine . . .
    1/4 cup olive oil
    1/4 cup lemon juice
    1/4 cup dill
    dash hot pepper sauce
Marinate for 2 hours:
    2 (8-oz.) salmon steaks
Place steaks in 9" round or oval glass baking dish.

Cover with vented plastic wrap.
Microcook on high 5 to 7 minutes.

Turn once.
Stand 3 minutes.
Hint: Fish should flake easily with a fork.

- 1/4 cup olive oil
- 1/4 cup lemon juice
- 1/4 cup dill
- dash hot pepper sauce
- 2 (8-oz.) salmon steaks

Oriental Swordfish

Swordfish prepared with rich Oriental flavors.
Serves 4. Microcook Time: 10 minutes. Marinate: 10 hours.
Calories: 302. Fat: 20 g. Carbohydrates: 8 g. Protein: 23 g. Sodium: 690 mg.

- •*1/4 cup olive oil*
- •*1/4 cup teriyaki sauce*
- •*2 tablespoons garlic red wine vinegar*
- •*1 tablespoon honey*
- •*1 slice orange with peel*
- •*1 lb. swordfish fillet*

Combine . . .
>   1/4 cup olive oil
>   1/4 cup teriyaki sauce
>   2 tablespoons garlic red wine vinegar
>   1 tablespoon honey
>   1 slice orange with peel

Marinate for 2 hours:
>   1 lb. swordfish fillet

Place swordfish in 9" round microwave-safe baking dish.
Cover with vented plastic wrap.
Microcook on high 4 to 6 minutes.
Stand 3 minutes.
Hint: Fish should be very hot in center and flake easily with a fork.

Swordfish Fillet

The perfect fillet.
Serves 4. Microcook Time: 11 minutes.
Calories: 174. Fat: 4 g. Carbohydrates: 0 g. Protein: 28 g. Sodium: 102 mg.

- •*1 swordfish fillet (1 lb.)*
- •*freshly grated Parmesan cheese*

Preheat a browning skillet according to manufacturer's directions.
Place on hot browner:
>   1 swordfish fillet (1 lb.)

Microcook on high 3 to 4 minutes.
Turn after 1 minute.
Rotate once.
Stand 2 minutes on browner.
Sprinkle with:
>   freshly grated Parmesan cheese

Walleye Pike

Fresh from the land of 10,000 lakes.
Serves 6. Microcook Time: 15 minutes
Calories: 11. Fat: 1 g. Carbohydrates: 2 g. Protein: 20 g. Sodium: 58 mg.

Place in an 11x7x1 1/2" glass dish:
    1 (1 1/2-lb.) walleye pike fillets
Pour poaching mixture over fish (see below).
Cover with vented plastic wrap.
Microcook on high 8 to 10 minutes.
Hint: Fish should flake easily with a fork.
Stand 3 minutes.

> •*1 (1 1/2-lb.) walleye pike fillets*

Poaching Mixtures

Wine	Creamy
Combine . . .	**Combine . . .**
•1/2 cup white wine	•1/2 cup half-&-half (12% cream)
•6 mushrooms, sliced	•1/4 cup dry white wine
•1 tablespoon chopped onion	•1 tablespoon lemon juice
•1/4 teaspoon garlic powder	•1/4 teaspoon tarragon
•1/8 teaspoon dry mustard	•freshly ground pepper
•1/8 teaspoon grated lemon peel	•dash fennel

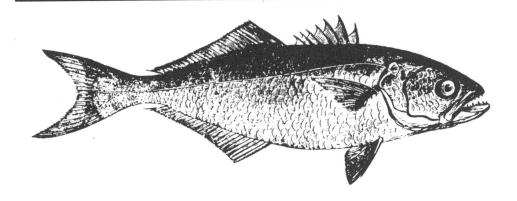

Warroad Minnesota's Walleye Pike

From Warroad, Minnesota, where they really know how to prepare Walleye.
Serves 2. Microcook Time: 10 minutes.
Calories: 282. Fat: 14 g. Carbohydrates: 5 g. Protein: 29 g. Sodium: 204 mg.

- 2 tablespoons butter
- 6 to 8 fresh mushrooms, sliced
- 1/4 onion, chopped
- 1 clove garlic, minced
- 1/4 cup white wine
- 2 (6 to 8-oz.) walleye fillets

Place in a 9" round glass baking dish:
    2 tablespoons butter
Microcook on high 1 minute.
Add . . .
    6 to 8 fresh mushrooms, sliced
    1/4 onion, chopped
    1 clove garlic, minced
    1/4 cup white wine
Top with:
    2 (6 to 8-oz.) walleye fillets
Cover with vented plastic wrap.
Microcook on high 3 to 4 minutes per lb.
Rotate once.
Hint: Fish should flake easily with a fork.

Tommy's Terrific Tuna

My grandson Tommy likes this casserole.
Serves 6. Microcook Time: 25 minutes.
Calories: 309. Fat: 14 g. Carbohydrates: 25 g. Protein: 21 g. Sodium: 781 mg.

- 2 cups (8 oz.) macaroni, cooked
- 2 (7 1/2-oz.) cans water-packed tuna, drained
- 1 (10 3/4-oz.) can low-sodium cream of mushroom soup
- 1 (4-oz.) can mushrooms, stems & pieces, drained
- 1/2 cup skim milk
- 1/3 cup shredded Cheddar cheese

Place in a 3-quart microwave-safe dish:
    2 cups (8 oz.) macaroni, cooked
    2 (7 1/2-oz.) cans water-packed tuna, drained
    1 (10 3/4-oz.) can low-sodium cream of mushroom soup
    1 (4-oz.) can mushrooms, stems & pieces, drained
    1/2 cup skim milk
    1/3 cup shredded Cheddar cheese
Cover with vented plastic wrap.
Microcook on high 3 to 5 minutes.
Stand.

White Fish Amandine

Great with Asparagus (page 103) and Honey Orange Carrots (page 105).
Serves 4. Microcook Time: 15 minutes.
Calories: 180. Fat: 8 g. Carbohydrates: 2 g. Protein: 23 g. Sodium: 96 mg.

Place in an 11x7x1 1/2" glass dish:
    1 lb. halibut
Add . . .
    2 tablespoons dry white wine
    1 tablespoon lemon juice
    freshly ground pepper.
Cover with vented plastic wrap.
Microcook on high 3 minutes.
Turn.
Microcook on high 2 to 3 minutes until fish flakes easily with a fork.
Add . . .
    1/4 cup toasted slivered almonds
Hint: Almonds may be toasted by placing them in a 9" glass pie plate and microcooking them on high for 2 to 3 minutes; **stir** twice.
Cover.
Stand 2 minutes.

- *1 lb. halibut*
- *2 tablespoons dry white wine*
- *1 tablespoon lemon juice*
- *freshly ground pepper*
- *1/4 cup toasted slivered almonds*

Crab Supreme

Rich and wonderful.
Serves 4. Microcook Time: 20 minutes.
Calories: 338. Fat: 19 g. Carbohydrates: 24 g. Protein: 21 g. Sodium: 809 mg.

- 2 tablespoons margarine
- 2 tablespoons flour
- 3/4 teaspoon white pepper
- 1 cup half-&-half (12% cream)*
- 1 teaspoon lemon juice
- 2 teaspoons low-sodium Worcestershire sauce
- 2 tablespoons minced green pepper
- 2 tablespoons minced onion
- 1 egg, beaten
- 1 (6-oz.) can crabmeat, drained and flaked
- 1/2 cup crushed croutons
- 2 tablespoons freshly grated Parmesan cheese

Place in a 1 1/2-quart casserole:
>2 tablespoons margarine

Microcook on high 30 seconds.
Add . . .
>2 tablespoons flour
>3/4 teaspoon white pepper

Stir.
Add . . .
>1 cup half-&-half (12% cream)*

Stir.
Add . . .
>1 teaspoon lemon juice
>2 teaspoons low-sodium Worcestershire sauce
>2 tablespoons minced green pepper
>2 tablespoons minced onion

Microcook on high 3 to 3 1/2 minutes, until thickened.
Stir twice.
Stir a little of the hot mixture into
>1 egg, beaten

Add egg to rest of sauce.
Stir.
Microcook on medium low 1 minute.
Stir into sauce
>1 (6-oz.) can crabmeat, drained and flaked

Divide mixture among 4 microwave-safe serving dishes.
Combine . . .
>1/2 cup crushed croutons
>2 tablespoons freshly grated Parmesan cheese

Sprinkle over top.
Microcook on high 3 to 4 minutes.
*Skim milk lowers fat.

Scallops St. Jacques Au Gratin

Perfectly elegant.
Serves 4. Microcook Time: 25 minutes.
Calories: 245. Fat: 18 g. Carbohydrates: 9 g. Protein: 13 g. Sodium: 268 mg.

Place in an 8" round glass dish:
    8 oz. bay scallops
Top with:
    2 tablespoons white wine
Cover with vented plastic wrap.
Microcook on high 2 to 4 minutes.
Place in 4-cup glass measure:
    3 tablespoons margarine
Microcook on high 30 to 45 seconds.
Add . . .
    6 fresh mushrooms, sliced
    1 teaspoon lemon juice
    1/2 teaspoon onion powder
Microcook on high 2 to 3 minutes.
Stir in:
    3 tablespoons flour
Add . . .
    3/4 cup half-&-half (12% cream)
    1/2 teaspoon nutmeg
Stir.
Microcook on medium 2 to 3 minutes.
Add . . .
    1/4 cup shredded Swiss cheese
Microcook on medium 2 minutes.
Divide scallops among four (10-oz.) custard cups.
Top with cheese sauce.
Sprinkle with:
    2 tablespoons grated Parmesan cheese
Microcook on high 1 1/2 to 2 1/2 minutes.

- 8 oz. bay scallops
- 2 tablespoons white wine
- 3 tablespoons margarine
- 6 fresh mushrooms, sliced
- 1 teaspoon lemon juice
- 1/2 teaspoon onion powder
- 3 tablespoons flour
- 3/4 cup half-&-half (12% cream)
- 1/2 teaspoon nutmeg
- 1/4 cup shredded Swiss cheese
- 2 tablespoons grated Parmesan cheese

Shrimp in Cheese Sauce

A divine way to prepare shrimp.
Serves 4. Microcook Time: 35 minutes.
Calories: 319. Fat: 6 g. Carbohydrates: 45 g. Protein: 20 g. Sodium: 1226 mg.

- *2 cups very hot water*
- *1 cup uncooked long-grain rice*
- *1 (10 3/4-oz.) can Cheddar cheese soup*
- *2 tablespoons white wine*
- *6 large fresh mushrooms, sliced*
- *8 oz. frozen cooked shrimp, thawed*
- *1/2 teaspoon lemon pepper*
- *dash celery seed*

Combine in 2-quart casserole:
    2 cups very hot water
    1 cup uncooked long-grain rice,
Cover with vented plastic wrap.
Microcook on high 5 minutes.
Microcook on medium low 15 to 17 minutes.
Stand 6 minutes.
Fluff with fork when ready to serve.
Re-cover.
Combine in 1 1/2-quart casserole:
    1 (10 3/4-oz.) can Cheddar cheese soup
    2 tablespoons white wine
    6 large fresh mushrooms, sliced
    8 oz. frozen cooked shrimp, thawed
    1/2 teaspoon lemon pepper
    dash celery seed
Microcook on high 4 to 6 minutes.
Serve over rice.

`100%` `30%` `100%`

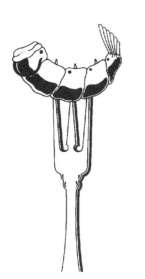 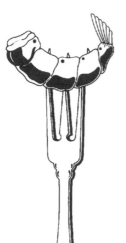 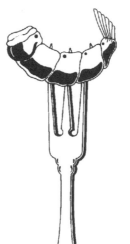 

Shrimp Creole

Shrimp served the only way - Creole style!
Serves 8. Microcook Time: 15 minutes.
Calories: 91. Fat: 1 g. Carbohydrates: 4 g. Protein: 14 g. Sodium: 174 mg.

Combine in a 2-quart glass casserole:
    2 fresh tomatoes, chopped
    6 fresh mushrooms, sliced
    1/2 cup chopped green pepper
    1 rib celery, sliced
    1/2 cup sliced onion
    1 clove garlic, minced
    3/4 teaspoon thyme
    1/2 cup white grape juice or white wine
    1 teaspoon instant low-sodium chicken
      bouillon granules
    3 drops hot pepper sauce
Cover with vented plastic wrap.
Microcook on high 8 to 10 minutes.
Add . . .
    1 lb. raw shrimp, shelled and deveined
Re-cover.
Microcook on high 3 to 5 minutes, until shrimp is
pink and opaque.
Stand 5 minutes.
Serve over White Rice, page 194.

- 2 fresh tomatoes, chopped
- 6 fresh mushrooms, sliced
- 1/2 cup chopped green pepper
- 1 rib celery, sliced
- 1/2 cup sliced onion
- 1 clove garlic, minced
- 3/4 teaspoon thyme
- 1/2 cup white grape juice or white wine
- 1 teaspoon instant low-sodium chicken bouillon granules
- 3 drops hot pepper sauce
- 1 lb. raw shrimp, shelled and deveined

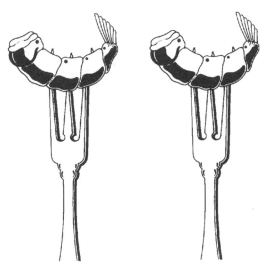
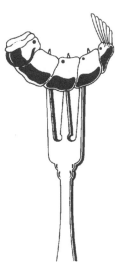
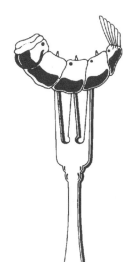

Broccoli & Chicken

A quick, easy and satisfying combination.
Serves 2. Microcook Time: 10 minutes.
Calories: 352. Fat: 22 g. Carbohydrates: 12 g. Protein: 29 g. Sodium: 282 mg.

- 1 (10-oz.) pkg. chopped broccoli, thawed
- 1 (5 1/2-oz.) can chicken chunks
- 1 tablespoon margarine
- 1/2 cup skim milk
- 1 tablespoon flour
- 1/2 teaspoon low-sodium chicken bouillon granules
- 1/4 teaspoon dry mustard
- dash paprika
- dash pepper
- 1/2 cup shredded Cheddar cheese

Spread in a 1-quart glass casserole:
> 1 (10-oz.) pkg. chopped broccoli, thawed

Top with:
> 1 (5 1/2-oz.) can chicken chunks

Cover lightly with plastic wrap.

Microcook on high 1 1/2 minutes.

Place in 2-cup measure:
> 1 tablespoon margarine

Microcook on high 10 seconds.

Stir in:
> 1/2 cup skim milk
> 1 tablespoon flour
> 1/2 teaspoon low-sodium chicken bouillon granules
> 1/4 teaspoon dry mustard
> dash paprika
> dash pepper

Microcook on medium 2 1/2 to 3 minutes until thickened; do not boil.

Stir in:
> 1/2 cup shredded Cheddar cheese

Pour mixture over chicken and broccoli.

Cover loosely with vented plastic wrap.

Microcook on medium 3 to 4 minutes or until heated through.

Cajun Chicken with Rice

Try serving with a spinach salad and Pepper Cream Dressing (page 97).
Serves 2. Microcook Time: 10 minutes.
Calories: 314. Fat: 7 g. Carbohydrates: 32 g. Protein: 30 g. Sodium: 464 mg.

Place between 2 pieces of waxed paper:
      1 whole boned, skinless chicken breast
Pound with a mallet until approximately 1/4" thick.
Sprinkle with:
      1 tablespoon Cajun seasoning*
Turn.
Cover with waxed paper.
Pound with mallet.
Remove waxed paper.
Roll chicken into a cylinder lengthwise.
Place in a microwave-safe 9" round baking dish:
      1 cup cooked seasoned rice**
Top with chicken.
Cover with vented plastic wrap.
Microcook on medium high 3 to 4 minutes until chicken is no longer pink.
*Cajun seasoning may be purchased or you may make your own, page 160.
**Season rice with onion and garlic powder.

> •1 whole boned, skinless chicken breast
> •2 tablespoons Cajun seasoning*
> •1 cup cooked seasoned rice

Chicken Divan

An excellent company dish.
Serves 4. Microcook Time: 25 minutes.
Calories: 583. Fat: 29 g. Carbohydrates: 34 g. Protein: 48 g. Sodium: 1396 mg.

- 2 whole boned, skinless chicken breasts
- 2 (10-oz.) pkgs. chopped broccoli, thawed
- 8 oz. sliced process cheese*
- 1 (10 1/2-oz.) can low-sodium cream of mushroom soup
- 1 (4-oz.) can whole mushrooms, drained
- 1 teaspoon low-sodium Worcestershire sauce
- 2 tablespoons white grape juice
- dash white pepper
- 1 cup crushed seasoned croutons**

Place on a 9" round glass plate:
> 2 whole boned, skinless chicken breasts

Cover with waxed paper.

Microcook on medium high 8 minutes.

Line a 12x8x2" casserole dish with:
> 2 (10-oz.) pkgs. chopped broccoli, thawed

Top broccoli with cooked chicken.

Top chicken with:
> 8 oz. sliced process cheese*

Combine . . .
> 1 (10 1/2-oz.) can low-sodium cream of mushroom soup
> 1 (4-oz.) can whole mushrooms, drained
> 1 teaspoon low-sodium Worcestershire sauce
> 2 tablespoons white grape juice
> dash white pepper

Pour soup mixture over chicken.

Sprinkle with:
> 1 cup crushed seasoned croutons**

Microcook on high 8 minutes.

Microcook on medium 4 to 6 minutes.

*Low-fat and low-sodium cheese is available.

**Use unseasoned croutons for lower sodium.

Chicken Royal

Mother always served Chicken Royal on my birthday.
Serves 6. Microcook Time: 20 minutes.
Calories: 249. Fat: 7 g. Carbohydrates: 32 g. Protein: 15 g. Sodium: 536 mg.

Combine in a 3-quart microwave-safe casserole:
    2 cups cooked rice
    1 whole chicken breast, cooked and cubed
    1 (10 3/4-oz.) can low-sodium cream of
      chicken soup
    1 (8-oz.) can sliced water chestnuts,
      drained
    1 (4-oz.) jar whole mushrooms, drained
    1/4 cup chopped celery
    1/4 cup chopped green pepper
    1/4 cup frozen peas
    1 (2-oz.) jar pimiento, drained
    3/4 teaspoon onion powder
    dash pepper
Cover with vented plastic wrap.
Microcook on high 12 to 14 minutes.
Stand 5 minutes.

100%

- *2 cups cooked rice*
- *1 whole chicken breast, cooked and cubed*
- *1 (10 3/4-oz.) can low-sodium cream of chicken soup*
- *1 (8-oz.) can sliced water chestnuts, drained*
- *1 (4-oz.) jar whole mushrooms, drained*
- *1/4 cup chopped celery*
- *1/4 cup chopped green pepper*
- *1/4 cup frozen peas*
- *1 (2-oz.) jar pimiento, drained*
- *3/4 teaspoon onion powder*
- *dash pepper*

Chicken in Lemon Sauce

Fresh lemon will give a tangy, fascinating flavor!
Serves 4. Microcook Time: 35 minutes.
Calories: 359. Fat: 13 g. Carbohydrates: 9 g. Protein: 50 g. Sodium: 203 mg.

- 2 carrots, sliced
- 2 ribs celery, sliced
- 3 green onions, sliced
- 1 tablespoon fresh parsley
- 2 tablespoons white wine
- 2 tablespoons lemon juice
- 1 teaspoon low-sodium chicken bouillon granules
- 1/2 teaspoon teriyaki sauce
- 1/2 teaspoon dill weed
- 1/2 teaspoon basil
- dash thyme
- dash pepper
- 1 fryer chicken, cut up
- 1 lemon, thinly sliced

Combine in an 8-cup glass measure:
    2 carrots, sliced
    2 ribs celery, sliced
    3 green onions, sliced
    1 tablespoon fresh parsley
    2 tablespoons white wine
    2 tablespoons lemon juice
    1 teaspoon low-sodium chicken bouillon granules
    1/2 teaspoon teriyaki sauce
    1/2 teaspoon dill weed
    1/2 teaspoon basil
    dash thyme
    dash pepper
Cover with vented plastic wrap.
Microcook on high 2 minutes.
Stir once.

Arrange in 8x12x2" glass dish:
    1 fryer chicken, cut up
Hint: Remove skin to reduce fat and calories.
Hint: Place largest pieces toward outside.
Place on top of chicken:
    1 lemon, thinly sliced

Pour sauce over chicken.
Cover with waxed paper.
Microcook on high 15 to 18 minutes; **rearrange** and **baste** every 4 minutes.

Microcook on medium 5 to 10 minutes, until vegetables are tender.

Stand 5 to 8 minutes.
Hint: Chicken is done when juices run clear.

Stir-Fry Chicken

This recipe uses a special browning dish.
Serves 4. Microcook Time: 15 minutes. Marinate: 12 hours.
Calories: 177. Fat: 4 g. Carbohydrates: 17 g. Protein: 16 g. Sodium: 768 mg.

Combine in a mixing bowl:
    1 whole boned, skinless chicken breast, cut
      into 1/4" strips
    1/4 cup teriyaki marinade
    1/4 cup dry sherry
    1 teaspoon grated fresh gingerroot
    2 cloves garlic, minced
    1/4 teaspoon crushed red pepper
Marinate 2 hours or overnight, in refrigerator.
Preheat microwave browning dish according to manufacturer's directions.
Add chicken strips to browning dish.
Microcook on high for 2 minutes.
Stir twice.
Add . . .
    1 large rib celery, sliced
    1/2 green pepper, chopped
    1 (8-oz.) can sliced water chestnuts,
      drained
    2 cups fresh spinach, torn into pieces
Microcook on high 2 to 4 minutes.
Serve with rice and top with cashew nuts, if desired.

- *1 whole boned, skinless chicken breast, cut into 1/4" strips*
- *1/4 cup teriyaki marinade*
- *1/4 cup dry sherry*
- *1 teaspoon grated fresh gingerroot*
- *2 cloves garlic, minced*
- *1/4 teaspoon crushed red pepper*
- *1 large rib celery, sliced*
- *1/2 green pepper, chopped*
- *1 (8-oz.) can sliced water chestnuts, drained*
- *2 cups fresh spinach, torn into pieces*

Sweet & Sour Chicken

Surprisingly easy to prepare.
Serves 4. Microcook Time: 10 minutes. Marinate: 2 hours.
Calories: 275. Fat: 7 g. Carbohydrates: 26 g. Protein: 27 g. Sodium: 87 mg.

•2 whole boned, skinless chicken breasts, cut into 1/4" strips
•1 (8-oz.) can pineapple chunks, drained
•1/4 cup lemon juice
•1 tablespoon honey
•juice from 1 orange
•1/2 teaspoon garlic powder
•1/2 teaspoon ginger
•1/4 teaspoon minced onion
 •1/2 green pepper, sliced
•1 (8-oz.) can sliced water chestnuts, drained

Combine in mixing bowl :
> 2 whole boned, skinless chicken breasts, cut into 1/4" strips
> 1 (8-oz.) can pineapple chunks, drained
> 1/4 cup lemon juice
> 1 tablespoon honey
> juice from 1 orange
> 1/2 teaspoon garlic powder
> 1/2 teaspoon ginger
> 1/4 teaspoon minced onion

Marinate at least 2 hours.
Remove chicken and pineapple chunks from marinade.
Place chicken around the edge of a 12" microwave plate.
Pour marinade over chicken.
Place in the center of the plate:
> 1/2 green pepper, sliced
> 1 (8-oz.) can sliced water chestnuts, drained
> pineapple chunks

Cover with waxed paper.
Microcook on high 5 minutes.
Rotate.
Re-cover.
Microcook on high 2 to 3 minutes.

Bob's Cajun Chicken

My son, Bob, loves this spicy chicken recipe.
Serves 2. Microcook Time: 10 minutes.
Calories: 187. Fat: 7 g. Carbohydrates: 3 g. Protein: 27 g. Sodium: 78 mg.

Preheat microwave browning skillet according to manufacturer's directions.
Flatten between 2 sheets of waxed paper using a mallet:

  1 whole boned chicken breast, halved

Hint: Chicken should be about 1/4" thick.
Cut into 1" strips.
Coat in a plastic bag with:

  1 tablespoon Cajun seasoning*

Microcook on browner on high 4 to 6 minutes.
Turn once.
Stand 3 minutes on browner.
Hint: You may want to add a few drops of red pepper sauce for a hotter flavor.
*Cajun seasoning may be purchased or you may make your own, page 160.

> • 1 whole boned chicken breast, halved
> • 1 tablespoon Cajun seasoning*

Turkey Hints

- When microcooking turkey, it is necessary to turn and rotate the bird for even cooking.
- Standing time is needed to allow turkey to finish cooking.
- If turkey is frozen, defrost in the refrigerator or use cold water defrosting.
- An 8 to 12-lb. turkey is best suited for the microwave oven.
- Always remove plastic pop-out timer and metal holder for legs.
- Juices will run clear and meat should not be pink when done.
- Temperature in the thigh should be 175 to 180 degrees; in the breast 170 degrees.
- Plastic cooking bags work well for microcooking turkey pieces.
- Coat plastic cooking bags with 1 tablespoon flour or seasoning mix before adding poultry.
- Always use nylon ties to close bags.
- Make 1/2" slits in the top of the bag to let steam escape.
- When using plastic cooking bags use medium power.

12-Lb. Whole Turkey

Not only a Thanksgiving Day meal.
Serves 12. Microcook Time: 2 hours, 48 minutes.
Calories: 300. Fat: 7 g. Carbohydrates: 0 g. Protein: 56 g. Sodium: 140 mg.

Prepare browning sauce:
Microcook on high 40 seconds:
    1/4 cup butter*
Add . . .
    1/4 teaspoon paprika
Place turkey on large microwave-safe baking dish, breast side down. Tie legs and wings together with string.
Brush with browning sauce.
Remove plastic pop-out timer and metal holder for legs from turkey.
Microcook on high 24 minutes.
Rotate turkey 1/2 turn.**
Microcook on high 24 minutes.
Remove all drippings with baster and discard.***
Turn turkey breast side up.
Microcook on medium power 24 minutes.
Rotate 1/4 turn.
Microcook on medium power 24 minutes.
Rotate 1/4 turn.
Microcook on medium power 24 minutes.
Check temperature to indicate completeness of cooking; in thigh area, it should be **175 to 180 degrees,** in breast area **170 degrees,** stuffing should be **160 to 165 degrees.**
Rotate 1/4 turn.
Microcook on medium 24 minutes.
Check temperature.
Stand tented with foil 12 minutes.
Hint: During standing time, place turkey on a smoky grill to give it a wood-smoked flavor.
* Margarine may be substituted.
**Use pot holders, turket is hot!
***Important to do this - high fat content of drippings wastes microwave energy and will increase cooking time.

> •*1/4 cup butter**
> •*1/4 teaspoon paprika*
> •*12-lb. turkey*

Vegetable Stuffing

A heart-watcher delight.
Serves 12. Microcook Time: 15 minutes.
Calories: 61. Fat: 0 g. Carbohydrates: 14 g. Protein: 3 g. Sodium: 12 g.

- *3 potatoes, shredded*
- *3 carrots, shredded*
- *1 (10-oz.) pkg. frozen whole kernel corn*
- *1 (20-oz.) pkg. frozen chopped broccoli*
- *1 tablespoon poultry seasoning*

Place in a microwave steamer:
    3 potatoes, shredded
    3 carrots, shredded
    1 (10-oz.) pkg. frozen whole kernel corn
    1 (20-oz.) pkg. frozen chopped broccoli
Microcook on high 6 to 8 minutes.
Add . . .
    1 tablespoon poultry seasoning
Stir.
Stuff neck and body cavity of a 12-lb. turkey with mixture.

Boneless Turkey Breast

Perfect for sandwiches the next day.
Serves 4 per lb. Microcook Time: 10 minutes.
Calories: 200 Fat: 5 g. Carbohydrates: 0 g. Protein: 37 g. Sodium: 93 mg.

- *1 boned, skinless turkey breast*

Place on a microwave-safe rack and dish:
    1 boned, skinless turkey breast
Cover with waxed paper.
Microcook on medium high 8 minutes per lb., until the internal temperature reaches 170 degrees and juices should run clear.
Turn the breast over and **rotate** during cooking.
Stand tented with foil 5 to 7 minutes.

Individual Turkey Loaf

Another super heart-watcher.
Serves 2. Microcook Time: 10 minutes.
Calories: 278 Fat: 14 g. Carbohydrates: 14 g. Protein: 25 g. Sodium: 64 mg.

Combine in a bowl:
    1/2 lb. ground turkey
    1/2 cup oat bran
    1/2 teaspoon poultry seasoning
    1/2 teaspoon onion powder
Mix well.
Divide mixture into 3 portions.
Place in 3 (10-oz.) custard cups.
Push mixture to form a flat patty and **push** thumb
into center to make a hole (donut shape).
Cover with waxed paper.
Microcook on high for 3 1/2 to 4 1/2 minutes.
Stand 4 minutes.

- 1/2 lb. ground turkey
- 1/2 cup oat bran
- 1/2 teaspoon poultry seasoning
- 1/2 teaspoon onion powder

Duck

If you know duck hunters, this juicy recipe will come in handy.
Serves 2. Microcook Time: 9 minutes/lb.
Calories: 285. Fat: 16 g. Carbohydrates: 0 g. Protein: 32 g. Sodium: 92 mg.

Remove fat and giblets, **prick** skin of a:
    3-lb. duck
Stuff lightly with any of the following stuffing
combinations:*
    apple & onion with apple jelly
    raisins (soaked in brandy) and sliced
      apples
    onion, apples and bacon bits
Place breast side down in microwave-safe dish .
Cover lightly with waxed paper.
Microcook on medium high for 9 minutes per lb.
Turn and **rotate.**
Drain fat during cooking.
Stand 5 to 7 minutes tented with foil.
*Cook dressing separately for less fat.

- 3-lb. duck
- stuffing combinations (see recipe)

Duck Sauce

The "only" duck sauce..
Serves 2. Microcook Time: 5 minutes.
Calories: 231. Fat: 0 g. Carbohydrates: 59 g.. Protein: 0 g. Sodium: 42 mg.

- 1/2 (21-oz.) can cherry pie filling
- 1/4 cup apricot jam
- 2 tablespoons orange marmalade

Place in a 4-cup glass measure:
> 1/2 (21-oz.) can cherry pie filling
> 1/4 cup apricot jam
> 2 tablespoons orange marmalade

Microcook on high for 2 to 2 1/2 minutes.
Serve with Duck, page 181.

Oriental Game Hens

Wild rice makes a faultless complement!
Serves 2. Microcook Time: 24 minutes. Marinate: 6 to 12 hours.
Calories: 437. Fat: 13 g. Carbohydrates: 18 g. Protein: 52 g. Sodium: 1960 mg.

- 2 Cornish game hens
- 1/4 cup soy sauce
- 1/4 cup dry sherry
- 1/4 cup pineapple juice
- 1 tablespoon brown sugar
- 1/2 teaspoon curry powder
- 1/4 teaspoon dry mustard
- pinch garlic powder

Place in a 12x8x2" microwave-safe dish, skin side down:
> 2 Cornish game hens

Combine . . .
> 1/4 cup soy sauce
> 1/4 cup dry sherry
> 1/4 cup pineapple juice
> 1 tablespoon brown sugar
> 1/2 teaspoon curry powder
> 1/4 teaspoon dry mustard
> pinch garlic powder

Pour over hens.
Refrigerate 4 hours or overnight.
Turn skin side up and **baste** with marinade.
Cover with waxed paper.
Microcook on high 6 to 8 minutes per pound.
Turn over, **rotate** and **baste** during cooking.
Hint: Hens are done when juices run clear and legs move freely.
Stand 5 to 7 minutes.
Hint: To lower sodium omit soy sauce.

PASTA &RICE

Pasta Hints

- Pasta is best cooked on top of the range but may be cooked in the microwave.
- Do not cook more than 8 oz. at one time.
- Cook pasta the minimum time and test for doneness.
- Pasta is usually cooked "al dente" (just firm to the bite).
- Do not cover during cooking as this makes pasta too soft.
- Drain immediately; it becomes soft during standing time.
- Some pasta recipes (lasagna for example) call for placing uncooked pasta in baking dish and increasing liquid.
- AVOID adding oil to the water as microwaves are attracted to fat and could cause a sudden boilover.
- You do not save time cooking pasta in the microwave.
- Use large containers to avoid boilovers.
- Use pot holders to avoid burns.

Macaroni

Neither Macaroni nor Spaghetti saves time over conventional cooking.
Serves 2. Microcook Time: 3 hrs.
Calories: 95. Fat: 0 g. Carbohydrates: 40 g. Protein: 7 g. Sodium: 0 mg.

• 4 cups very hot water
• 2 cups macaroni
	Place in a 3-quart casserole:
	    4 cups very hot water
	Microcook on high 6 to 8 minutes.
	Add . . .
	    2 cups macaroni.
	Microcook on high 10 to 12 minutes.
	Drain.

Spaghetti

Neither Spaghetti nor Macaroni saves time over conventional cooking.
Serves 2. Microcook Time: 3 hrs.
Calories: 190. Fat: 1 g. Carbohydrates: 40 g. Protein: 7 g. Sodium: 1 mg.

• 4 cups very hot water
• 7 oz. spaghetti
	Place in a 3-quart casserole:
	    4 cups very hot water
	Microcook on high 6 to 8 minutes.
	Add . . .
	    7 oz. spaghetti.
	Microcook on high 10 to 12 minutes.
	Drain.

Chicken Pasta Salad

Delicious on a summer picnic or anytime!
Serves 12. Microcook Time: 18 minutes.
Calories: 333. Fat: 18 g. Carbohydrates: 29 g. Protein: 14 g. Sodium: 113 mg.

Place on a microwave-safe meat rack and dish:
    2 whole boned, skinless chicken breasts
Cover with waxed paper.
Microcook on high 7 to 10 minutes, depending on size.

Cool slightly.
Cut into bite-size pieces.
Cook:
    1 (12-oz.) pkg. rotini
Place in a 4-cup glass measure:
    1 (10-oz.) pkg. frozen peas
Microcook on high 3 to 4 minutes.
Combine chicken, pasta and peas in large bowl with:
    1 (15-oz.) can garbanzo beans, drained
    1 (2 1/2-oz.) can sliced black olives, drained
    1 (4-oz.) jar chopped pimiento, drained
Combine in a 4-cup measure:
    1/2 cup oil
    1/4 cup safflower oil
    1/4 cup red wine vinegar
    2 tablespoons Dijon mustard
    1/2 teaspoon mild curry powder
    1 clove garlic, minced
    freshly ground pepper
Pour over chicken mixture.
Refrigerate until serving.
Hint: For more intense flavor, refrigerate overnight.

- 2 whole boned, skinless chicken breasts
- 1 (12-oz.) pkg. rotini
- 1 (10-oz.) pkg. frozen peas
- 1 (15-oz.) can garbanzo beans, drained
- 1 (2 1/2-oz.) can sliced black olives, drained
- 1 (4-oz.) jar chopped pimiento, drained
- 1/2 cup oil (olive gives good flavor)
- 1/4 cup safflower oil
- 1/4 cup red wine vinegar
- 2 tablespoons Dijon mustard
- 1/2 teaspoon mild curry powder
- 1 clove garlic, minced
- freshly ground pepper

Couscous

Fabulous! And fun to serve!
Serves 6. Microcook Time: 10 minutes.
Calories: 322. Fat: 3 g. Carbohydrates: 75 g. Protein: 15 g. Sodium: 105 mg.

- 1 (10-oz.) pkg. couscous (Moroccan pasta)
- 1 1/2 cups water
- 1 tablespoon low-sodium instant chicken bouillon
- 1 tablespoon margarine
- 2 tablespoons flour
- 1/4 cup grated Parmesan cheese
- 1 1/2 cups skim milk
- 1/4 teaspoon garlic powder
- 1/4 teaspoon instant onion
- 1/4 teaspoon pesto seasoning*
- 6 drops hot pepper sauce
- 1/4 teaspoon salt-free extra spicy seasoning

Combine in a 4-cup glass measure:
> 1 (10-oz.) pkg. couscous (Moroccan pasta)
> 1 1/2 cups water
> 1 tablespoon low-sodium instant chicken bouillon

Cover with vented plastic wrap.
Microcook on high 3 to 4 minutes.
Allow standing time.
Lift with fork.
Set aside.
Place in a 2-cup glass measure:
> 1 tablespoon margarine

Microcook on high 45 seconds.
Add . . .
> 2 tablespoons flour

Stir.
Add . . .
> 1/4 cup grated Parmesan cheese
> 1 1/2 cups skim milk
> 1/4 teaspoon garlic powder
> 1/4 teaspoon instant onion
> 1/4 teaspoon pesto seasoning*
> 6 drops hot pepper sauce
> 1/4 teaspoon salt-free extra spicy seasoning

Microcook on high 2 to 3 minutes.
Stir.
Pour over couscous.
Stir.
*Basil, garlic & parsley

Polka-Dot Pasta

Heart-watcher recipe; my favorite pasta.
Serves 8. Microcook Time: 15 minutes.
Calories: 176. Fat: 8 g. Carbohydrates: 23 g. Protein: 5 g. Sodium: 61 mg.

Combine in microwave steamer:
    1 cup broccoli flowerettes
    1 cup sliced carrots
    1 cup cauliflower flowerettes
    1/2 cup sliced green pepper
    1 cup frozen green peas
    1/4 cup water
Microcook on high 8 to 10 minutes.
Hint: Vegetables do not have to be soft.
Drain water.
Add vegetables to:
    6 oz. mixed vegetable rotini, cooked
Add . . .
    10 mushrooms, halved
Place in a 2-cup glass measure:
    3/4 cup garlic wine vinegar
    1/4 cup safflower oil or olive oil
    1 tablespoon Dijon mustard
    1 clove garlic, minced
    2 teaspoons mild curry powder
    freshly ground pepper
Pour over pasta-vegetable mixture.
Toss.
Chill.
Hint: In place of oil and vinegar dressing,
try 1 cup Ranch buttermilk dressing.

`100% !`

- 1 cup broccoli flowerettes
- 1 cup sliced carrots
- 1 cup cauliflower flowerettes
- 1/2 cup sliced green pepper
- 1 cup frozen green peas
- 1/4 cup water
- 6 oz. mixed vegetable rotini, cooked
- 10 mushrooms, halved
- 3/4 cup garlic wine vinegar
- 1/4 cup safflower oil or olive oil
- 1 tablespoon Dijon mustard
- 1 clove garlic, minced
- 2 teaspoons mild curry powder
- freshly ground pepper

Creamy Vegetable Pasta

A meal in itself.
Serves 12. Microcook Time: 20 minutes.
Calories: 268 g. Fat: 16 g. Carbohydrates: 20 g. Protein: 12 g. Sodium: 297 mg.

- 1 onion, chopped
- 1 clove garlic, minced
- 1/4 cup margarine
- 1/4 cup flour
- 1 cup skim milk
- 1 cup ricotta cheese
- 1 (2 1/2-oz.) can sliced ripe olives, drained
- 1/2 teaspoon pepper
- 1 cup 2% cottage cheese
- 1 (8-oz.) pkg. cream cheese
- 3/4 cup grated Parmesan cheese
- 1 cup broccoli flowerettes
- 1 cup sliced carrot
- 1 cup cauliflower flowerettes
- 1 cup mushrooms, halved
- 1 (8-oz.) pkg. rotini, or pasta of your choice, cooked

Combine in an 8-cup glass measure:
>   1 onion, chopped
>   1 clove garlic, minced
>   1/4 cup margarine

Microcook on high 3 to 4 minutes.
Stir in:
>   1/4 cup flour

Add gradually:
>   1 cup skim milk

Stir.
Microcook on high 3 to 4 minutes.
Stir once.
Hint: Mixture should thicken.
Add . . .
>   1 cup ricotta cheese
>   1 (2 1/2-oz.) can ripe black olives, drained
>   1/2 teaspoon pepper

Stir.
Blend together until smooth:
>   1 cup 2% cottage cheese
>   1 (8-oz.) pkg. cream cheese
>   3/4 cup grated Parmesan cheese

Add to creamed mixture.
Microcook on high 4 to 5 minutes.
Combine in an 8-cup glass measure or microwave steamer:
>   1 cup broccoli flowerettes
>   1 cup sliced carrot
>   1 cup cauliflower flowerettes
>   1 cup mushrooms, halved

Cover with vented plastic wrap or steamer cover.
Microcook vegetables on high 3 to 4 minutes.
Toss vegetables with:
>   1 (8-oz.) pkg. rotini, or pasta of your choice, cooked

Pour sauce over pasta and toss.
Serve immediately or **chill** overnight.

Lasagna

Because it's made with uncooked noodles, it's a real time-saver.
Serves 8. Microcook Time: 55 minutes.
Calories: 393. Fat: 20 g. Carbohydrates: 61 g. Protein: 32 g. Sodium: 502 mg.

Place in a microwave-safe colander over a 2-quart casserole:

    1 lb. ground beef

Cover with waxed paper.
Microcook on high 5 to 6 minutes.
Drain fat.
Place meat in casserole.
Stir in:

    1 (14 1/2-oz.) can tomatoes, undrained
    1 (6-oz.) can low-sodium tomato paste
    1/2 cup water
    1 1/2 teaspoons basil
    1/2 teaspoon oregano
    1/4 teaspoon garlic powder

Cover with waxed paper.
Microcook on high 5 minutes.
Combine in a mixing bowl:

    2 cups low-fat cottage cheese
    1 1/4 cups grated Parmesan cheese
    1 egg
    1 tablespoon parsley flakes

Pour on bottom of 12x8x2" glass dish:

    1 1/2 cups tomato-meat mixture

Top with:

    3 uncooked lasagna noodles

Sprinkle with:

    1 cup shredded mozzarella cheese

Spoon 1 cup of tomato-meat mixture over the cheese.
Add . . .

    3 uncooked lasagna noodles

Top with remaining tomato-meat mixture and:

    1/2 cup grated Parmesan cheese

Cover with vented plastic wrap.
Microcook on medium 25 to 30 minutes.
Rotate.
Stand 15 minutes.

- 1 lb. ground beef
- 1 (14 1/2-oz.) can tomatoes, undrained
- 1 (6-oz.) can low-sodium tomato paste
- 1/2 cup water
- 1 1/2 teaspoons basil
- 1/2 teaspoon oregano
- 1/4 teaspoon garlic powder
- 2 cups low-fat cottage cheese
- 1 1/4 cups grated Parmesan cheese
- 1 egg
- 1 tablespoon parsley flakes
- 6 uncooked lasagna noodles
- 1 cup shredded mozzarella cheese
- 1/2 cup grated Parmesan cheese

Vegetable Lasagna

Even if you're not a vegetarian, you'll love this rich-tasting lasagna.
Serves 6. Microcook Time: 25 minutes.
Calories: 263. Fat: 9 g. Carbohydrates: 28 g. Protein: 18 g. Sodium: 540 mg.

- 4 oz. lasagna noodles, cooked
- 1 (8-oz.) pkg. chopped spinach
- 1 (8-oz.) carton low-fat cottage cheese
- 1 cup shredded mozzarella cheese
- 3 cloves garlic, chopped
- 3/4 teaspoon basil
- 1 teaspoon oregano
- 1 egg
- 1 zucchini, sliced
- 1 carrot, sliced
- 5 fresh mushrooms, sliced
- 1 onion, chopped
- 1 tomato, sliced
- 1 (8-oz.) can tomato puree or 1 cup spaghetti sauce
- 1/2 cup grated Parmesan cheese

Place in an 11x7x1 1/2" glass casserole:
    4 oz. lasagna noodles, cooked
Microcook on high 4 minutes:
    1 (8-oz.) pkg. chopped spinach

Drain.
Combine spinach and:
    1 (8-oz.) carton low-fat cottage cheese
    1 cup shredded mozzarella cheese
    3 cloves garlic, chopped
    3/4 teaspoon basil
    1 teaspoon oregano
    1 egg
Spread over pasta.
Layer over spinach-cheese mixture:
    1 zucchini, sliced
    1 carrot, sliced
    5 fresh mushrooms, sliced
    1 onion, chopped
    1 tomato, sliced
Top with:
    1 (8-oz.) can tomato puree or 1 cup spaghetti
      sauce
    1/2 cup grated Parmesan cheese
Cover with vented plastic wrap.
Microcook on medium 15 to 17 minutes.
Stand 5 to 10 minutes.

Spaghetti Pizza

Two of kids' favorite foods in one!.
Serves 6. Microcook Time: 35 minutes.
Calories: 444. Fat: 21 g. Carbohydrates: 85 g. Protein: 31 g. Sodium: 424 mg.

Combine in mixing bowl:
      6 oz. spaghetti noodles, cooked
      2 eggs
      1/4 cup grated Parmesan cheese
      1 tablespoon margarine
Form a spaghetti crust on a 12" glass pie plate.
Microcook on high 2 minutes.
Place in a plastic microwave-safe colander on top
of a 2 -quart glass casserole:
      1 lb. lean ground beef
      1/2 onion, chopped
Cover with waxed paper.
Microcook on high 3 to 4 minutes.
Drain fat.
Place meat in casserole.
Add . . .
      1 (16-oz.) can tomatoes, undrained
      1 (6-oz.) can low-sodium tomato paste
      1 teaspoon oregano
      1/4 teaspoon garlic powder
Microcook on high 2 minutes.
Pour over spaghetti crust:
      1 cup small curd cottage cheese
Add 1/2 meat mixture.
Top with:
      1/2 cup small curd cottage cheese
Add remaining meat mixture.
Top with:
      1/2 cup shredded mozzarella cheese
      1/4 cup grated Parmesan cheese
Microcook on medium 4 to 5 minutes.
Stand 5 minutes.

- 6 oz. spaghetti noodles, cooked
- 2 eggs
- 1/4 cup grated Parmesan cheese
- 1 tablespoon margarine
- 1 lb. lean ground beef
- 1/2 onion, chopped
- 1 (16-oz.) can tomatoes, undrained
- 1 (6-oz.) can low-sodium tomato paste
- 1 teaspoon oregano
- 1/4 teaspoon garlic powder
- 1 1/2 cups small curd cottage cheese
- 1/2 cup shredded mozzarella cheese
- 1/4 cup grated Parmesan cheese

White Rice

Perfect, basic, easy!
Serves 4. Microcook Time: 20 minutes.
Calories: 169. Fat: 0 g. Carbohydrates: 39 g. Protein: 3 g. Sodium: 535 mg.

> •*1 cup uncooked rice*
> •*2 cups liquid (water,*
> *chicken or beef broth)**

Combine in an 8-cup glass measure:
    1 cup uncooked rice
    2 cups liquid (water, chicken or beef broth)*
Cover with vented plastic wrap.
Microcook on high 5 minutes.
Reduce power to medium for regular and par-boiled rice, and **microcook** 15 minutes.
To re-heat cooked rice, **cover** with plastic wrap and **microcook** on high 1 minute for 1 cup rice.
*Low-sodium broth is available.

Brown Rice

See rice chart for quick-cooking rice (page 196).
Serves 4. Microcook Time: 50 minutes.
Calories: 180 g. Fat: 1 g. Carbohydrates: 39 g. Protein: 4 g. Sodium: 180 mg.

> •*1 cup uncooked rice*
> •*2 cups liquid (water,*
> *chicken or beef broth)**
> •*1 teaspoon salt*

Combine in an 8-cup glass measure:
    1 cup uncooked rice
    2 cups liquid (water, chicken or beef broth)*
    1 teaspoon salt
Cover with vented plastic wrap.
Microcook on high 5 minutes, reduce power to medium low and **microcook** 45 minutes.
To re-heat cooked rice, **cover,** and **microcook** on high 1 minute for 1 cup rice.
    *Low-sodium broth is available.

Rice with Olives

A savory twist to your rice dish.
Serves 4. Microcook Time: 30 minutes.
Calories: 305 g. Fat: 9 g. Carbohydrates: 47 g. Protein: 11 g. Sodium: 1645 g.

Combine in a 2-quart glass casserole:
    1 cup uncooked white rice
    1 (14 1/2-oz.) can low-sodium chicken
      broth
    1 cup chopped onion
    1/4 cup chopped celery
    dash pepper
Cover with plastic wrap or glass cover.
Microcook on high 5 minutes.
Stir twice.
Microcook on medium 15 minutes.
Add . . .
    1 (4 1/2-oz.) can sliced ripe olives, drained
    1 (2-oz.) bottle pimiento-stuffed olives,
      sliced
    1 (4-oz.) can mushrooms, drained
    1/2 cup grated Parmesan cheese
Mix well.
Cover with vented plastic wrap or glass cover.
Microcook on high 4 to 5 minutes.
Stand 4 to 5 minutes.

- *1 cup uncooked white rice*
- *1 (14 1/2-oz.) can low-sodium chicken broth*
- *1 cup chopped onion*
- *1/4 cup chopped celery*
- *dash pepper*
- *1 (4 1/2-oz.) can sliced ripe olives, drained*
- *1 (2-oz.) bottle pimiento-stuffed olives, sliced*
- *1 (4-oz.) can mushrooms, drained*
- *1/2 cup grated Parmesan cheese*

Quick-Cooking Rice

Rice/Amount	Add Water	Microcooking Time
Regular long grain 1 cup	**1 3/4 to 2 cups**	**High 5 minutes** **Medium 15 minutes** **Stand 5 minutes**
Medium short grain 1 cup	**1 1/2 cups**	**High 5 minutes** **Medium 15 minutes** **Stand 5 minutes**
Brown Rice 1 cup	**2 to 2 1/2 cups**	**High 5 minutes** **Medium low 45 minutes** **Stand 5 minutes**
Wild Rice 1 cup	**3 cups**	**High 5 minutes** **Medium low 40 minutes** **Stand 15 minutes**

Cover during cooking and standing time.
Stir once.

Carol's Heart-Watcher Lasagna

This is my favorite recipe!
Serves 8. Microcook Time: 50 minutes.
Calories: 258. Fat: 3 g. Carbohydrates: 42 g. Protein: 18 g. Sodium: 313 mg.

Place in a 12x8x2" glass baking dish:
  1 tomato, sliced into 6 circles
Top with:
  1/2 (15-oz.) can no salt added tomato puree
  3 uncooked lasagna noodles
Add . . .
  1 zucchini, sliced
  6 spears asparagus, sliced into 1" pieces
  6 mushrooms, sliced
Combine in a blender:
  1 (10-oz.) pkg. frozen spinach
  1 (16-oz.) pkg. low-salt, low-fat cottage
    cheese
  1 egg
  1 clove garlic
  3 basil leaves, minced
  2 tablespoons lemon juice
  1/2 teaspoon onion powder
  1/2 teaspoon oregano
  1/2 teaspoon freshly ground pepper
  1/4 teaspoon fennel
  1/4 teaspoon garlic powder
  6 drops hot pepper sauce
Spread on vegetables.
Add . . .
  remaining 3 uncooked lasagna noodles
Top with:
  remaining 1/2 (15-oz.) can no salt added
    tomato puree
Cover with vented plastic wrap.
Microcook on medium high 35 minutes.
Rotate 4 times.
Stand 10 minutes.
Sprinkle on top:
  1/4 cup freshly grated Parmesan cheese

- 1 tomato, sliced into 6 circles
- 1 (15-oz.) can no salt added tomato puree
- 6 uncooked lasagna noodles
- 1 zucchini, sliced
- 6 spears asparagus, sliced into 1" pieces
- 6 mushrooms, sliced
- 1 (10-oz.) pkg. frozen spinach
- 1 (16-oz.) pkg. low-salt, low-fat cottage cheese
- 1 egg
- 1 clove garlic
- 3 basil leaves, minced
- 2 tablespoons lemon juice
- 1/2 teaspoon onion powder
- 1/2 teaspoon oregano
- 1/2 teaspoon freshly ground pepper
- 1/4 teaspoon fennel
- 1/4 teaspoon garlic powder
- 6 drops hot pepper sauce
- 1/4 cup freshly grated Parmesan cheese

SAUCES

Mike's Barbecue Sauce

My son Mike's absolute favorite. Try on ribs or chicken.
Serves 40. Microcook Time: 10 minutes.
*Calories: 19. Fat: 0 g. Carbohydrates: 5 g. Protein: 0 g. Sodium: 92 mg.

- •1 cup chili sauce
- •1/2 cup red wine vinegar
- •1/2 cup brown sugar
- •1/4 cup chopped onion
- •1 tablespoon dry mustard
- •1 tablespoon lemon juice
- •8 drops hot pepper sauce
- •freshly ground pepper
- •liquid smoke, if desired

Combine in a 4-cup glass measure:
1 cup chili sauce
1/2 cup red wine vinegar
1/2 cup brown sugar
1/4 cup chopped onion
1 tablespoon dry mustard
1 tablespoon lemon juice
8 drops hot pepper sauce
freshly ground pepper
liquid smoke, if desired
Cover with waxed paper.
Microcook on high 6 minutes.
*Calories per teaspoon.

Butterscotch Sauce

Scrumptious on chocolate ice cream.
Serves 36 . Microcook Time: 10 minutes.
*Calories: 60. Fat: 3 g. Carbohydrates: 9 g. Protein: 0 g. Sodium: 39 mg.

- •1 cup dark brown sugar
- •1/2 cup margarine
- •1/2 cup dark corn syrup
- •1/4 cup milk or cream
- •1 teaspoon vanilla

Combine in a 4-cup glass measure:
1 cup dark brown sugar
1/2 cup margarine
1/2 cup dark corn syrup
1/4 cup milk or cream
Cover with vented plastic wrap.
Microcook on high 5 to 6 minutes.
Stir well.
Add . . .
1 teaspoon vanilla
Stir and **cool.**
*Calories per teaspoon.

Cheese Sauce

A richly flavored standard to be tried with so many foods.
Serves 40. Microcook Time: 5 minutes.
*Calories: 23. Fat: 2 g. Carbohydrates: 1 g. Protein: 1 g. Sodium: 27 mg.

Place in a 4-cup glass measure:
    2 tablespoons margarine
Microcook on high 30 seconds.
Stir in:
    2 tablespoons flour
Stir in:
    1 cup skim milk
Microcook on high 3 to 3 1/2 minutes.
Stir twice.
Add . . .
    1/2 cup shredded Swiss cheese
    3/4 cup shredded Cheddar cheese
    1/2 teaspoon white pepper
    1 tablespoon lemon juice
    1 teaspoon dry mustard
    4 drops hot pepper sauce
Stir.
Cover until cheese melts.
*Calories per teaspoon.

- *2 tablespoons margarine*
- *2 tablespoons flour*
- *1 cup skim milk*
- *1/2 cup shredded Swiss cheese*
- *3/4 cup shredded Cheddar cheese*
- *1/2 teaspoon white pepper*
- *1 tablespoon lemon juice*
- *1 teaspoon dry mustard*
- *4 drops hot pepper sauce*

"As Green as Ireland" Sauce

Try this with steamed vegetables or fish.
Serves 24. Prep Time: 10 minutes.
*Calories: 24 Fat: 2 g. Carbohydrates: 2 g. Protein: 0 g. Sodium: 26 mg.

Place in a blender and puree:
    1 cup fresh spinach, stems removed
Add . . .
    1 cup low-fat sour cream
    1/4 cup light mayonnaise
    juice of 1 large lemon
    2 teaspoons dehydrated shallots or onion
Mix well.
*Calories per teaspoon.

- *1 cup fresh spinach, stems removed*
- *1 cup low-fat sour cream*
- *1/4 cup light mayonnaise*
- *juice of 1 large lemon*
- *2 teaspoons dehydrated shallots or onion*

Hollandaise Sauce

A delectable Hollandaise. Serve with Eggs Benedict (page 63) and more.
Serves 32. Microcook Time: 3 minutes.
*Calories: 19. Fat: 2 g. Carbohydrates: 2 g. Protein: 0 g. Sodium: 20 mg.

- 1/4 cup margarine
- 2 egg yolks
- 1/4 cup milk
- 1 tablespoon lemon juice
- 1/4 teaspoon dry mustard
- dash paprika

Place in a 2-cup glass measure:
 1/4 cup margarine
Microcook on high 30 to 60 seconds.
Add . . .
 2 egg yolks
 1/4 cup milk
 1 tablespoon lemon juice
 1/4 teaspoon dry mustard
 dash paprika
Stir.
Microcook on high 1 to 2 minutes.
Stir and **serve** over eggs.
Hint: Overcooking will toughen protein and produce a rubbery egg. Watch closely.
*Calories per tablespoon.

Curry Sauce

Use this to rev up potato salad.
Serves 32. Microcook Time: 5 minutes.
*Calories: 34. Fat: 3 g. Carbohydrates: 1 g. Protein: 0 g. Sodium: 63 mg.

- 1/2 cup water
- 3/4 teaspoon low-sodium chicken bouillon granules
- 1 1/2 tablespoons curry powder
- 1 tablespoon honey
- 1/2 teaspoon coriander
- 6 drops hot pepper sauce
- freshly ground pepper
- 1 1/4 cups light mayonnaise
- 1/4 teaspoon Dijon mustard

Combine in a 2-cup glass measure:
 1/2 cup water
 3/4 teaspoon low-sodium chicken bouillon
 granules
Stir.
Add . . .
 1 1/2 tablespoons curry powder
 1 tablespoon honey
 1/2 teaspoon coriander
 6 drops hot pepper sauce
 freshly ground pepper
Microcook on medium 4 minutes.
Stir in:
 1 1/4 cups light mayonnaise
 1/4 teaspoon Dijon mustard
*Calories per tablespoon.

Oriental Sweet & Sour Sauce

Especially tasty with chicken.
Serves 20. Microcook Time: 5 minutes.
*Calories: 14. Fat: 0 g. Carbohydrates: 3 g. Protein: 0 g. Sodium: 35 mg.

Combine in a 4-cup glass measure:
    1 teaspoon low-sodium instant chicken
      bouillon granules
    1/2 cup water
    1 tablespoon teriyaki sauce
    2 tablespoons orange marmalade
    2 tablespoons crushed pineapple
    2 tablespoons apricot jam
    3 tablespoons raspberry vinegar
    1/2 teaspoon hot dry mustard
    1/2 teaspoon cornstarch
Microcook on high 3 minutes.
Stir 3 times.
Serve with chicken breast.
*Calories per tablespoon.

- 1 teaspoon low-sodium chicken bouillon granules
- 1/2 cup water
- 1 tablespoon teriyaki sauce
- 2 tablespoons orange marmalade
- 2 tablespoons crushed pineapple
- 2 tablespoons apricot jam
- 3 tablespoons raspberry vinegar
- 1/2 teaspoon hot dry mustard
- 1/2 teaspoon cornstarch

Wine Sauce for Pasta

If you're a pasta lover, you must try this one!
Serves 8, 1/2-cup servings. Microcook Time: 15 minutes.
Calories: 216. Fat: 18 g. Carbohydrates: 6 g. Protein: 5 g. Sodium: 233 mg.

- 1/2 cup unsalted butter
- 2 cloves garlic, minced
- 8 fresh mushrooms, sliced
- 3/4 cup dry white wine
- 3/4 teaspoon crushed red pepper
- 1 cup half-and-half (12% cream)
- 1/2 cup tomato paste
- 6 ripe olives, sliced
- 1/2 cup freshly grated Parmesan cheese
- 1/4 cup freshly grated Romano cheese
- 2 tablespoons capers
- freshly ground pepper

Place in an 8-cup glass measure:

    1/2 cup unsalted butter

Microcook on high 2 minutes.

Add . . .

    2 cloves garlic, minced
    8 fresh mushrooms, sliced
    3/4 cup dry white wine
    3/4 teaspoon crushed red pepper

Cover with vented plastic wrap.

Microcook on high 2 to 3 minutes.

Add . . .

    1 cup half-and-half (12% cream)
    1/2 cup tomato paste

Stir.

Microcook on medium 6 minutes.

Add . . .

    6 ripe olives, sliced
    1/2 cup freshly grated Parmesan cheese
    1/4 cup freshly grated Romano cheese
    2 tablespoons capers
    freshly ground pepper

Stir.

Pour over cooked pasta, **mix** and **serve** immediately.

Spaghetti Sauce

Make your own and taste the difference.
Serves 6, 1/2-cup servings. Microcook Time: 12 minutes.
Calories: 315. Fat: 23 g. Carbohydrates: 7 g. Protein: 19 g. Sodium: 901 mg.

Place in a microwave-safe colander over a 2-quart casserole:

> 1 lb. ground beef, crumbled
> 1/2 onion, chopped

Cover with waxed paper.
Microcook on high 5 minutes.
Stir after 2 minutes.
Drain fat.
Place meat in glass casserole.
Add . . .

> 6 thin slices pepperoni, quartered
> 1 (15-oz.) can tomato sauce
> 1 clove garlic, minced
> 1/2 teaspoon oregano
> 1 teaspoon crushed red pepper
> 1/2 teaspoon freshly ground pepper

Stir.
Cover with waxed paper.
Microcook on high 2 to 3 minutes.
Serve over cooked pasta.

- •1 lb. ground beef, crumbled
- •1/2 onion, chopped
- •6 thin slices pepperoni, quartered
- •1 (15-oz.) can tomato sauce
- •1 clove garlic, minced
- •1/2 teaspoon oregano
- •1 teaspoon crushed red pepper
- •1/2 teaspoon freshly ground pepper

Peanut Sauce for Chicken

A wonderful Oriental accompaniment for chicken.
Serves 9, 2 tablespoons per serving. Microcook Time: 5 minutes.
Calories: 135. Fat: 11 g. Carbohydrates: 5 g. Protein: 6 g. Sodium: 137 mg.

- *3/4 cup fresh creamy peanut butter*
- *3 green onions, chopped*
- *2 tablespoons sherry*
- *1/4 teaspoon grated fresh gingerroot*
- *1 clove garlic, sliced*
- *1 teaspoon low-sodium chicken bouillon granules*
- *1/2 teaspoon red pepper flakes*

Combine in a 4-cup glass measure:
    3/4 cup fresh creamy peanut butter
    3 green onions, chopped
    2 tablespoons sherry
    1/4 teaspoon grated fresh ginger root
    1 clove garlic, sliced
    1 teaspoon low-sodium chicken bouillon granules
    1/2 teaspoon red pepper flakes
Cover with plastic wrap.
Microcook on high 2 to 3 minutes.

Orange & Ginger Sauce

Great with all poultry.
Serves 5, 1/4 cup servings. Microcook Time: 8 minutes.
Calories: 50. Fat: 0 g. Carbohydrates: 13 g. Protein: 0 g. Sodium: 2 mg.

- *1 cup cold orange juice*
- *1 tablespoon cornstarch*
- *1/4 cup orange marmalade*
- *1/4 cup crushed pineapple*
- *1 tablespoon low-sodium chicken bouillon granules*
- *1/2 teaspoon grated fresh gingerroot*
- *1 teaspoon instant minced onion*

Place in a 4-cup glass measure:
    1 cup cold orange juice
    1 tablespoon cornstarch
Stir.
Add . . .
    1/4 cup orange marmalade
    1/4 cup crushed pineapple
    1 tablespoon low-sodium chicken bouillon granules
    1/2 teaspoon grated fresh gingerroot
    1 teaspoon instant minced onion
Microcook on high 4 to 5 minutes.
Stir 3 times.
Hint: Sauce should thicken.

Raspberry Sauce

Makes a savory and pretty addition to chicken.
Serves 5, 1/4-cup servings. Microcook Time: 5 minutes.
Calories: 62. Fat: 2 g. Carbohydrates: 13 g. Protein: 0 g. Sodium: 2 mg.

Place in a 4-cup glass measure:
  1/4 cup cold water
Stir in:
  1 tablespoon cornstarch
Add . . .
  1/2 cup frozen raspberries, thawed
  1/4 cup raspberry vinegar
  2 tablespoons black currant syrup or
    liqueur
  2 tablespoons black currant preserves
  1 teaspoon grated lemon peel
  1 teaspoon low-sodium chicken bouillon
    granules
Microcook on high 3 to 4 minutes.
Stir 3 times.
Hint: Sauce should thicken.
Serve with chicken breast.

- 1/4 cup cold water
- 1 tablespoon cornstarch
- 1/2 cup frozen raspberries, thawed
- 1/4 cup raspberry vinegar
- 2 tablespoons black currant syrup or liqueur
- 2 tablespoons black currant preserves
- 1 teaspoon grated lemon peel
- 1 teaspoon low-sodium chicken bouillon granules

Sauce for Bread Pudding

Try with Pineapple Bread Pudding (page 232).
Serves 7, 1/4-cup servings. Microcook Time: 10 minutes.
Calories: 212. Fat: 13 g. Carbohydrates: 19 g. Protein: 0 g. Sodium: 139 mg.

- •*1/2 cup butter or margarine*
- •*1 cup sifted powdered sugar*
- •*1 egg yolk*
- •*3 tablespoons pineapple juice from drained pineapple*
- •*1 or 2 tablespoons light rum to taste or 1 teaspoon rum extract*

Place in a 4-cup glass measure:
　　　1/2 cup butter or margarine
Microcook on high 45 seconds.
Add . . .
　　　1 cup sifted powdered sugar
Stir well.
Add . . .
　　　1 egg yolk
Microcook on medium high 2 minutes.
Stir.
Add . . .
　　　3 tablespoons pineapple juice from
　　　　　drained pineapple
Microcook on high 1 to 2 minutes, until
slightly thick.
Stir.
Add . . .
　　　1 or 2 tablespoons light rum to taste
　　　　　or 1 teaspoon rum extract
Pour over warm pudding.

Primavera for Pasta

A creamy cheese sauce that makes your pasta.
Serves 5, 1/2-cup servings. Microcook Time: 10 minutes.
Calories: 216. Fat: 18 g. Carbohydrates: 2 g. Protein: 11 g. Sodium: 475 mg.

Place in a 4-cup glass measure:
    2 tablespoons butter
Microcook on high 45 seconds.
Add . . .
    1/2 cup half-and-half (12% cream)
Microcook on medium 2 to 3 minutes.
Add . . .
    3/4 cup crumbled Gorgonzola cheese
    1/2 cup grated Fontina cheese
    1/2 cup grated Parmesan cheese
    1/4 teaspoon dry mustard
    dash nutmeg
Stir.
Cover with plastic wrap.
Stand 4 to 5 minutes, until cheeses melt.
Stir.
Pour over cooked pasta.

- *2 tablespoons butter*
- *1/2 cup half-and-half (12% cream)*
- *3/4 cup crumbled Gorgonzola cheese*
- *1/2 cup grated Fontina cheese*
- *1/2 cup grated Parmesan cheese*
- *1/4 teaspoon dry mustard*
- *dash nutmeg*

Raspberry-Apricot Sauce

Fabulous on chicken breast.
Serves 4, 1/2 cup servings. Microcook Time: 10 minutes.
Calories: 89. Fat: 1 g. Carbohydrates: 21 g. Protein: 2 g. Sodium: 2 mg.

Combine in an 8-cup glass measure:
    1 (10-oz.) pkg. frozen raspberries, thawed
    2 fresh apricots, chopped
    1/2 cup orange juice
    1 tablespoon cornstarch
Stir.
Microcook on high 4 minutes.
Stir twice.
Microcook on high 1 to 2 minutes until thick.

- *1 (10-oz.) pkg. frozen raspberries, thawed*
- *2 fresh apricots, chopped*
- *1/2 cup orange juice*
- *1 tablespoon cornstarch*

DESSERTS

Beret's Best Company Cake

Friend Beret Hagen would rather eat this cake than do anything else.
Serves 12. Microcook Time: 45 minutes.
Calories: 252. Fat: 15 g. Carbohydrates: 31 g. Protein: 1 g. Sodium: 55 mg.

- *1 cup butterscotch caramel fudge topping*
- *1 cup whipping cream*
- *1/2 cup almond brickle chips*

Prepare Chocolate Cake recipe on page 219.
When warm, pierce surface with fork 12 times.
Pour over the cake:
    1 cup butterscotch caramel fudge topping
Whip...
    1 cup whipping cream
Fold in:
    1/2 cup almond brickle chips
Spread over cake.
Chill overnight.

Cheri's Strawberry Fun Cake

Daughter-in-law Cheri Trench says it's always fun to serve this cake.
Serves 12. Microcook Time: 45 minutes.
Calories: 301. Fat: 12 g. Carbohydrates: 46 g. Protein: 4 g. Sodium: 326 mg.

- *1 (18 1/2-oz.) pkg. white cake mix*
- *3 eggs*
- *1 (6-oz.) can frozen bacardi concentrate*
- *1 (10-oz.) pkg. frozen straw-berries, thawed*
- *1/3 cup oil*

Combine in a mixing bowl:
    1 (18 1/2-oz.) pkg. white cake mix
    3 eggs
    1 (6-oz.) can frozen bacardi concentrate
    1 (10-oz.) pkg. frozen strawberries, thawed
    1/3 cup oil
Mix by hand for 3 minutes.
Pour into greased microwave bundt pan.
Microcook on an inverted microwave-safe saucer on medium low 13 minutes.
Microcook on high 6 to 7 minutes.
Cool on counter 10 minutes.
invert to dish.

Carrot Cake

A delicious, full-bodied cake.
Serves 8. Microcook Time: 27 minutes.
Calories: 268. Fat: 15 g. Carbohydrates: 36 g. Protein: 3 g. Sodium: 101 mg.

Combine in a mixing bowl:
    3/4 cup all-purpose flour
    3/4 cup sugar
    1/2 teaspoon baking powder
    1/2 teaspoon baking soda
    1 teaspoon cinnamon
    1/2 cup oil
    1 cup shredded carrots
    2 eggs
Beat for 2 minutes.
Stir in:
    1/2 cup golden raisins
Pour into a greased 9" round microwave cake dish.
Place on an inverted microwave-safe saucer.
Microcook on medium 6 minutes.
Rotate once.
Microcook on high 3 1/2 to 5 minutes.
Stand 10 minutes.

- *3/4 cup all-purpose flour*
- *3/4 cup sugar*
- *1/2 teaspoon baking powder*
- *1/2 teaspoon baking soda*
- *1 teaspoon cinnamon*
- *1/2 cup oil*
- *1 cup shredded carrots*
- *2 eggs*
- *1/2 cup golden raisins*

Cream Cheese Frosting

*The **best** carrot cake frosting.*
Serves 8. Microcook Time: 5 minutes.
Calories: 219. Fat: 7 g. Carbohydrates: 40 g. Protein: 1 g. Sodium: 68 mg.

Combine in a 4-cup glass measure:
    1 (3-oz.) pkg. cream cheese
    2 tablespoons margarine
    1 teaspoon vanilla
    a few drops of coconut extract
Microcook on medium 1 minute.
Blend well.
Add . . .
    2 1/2 cups sifted powdered sugar
Stir until spreading consistency.

- *1 (3-oz.) pkg. cream cheese*
- *2 tablespoons margarine*
- *1 teaspoon vanilla*
- *a few drops of coconut extract*
- *2 1/2 cups sifted powdered sugar*

Lemon Yogurt Cake

Yogurt cake with a delicate lemon flavor.
Serves 12. Microcook Time: 35 minutes.
Calories: 271. Fat: 8 g. Carbohydrates: 43 g. Protein: 5 g. Sodium: 324 mg.

- *1 (18 1/2-oz.) pkg. white cake mix*
- *1 cup low-fat vanilla yogurt*
- *1 (6-oz.) can frozen lemonade concentrate, thawed*
- *2 tablespoons fresh lemon juice*
- *3 eggs*

Combine in a mixing bowl:
> 1 (18 1/2-oz.) pkg. white cake mix
> 1 cup low-fat vanilla yogurt
> 1 (6-oz.) can frozen lemonade concentrate, thawed
> 2 tablespoons fresh lemon juice
> 3 eggs

Beat with mixer until creamy, 3 to 4 minutes.
Pour into well-greased microwave bundt pan.
Place on an inverted microwave-safe saucer.
Microcook on medium low 12 minutes.
Microcook on high 6 minutes.
Cool on counter 10 minutes.
Invert onto serving plate.

Terri's Rhubarb Cake

This is my daughter's favorite.
Serves 8. Microcook Time: 19 minutes.
Calories: 447. Fat: 13 g. Carbohydrates: 79 g. Protein: 5 g. Sodium: 318 mg.

- *2 cups brown sugar*
- *1/2 cup margarine*
- *1 egg*
- *1 1/2 teaspoons vanilla*
- *2 cups all-purpose flour*
- *1 cup buttermilk (with 1 teaspoon baking soda)*
- *2 cups chopped rhubarb*
- *1 1/2 teaspoons cinnamon*

Cream together in a mixing bowl:
> 2 cups brown sugar
> 1/2 cup margarine

Add . . .
> 1 egg
> 1 1/2 teaspoons vanilla

Add alternately:
> 2 cups all-purpose flour
> 1 cup buttermilk (with 1 teaspoon baking soda)

Stir in:
> 2 cups chopped rhubarb
> 1 1/2 teaspoons cinnamon

Pour into greased 9" microwave ring mold.
Microcook on elevated rack on medium 8 minutes.
Rotate twice.
Microcook on high 4 to 5 minutes.
Cool on flat surface.
Hint: Excellent served without topping, but whipped topping may be added, if desired.

Cheesecake

Made famous in New York. Made better in your kitchen!
Serves 8. Microcook Time: 35 minutes.
Calories: 493. Fat: 36 g. Carbohydrates: 32 g. Protein: 9 g. Sodium: 431 mg.

Place in a 9" round glass pie plate:
      1/3 cup margarine
Microcook on high 45 to 60 seconds.
Stir in:
      1 pack graham crackers, crushed (11
         double crackers)
      1/4 teaspoon cinnamon
Press firmly into the pie plate.
Place in an 8-cup glass measure:
      2 (8-oz.) pkgs. cream cheese
Microcook on medium 1 minute.
Stir.
Add . . .
      1/2 cup sugar
      2 tablespoons lemon juice
      4 eggs
Stir well until combined.
Microcook on high 3 to 4 minutes.
Stir every 2 minutes.
Pour over crust.
Microcook on medium 6 to 9 minutes until almost
set in center.
Rotate every 3 minutes.
Spread with:
      1 cup sour cream
      1 tablespoon vanilla
Chill.
Top with:
      fresh berries or 1 (21-oz.) can cherry pie
         filling

- 1/3 cup margarine
- 1 pack graham crackers, crushed (11 double crackers)
- 1/4 teaspoon cinnamon
- 2 (8-oz.) pkgs. cream cheese
- 1/2 cup sugar
- 2 tablespoons lemon juice
- 4 eggs
- 1 cup sour cream
- 1 tablespoon vanilla
- fresh berries or 1 (21-oz.) can cherry pie filling

Mike's Cheesecake

Created for my son, Mike, who loves cheesecake.
Serves 10. Microcook Time: 20 minutes.
Calories: 499. Fat: 39 g. Carbohydrates: 28 g. Protein: 8 g. Sodium: 376 mg.

- 1/2 cup unsalted butter
- 9 double graham crackers, crushed
- 1 teaspoon cinnamon
- 3 (8-oz.) pkgs. cream cheese
- 4 eggs
- 3/4 cup sugar
- 3 teaspoons vanilla
- 1 cup sour cream
- 1 tablespoon sugar
- 1 teaspoon vanilla

Place in a 10" quiche dish:
> 1/2 cup unsalted butter

Microcook on high 30 to 45 seconds until melted.
Combine . . .
> 9 double graham crackers, crushed
> 1 teaspoon cinnamon

Press to form a crust on bottom and sides of dish.
Place in an 8-cup measure:
> 3 (8-oz.) pkgs. cream cheese
> 4 eggs
> 3/4 cup sugar
> 2 teaspoons vanilla

Beat with a mixer until light and fluffy.
Microcook on high 3 to 6 minutes.
Stir 3 times.

Pour into prepared crust.
Microcook on medium 7 to 10 minutes.
Rotate twice.
Combine . . .
> 1 cup sour cream
> 1 tablespoon sugar
> 1 teaspoon vanilla

Pour over cheesecake.
Chill.
Top with sweetened fruit topping or serve plain.

Amaretto Cheesecake

Almond paste is the secret to this luscious recipe.
Serves 10. Microcook Time: 30 minutes.
Calories: 575. Fat: 44 g. Carbohydrates: 35 g. Protein: 11 g. Sodium: 424 mg.

Place in a 10" quiche dish:
  1/2 cup unsalted butter
Microcook on high 1 minute.
Mix together:
  1 pack graham crackers, crushed (11
    double crackers)
  1 teaspoon cinnamon
Press to form a crust on bottom and sides of dish.
Combine in blender:
  3 (8-oz.) pkgs. cream cheese
  1/2 cup almond paste
  1/2 cup sugar
  4 eggs
  1/2 teaspoon almond extract
  2 tablespoons coconut amaretto liqueur
Pour into an 8-cup glass measure.
Microcook on high 3 to 5 minutes.
Stir 3 times.
Pour into prepared crust.
Microcook on medium 7 to 10 minutes.
Rotate.
Stand 10 minutes.
Top with:
  1 cup sour cream
Chill.

- 1/2 cup unsalted butter
- 1 pack graham crackers, crushed (11 double crackers)
- 1 teaspoon cinnamon
- 3 (8-oz.) pkgs. cream cheese
- 1/2 cup almond paste
- 1/2 cup sugar
- 4 eggs
- 1/2 teaspoon almond extract
- 2 tablespoons coconut amaretto liqueur
- 1 cup sour cream

Coconut Amaretto Cheesecake

Coconut and almond are a great duo.
Serves 8. Microcook Time: 30 minutes.
Calories: 425. Fat: 28 g. Carbohydrates: 29 g. Protein: 8 g. Sodium: 282 mg.

- *1/2 cup milk*
- *1/4 cup coconut*
- *1 teaspoon almond extract*
- *2 eggs*
- *1/2 cup sugar*
- *1/2 cup buttermilk baking mix*
- *2 (8-oz.) pkgs. cream cheese, cubed*
- *1 cup sour cream*
- *2 tablespoons coconut amaretto liqueur*
- *2 tablespoons cream of coconut*
- *2 teaspoons sugar*

Blend together until smooth:
> 1/2 cup milk
> 1/4 cup coconut
> 1 teaspoon almond extract
> 2 eggs
> 1/2 cup sugar
> 1/2 cup buttermilk baking mix
> 2 (8-oz.) pkgs. cream cheese, cubed

Pour into a 10" quiche dish.
Microcook on a rack on medium high 18 to 20 minutes.

Combine in an 8-cup glass measure:
> 1 cup sour cream
> 2 tablespoons coconut amaretto liqueur
> 2 tablespoons cream of coconut
> 2 teaspoons sugar

Pour over cheesecake.
Refrigerate.

Chocolate Cake

A rich, heavy cake, almost like a candy bar.
Serves 9. Microcook Time: 30 minutes.
Calories: 341. Fat: 12 g. Carbohydrates: 54 g. Protein: 4 g. Sodium: 163 mg.

Place in a glass mixing bowl:
  1 oz. unsweetened chocolate
  1/4 cup margarine
Microcook on high 1 3/4 minutes.
Add . . .
  2/3 cup all-purpose flour
  2/3 cup sugar
  3/4 teaspoon baking soda
  1/4 teaspoon salt
  2 eggs
  1/3 cup sour cream
  1 teaspoon vanilla
Beat until well combined.
Pour batter into a 9" round glass baking dish.
Elevate on an inverted microwave-safe saucer.
Microcook on medium 6 minutes.
Rotate twice.
Microcook on high 2 to 4 minutes.
Stand on flat surface.

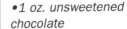
- 1 oz. unsweetened chocolate
- 1/4 cup margarine
- 2/3 cup all-purpose flour
- 2/3 cup sugar
- 3/4 teaspoon baking soda
- 1/4 teaspoon salt
- 2 eggs
- 1/3 cup sour cream
- 1 teaspoon vanilla
- 1 oz. unsweetened chocolate
- 1 tablespoon butter
- 1 tablespoon milk
- 1 cup sifted powdered sugar
- 1 teaspoon vanilla
- 20 miniature marshmallows

Chocolate Frosting

Combine in a 4-cup glass measure:
  1 oz. unsweetened chocolate
  1 tablespoon butter
  1 tablespoon milk
Microcook on medium 1 1/2 to 2 minutes.
Stir once.
Stir in:
  1 cup sifted powdered sugar
Cool slightly.
Add . . .
  1 teaspoon vanilla
Beat until smooth.
Hint: A drop or 2 of milk may be added for a smoother consistency.
Stir in:
  20 miniature marshmallows
Pour chocolate frosting over cake.

Melon Cake

Delicate melon flavor.
Serves 12. Microcook Time: 30 minutes.
Calories: 368. Fat: 15 g. Carbohydrates: 47 g. Protein: 4 g. Sodium: 453 mg.

- *1 (18 1/2-oz.) pkg. white cake mix*
- *3 eggs*
- *1/4 cup sour cream*
- *1/2 cup oil*
- *3/4 cup melon liqueur*
- *1 teaspoon coconut extract*

Combine in a mixing bowl:
    1 (18 1/2-oz.) pkg. white cake mix
    3 eggs
    1/4 cup sour cream
    1/2 cup oil
    3/4 cup melon liqueur
    1 teaspoon coconut extract
Beat with electric mixer for 4 minutes.
Pour into a greased microwave-safe bundt pan.
Microcook on medium low for 7 minutes.
Microcook on high for 7 to 8 minutes.
Rotate cake every 2 minutes.
Stand 10 minutes on counter.
Invert on cake dish.

Melon Glaze

Use on Melon Cake.
Serves 12. Prep Time: 5 minutes.
Calories: 115. Fat: 3 g. Carbohydrates: 16 g. Protein: 0 g. Sodium: 27 mg.

- *1 1/2 cups sifted powdered sugar*
- *1 (3-oz.) pkg. cream cheese*
- *1 tablespoon unsalted butter*
- *1/3 cup melon liqueur*

Combine in a mixing bowl:
    1 1/2 cups sifted powdered sugar
    1 (3-oz.) pkg. cream cheese
    1 tablespoon unsalted butter
    1/3 cup melon liqueur
Beat with mixer until smooth.
Pour over cake.

Snacking Cake

Tasty, informal, and a family favorite.
Serves 8. Microcook Time: 15 minutes.
Calories: 320. Fat: 15 g. Carbohydrates: 44 g. Protein: 3 g. Sodium: 190 mg.

Cream together in a mixing bowl:
      1/3 cup butter
      1/4 cup white sugar
      1/2 cup brown sugar
Add . . .
      1 cup all-purpose flour
      1 teaspoon baking powder
      1 egg
      1 teaspoon vanilla
Stir until well combined.
Stir in:
      1/2 (6-oz.) pkg. butterscotch chips
      1/2 (6-oz.) pkg. chocolate chips
Pour into an 8" round glass cake pan.
Place on an inverted microwave-safe saucer.
Microcook on medium 6 minutes.
Microcook on high 2 to 4 minutes.
Cool on counter.

- *1/3 cup butter*
- *1/4 cup white sugar*
- *1/2 cup brown sugar*
- *1 cup all-purpose flour*
- *1 teaspoon baking powder*
- *1 egg*
- *1 teaspoon vanilla*
- *1/2 (6-oz.) pkg. butter-scotch chips*
- *1/2 (6-oz.) pkg. chocolate chips*

Queen Kristine's Raspberry Cheesecake

Scrumptious and dainty, this cheesecake is fit for a queen.
Serves 12. Microcook Time: 25 minutes.
Calories: 273. Fat: 18 g. Carbohydrates: 20 g. Protein: 5 g. Sodium: 190 mg.

- *1 (10-oz.) pkg. frozen raspberries*
- *1/2 cup milk*
- *1/4 cup cassis syrup*
- *1/4 cup raspberry juice*
- *1/2 (14-oz.) can jellied cranberry-raspberry sauce*
- *2 eggs*
- *1/2 cup variety baking mix with buttermilk*
- *2 (8-oz.) pkgs. cream cheese, cubed*
- *1 cup sour cream*
- *1/4 cup raspberry liqueur*

Thaw . . .
>   1 (10-oz.) pkg. frozen raspberries

Drain and reserve juice.
Combine in blender:
>   1/2 cup milk
>   1/4 cup cassis syrup
>   1/4 cup raspberry juice
>   1/2 (14-oz.) can jellied cranberry-raspberry
>   sauce
>   2 eggs
>   1/2 cup variety baking mix with buttermilk
>   2 (8-oz.) pkgs. cream cheese, cubed

Blend until smooth.
Pour into a 10" quiche dish.
Elevate on a microwave-safe rack.
Microcook on medium high 19 to 21 minutes.
Rotate 3 times.
Combine thawed raspberries with:
>   1 cup sour cream
>   1/4 cup raspberry liqueur

Pour over cheesecake.

Brownies

Warm, homey and wonderful. Brownies microcooked on a plate are flat, like a cookie.
Serves 12. Microcook Time: 15 minutes.
Calories: 400. Fat: 17 g. Carbohydrates: 58 g. Protein: 4 g. Sodium: 291 mg.

Place in an 8-cup glass measure:
    1 (8-oz.) pkg. cream cheese
Microcook on medium 1 minute.
Beat in:

    1/4 cup sugar
    1 egg
    1 (6-oz). pkg. chocolate chips or candy-
       coated chocolate pieces
Prepare according to directions:
    1 (23-oz.) pkg. brownie mix
Pour into a 12" microwave-safe glass plate that has
been lined with waxed paper.
Microcook on high 9 minutes.
Rotate 3 times.
Spread cheese mixture over top.
Microcook on high 5 minutes.

- *1 (8-oz.) pkg. cream cheese*
- *1/4 cup sugar*
- *1 egg*
- *1 (6-oz.) pkg. chocolate chips or candy-coated chocolate pieces*
- *1 (23-oz.) pkg. brownie mix*

Choco-nut Balls

Grade schoolers have fun with this.
Serves 24. Microcook Time: 2 hours.
Calories: 278. Fat: 16 g. Carbohydrates: 29 g. Protein: 6 g. Sodium: 192 mg.

Combine in an 8-cup glass measure:
    2 cups sifted powdered sugar
    2 cups creamy peanut butter
    2 cups crushed graham crackers
Roll into balls the size of marbles.
Refrigerate 2 hours.
Place in a 4-cup glass measure:
    1 (12-oz.) pkg. chocolate chips
    1 tablespoon shortening
Microcook on high 1 to 2 minutes, until melted.
Stir.
Dip balls in melted chocolate.
Place on waxed paper.

- *2 cups sifted powdered sugar*
- *2 cups creamy peanut butter*
- *2 cups crushed graham crackers*
- *1 (12-oz.) pkg. chocolate chips*
- *1 tablespoon shortening*

Chow Mein Cookies

Another recipe kids will enjoy.
Serves 24. Microcook Time: 10 minutes.
Calories: 144. Fat: 9 g. Carbohydrates: 14 g. Protein: 3 g. Sodium: 67 mg.

- 1 (6-oz.) pkg. chocolate chips
- 1 (6-oz.) pkg. butterscotch chips
- 1 teaspoon vanilla
- 1 cup chopped cashew nuts
- 1 (3-oz.) pkg. chow mein noodles

Place in an 8-cup glass measure:
    1 (6-oz.) pkg. chocolate chips
    1 (6-oz.) pkg. butterscotch chips
Microcook on high 3 to 4 minutes, until melted.
Add . . .
    1 teaspoon vanilla
Stir.
Combine . . .
    1 cup chopped cashew nuts
    1 (3-oz.) pkg. chow mein noodles
Drop by teaspoonfuls on a waxed-paper-lined plate.
Chill.

Peanutty Crispy Bars

If you're a peanut butter fan, these are a must.
Serves 12. Microcook Time: 15 minutes.
Calories: 438. Fat: 16 g. Carbohydrates: 69 g. Protein: 6 g. Sodium: 348 mg.

- 1 cup sugar
- 1 cup corn syrup
- 3/4 cup chunky peanut butter
- 6 cups of favorite cold breakfast cereal
- 1 (6-oz.) pkg. chocolate chips
- 1 (6-oz.) pkg. butterscotch chips

Combine in an 8-cup glass measure:
    1 cup sugar
    1 cup corn syrup
    3/4 cup chunky peanut butter
Microcook on high 4 to 6 minutes.
Stir twice.
Pour into a 9x13" pan.
    6 cups of favorite cold breakfast cereal
Pour mixture over and stir.
Place in a 4-cup glass measure:
    1 (6-oz.) pkg. chocolate chips
    1 (6-oz.) pkg. butterscotch chips
Microcook on high 3 to 4 minutes, until melted.
Stir.
Spread over cereal.

Party Wreaths

Beautiful during the holiday season.
Serves 8. Microcook Time: 15 minutes.
Calories: 145. Fat: 5 g. Carbohydrates: 26 g. Protein: 1 g. Sodium: 185 mg.

Combine in an 8-cup measure:
    3 tablespoons margarine
    20 large marshmallows
Microcook on high 2 minutes.
Rotate and **stir.**
Hint: Mixture should be syrupy.
Stir in:
    1/2 teaspoon green food coloring
Add . . .
    3 cups corn cereal
Stir until well coated.
Butter fingers and **form** wreaths.
Hint: Use a 1/4-cup measure for each wreath.
Decorate with:
    red cinnamon candy (red-hots)
Makes 8 wreaths.
Hint: To make a large wreath, double recipe and form in greased ring mold.

- *3 tablespoons margarine*
- *20 large marshmallows*
- *1/2 teaspoon green food coloring*
- *3 cups corn cereal*
- *red cinnamon candy (red-hots)*

Pie Hints

- Pie shells may be made from scratch or purchased frozen. They all microcook well.
- Crusts will not brown. If color is desired, add spices, ground nuts or colored extracts.
- Be sure to use a fork to pierce the crust to prevent shrinking.
- A frozen crust may be thawed and transferred to glass plate before microcooking.
- Shells are microcooked on high 4 1/2 to 6 1/2 minutes.
- Avoid overcooking.
- Cooked pastry will look blistered on the surface.

 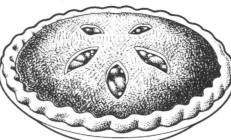 

Chocolate Cream Pie

The chocolate lover's favorite.
Serves 8. Microcook Time: 10 minutes.
Calories: 476. Fat: 41 g. Carbohydrates: 34 g. Protein: 2 g. Sodium: 33 mg.

- *2 (8-oz.) milk chocolate bars*
- *1/4 cup skim milk*
- *1/2 teaspoon vanilla*
- *1 pint whipping cream, whipped*
- *dash cinnamon*

Place in an 8-cup glass measure:
    2 (8-oz.) milk chocolate bars
    1/4 cup skim milk
    1/2 teaspoon vanilla
    dash cinnamon
Microcook on high 1 1/2 to 2 1/2 minutes, until chocolate is melted.
Cool.
Stir in:
    1 pint whipping cream, whipped
Pour into prepared shell.
Freeze.
Hint: Try adding a few drops of peppermint for a choco-mint flavor.

Open-face Apple Pie

The favorite dessert of the heartlands.
Serves 6. Microcook Time: 20 minutes.
Calories: 166. Fat: 1 g. Carbohydrates: 43 g. Protein: 1 g. Sodium: 3 mg.

Place in a baked pie shell:
> 5 to 6 cooking apples, sliced
> 3/4 teaspoon cinnamon
> 2 tablespoons all-purpose flour
> 1/4 cup golden raisins

Microcook on medium high 10 to 12 minutes.
Rotate.
Add . . .
> 1/2 cup caramel/butterscotch topping

Microcook on medium 4 minutes.

- 5 to 6 cooking apples, sliced
- 3/4 teaspoon cinnamon
- 2 tablespoons all-purpose flour
- 1/4 cup golden raisins
- 1/2 cup caramel/butter-scotch topping

Pecan Pie

Famous in the South for its rich, delectable taste.
Serves 8. Microcook Time: 20 minutes.
Calories: 327. Fat: 15 g. Carbohydrates: 46 g. Protein: 4 g. Sodium: 85 mg.

Combine in an 8-cup glass measure:
> 3 eggs
> 1/2 cup dark brown sugar
> 1 cup dark corn syrup
> 2 tablespoons butter
> 2 teaspoons vanilla

Mix well.
Microcook on medium 4 minutes.
Stir.
Pour into 9" baked pie shell.
Microcook on medium 9 to 13 minutes until almost set.
Rotate 3 times.
Top with:
> 1 cup pecans

Stand.
Refrigerate.

- 3 eggs
- 1/2 cup dark brown sugar
- 1 cup dark corn syrup
- 2 tablespoons butter
- 2 teaspoons vanilla
- 1 cup pecans

Chocolate Mousse Pie

When I want to make everyone happy, I serve this glorious pie.
Serves 12. Microcook Time: 3 1/4 hours.
Calories: 398. Fat: 28 g. Carbohydrates: 39 g. Protein: 4 g. Sodium: 147 mg.

- 25 vanilla wafers
- 1/4 cup butter
- 1 pint whipping cream
- 1 (16-oz.) can chocolate fudge syrup

Crush in a plastic bag:
    25 vanilla wafers
Place on a 9" glass pie plate:
    1/4 cup butter
Microcook on high 20 to 30 seconds.
Add crumbs and **press** to form a crust.
Whip using a mixer:
    1 pint whipping cream
Add . . .
    1 (16-oz). can chocolate fudge syrup
Pour into shell.
Refrigerate at least 3 hours or may be frozen.
Hint: Decorate with 1 oz. grated chocolate. Try adding 6 crushed peanut butter cups (candy).

`100%`

Creole Bread Pudding

This recipe was adapted from a Creole cooking class in New Orleans.
Serves 8. Microcook Time: 15 minutes.
Calories: 357. Fat: 17 g. Carbohydrates: 46 g. Protein: 8 g. Sodium: 196 mg.

- 6 to 7 slices day-old French bread, cubed
- 2 cups skim milk
- 2/3 cup sugar
- 1/2 cup golden raisins
- 1/4 cup coconut
- 1 (8-oz.) can crushed pineapple, drained
- 2 tablespoons butter
- 1 1/2 teaspoons vanilla
- 3 eggs
- 1 cup chopped pecans (optional)

Combine in a 2-quart glass casserole:
    6 to 7 slices day-old French bread, cubed
    2 cups skim milk
    2/3 cup sugar
    1/2 cup golden raisins
    1/4 cup coconut
    1 (8-oz.) can crushed pineapple, drained
    2 tablespoons butter
    1 1/2 teaspoons vanilla
    3 eggs
    1 cup chopped pecans (optional)
Stand in refrigerator 1 hour (if time permits).
Microcook on high 10 to 13 minutes.
Rotate.
Stir.
Top should start to dry slightly.

Fruit Bake

A light ending for a heavy meal.
Serves 6. Microcook Time: 10 minutes.
Calories: 94. Fat: 1 g. Carbohydrates: 19 g. Protein: 1 g. Sodium: 2 mg.

Combine in a bowl:
    2 large bananas, sliced
    2 oranges, peeled and cut into sections
    1/4 cup green or red grapes
Pour over the fruit:
    1/4 cup orange juice
    2 tablespoons lemon juice
    grated peel from both lemon and orange
Divide into 4 (10-oz.) custard cups.
Sprinkle with:
    2 teaspoons brown sugar
    2 tablespoons cream of coconut
Cover with waxed paper.
Microcook on high 2 1/2 to 3 minutes until bananas are soft.
Rotate once.
Serve warm.

- 2 large bananas, sliced
- 2 oranges, peeled and cut into sections
- 1/4 cup green or red grapes
- 1/4 cup orange juice
- 2 tablespoons lemon juice
- grated peel from both lemon and orange
- 2 teaspoons brown sugar
- 2 tablespoons cream of coconut

White Chocolate Mousse

When you really want an elegant dessert.
Serves 10. Microcook Time: 10 minutes.
Calories: 132. Fat: 12 g. Carbohydrates: 6 g. Protein: 1 g. Sodium: 16 mg.

Place in a 2-cup glass measure:
    1 (3 1/2-oz.) white chocolate bar
Microcook on high 2 minutes.
Stir.
Microcook on high 30 seconds until very smooth when stirred.
Add . . .
    1 teaspoon rum or rum extract
Cool slightly.
Stir in:
    2 cups whipped cream
Spoon into 4 small sherbet glasses and **chill.**

- 1 (3 1/2-oz.) white chocolate bar
- 1 teaspoon rum or rum extract
- 2 cups whipped cream

Capirotada

Mexican bread pudding; cheese is the surprise ingredient.
Serves 8. Microcook Time: 15 minutes.
Calories: 385. Fat: 17 g. Carbohydrates: 55 g. Protein: 6 g. Sodium: 359 mg.

- 1 cup brown sugar
- 3/4 cup water
- 1/2 cup margarine
- 1 teaspoon brandy
- 1/2 teaspoon cinnamon
- 1/4 teaspoon grated lemon peel
- 4 cups dry bread cubes
- 1 large cooking apple, chopped
- 1 banana, sliced
- 3/4 cup golden raisins
- 1/2 cup shredded Cheddar cheese

Combine in a 4-cup glass measure:
> 1 cup brown sugar
> 3/4 cup water
> 1/2 cup margarine
> 1 teaspoon brandy extract
> 1/2 teaspoon cinnamon
> 1/4 teaspoon grated lemon peel

Microcook on high 2 minutes.
Stir twice.
Place in a well-buttered 9" round glass dish:
> 4 cups dry bread cubes

Sprinkle over mixture:
> 1 large cooking apple, chopped
> 1 banana, sliced
> 3/4 cup golden raisins

Pour the liquid mixture over this.
Stand 5 to 10 minutes.
Microcook on high 4 to 5 minutes.
Rotate every 2 minutes.
Sprinkle top with:
> 1/2 cup shredded Cheddar cheese

Microcook on medium 1 minute or until cheese melts.
Serve warm with cinnamon ice cream.

Pie Crusts

If you want to "make your own", try one of these!
Microcook Time: 10 minutes.

One-Crust Pastry

Combine in a mixing bowl:
 1 1/4 cups all-purpose flour
 1/4 cup + 2 tablespoons vegetable oil
 2 1/2 tablespoons cold water
Stir and form a ball.
Place between two sheets of waxed paper and roll
flat to fit a 9" pie plate.
Trim & **fit** dough in pie plate.
Pierce crust with fork several times.
Microcook on high 5 to 6 minutes.

- *1 1/4 cups all-purpose flour*
- *1/4 cup + 2 tablespoons vegetable oil*
- *2 1/2 tablespoons cold water*

Graham Cracker Crust

Place in a 9" glass pie plate:
 1/3 cup margarine
Microcook on high 45 seconds.

Add . . .
 1 1/2 cups (16 crackers) crushed graham
  crackers
Press to form a crust.
Microcook on high 1 1/2 minutes.

Hint: try adding 1 teaspoon of cinnamon to
crushed crackers.

- *1/3 cup margarine*
- *1 1/2 cups (16 crackers) crushed graham crackers*

Chocolate Wafer Crust

Place in a 9" glass pie plate:
 1/4 cup margarine
Microcook on high 45 seconds.

Add . . .
 1/2 (8 1/4-oz.) box crushed chocolate
  wafers
Press to form a crust.
Microcook on high 1 minute.
Cool.

- *1/4 cup margarine*
- *1/2 (8 1/4-oz.) box crushed chocolate wafers*

Variation

Hint: Substitute 1 1/4 cups crushed vanilla wafers for chocolate.

Pineapple Bread Pudding

Serve with Sauce for Bread Pudding (page 208).
Serves 6. Microcook Time: 15 minutes.
Calories: 404. Fat: 21 g. Carbohydrates: 53 g. Protein: 7 g. Sodium: 355 mg.

- 1/2 cup margarine
- 3/4 cup sugar
- 4 eggs
- 1 (8-oz.) can crushed pineapple
- 3/4 teaspoon cinnamon
- 5 slices bread, cubed
- 1 teaspoon vanilla

Cream together in a 2-quart microwave-safe casserole:

> 1/2 cup margarine
> 3/4 cup sugar

Add . . .

> 4 eggs

Beat after each addition.

Add . . .

> 1 (8-oz.) can crushed pineapple
> 3/4 teaspoon cinnamon
> 5 slices bread, cubed
> 1 teaspoon vanilla

Stir.
Microcook on high 2 minutes.
Rotate.
Stir.
Microcook on medium 5 minutes.

Caramel Apple Dessert

McIntosh apples, when available, are great.
Serves 8. Microcook Time: 16 minutes.
Calories: 273. Fat: 10 g. Carbohydrates: 49 g. Protein: 2 g. Sodium: 80 mg.

Combine in an 8" round glass cake pan:
    4 medium cooking apples, sliced
    1/2 cup golden raisins
    1/4 cup whole wheat flour
    juice of 1 lemon
    2 teaspoons cinnamon
Place in a 4-cup glass measure:
    3 tablespoons margarine
    2 tablespoons brown sugar
Microcook on high 2 minutes.
Add . . .
    3/4 cup rolled oats
    1/2 cup caramel topping
Stir.
Pour over apple mixture and **combine** well.
Pour over the mixture:
    1/2 cup orange juice
Cover with vented plastic wrap.
Microcook on high 8 to 10 minutes.

- *4 medium cooking apples, sliced*
- *1/2 cup golden raisins*
- *1/4 cup whole wheat flour*
- *juice of 1 lemon*
- *2 teaspoons cinnamon*
- *3 tablespoons margarine*
- *2 tablespoons brown sugar*
- *3/4 cup rolled oats*
- *1/2 cup caramel topping*
- *1/2 cup orange juice*

Apple Crisp

Try this at harvest time when apples are plentiful and at their best.
Serves 8. Microcook Time: 25 minutes.
Calories: 320. Fat: 11 g. Carbohydrates: 54 g. Protein: 4 g. Sodium: 105 mg.

- *1/4 cup butter*
- *1/2 cup brown sugar*
- *1/2 cup rolled oats*
- *3/4 cup all-purpose flour*
- *4 cooking apples, sliced*
- *1/3 cup sugar*
- *1/4 cup golden raisins*
- *2 teaspoons all-purpose flour*
- *1 teaspoon lemon juice*
- *1 teaspoon cinnamon*
- *1 (3-oz.) pkg. cream cheese*
- *1/4 cup sugar*
- *1 egg*
- *1 tablespoon milk*
- *1 teaspoon vanilla*

Place in a 4-cup glass measure:

> 1/4 cup butter

Microcook on high 30 seconds.
Stir in:

> 1/2 cup brown sugar
> 1/2 cup rolled oats
> 3/4 cup all-purpose flour

Combine in an 8" square glass dish:

> 4 cooking apples, sliced
> 1/3 cup sugar
> 1/4 cup golden raisins
> 2 teaspoons all-purpose flour
> 1 teaspoon lemon juice
> 1 teaspoon cinnamon

Microcook on high 8 minutes.
Stir after 4 minutes.
Blend in a bowl:

> 1 (3-oz.) pkg. cream cheese
> 1/4 cup sugar
> 1 egg
> 1 tablespoon milk
> 1 teaspoon vanilla

Pour over apple mixture.
Sprinkle oat mixture over this.
Microcook on high 6 to 10 minutes.
Rotate twice.

Baked Apples

Not only taste delicious, but the aroma is marvelous.
Serves 2. Microcook Time: 10 minutes.
Calories: 171. Fat: 3 g. Carbohydrates: 39 g. Protein: 0 g. Sodium: 31 mg.

Wash and **core**:
    2 large Rome apples
Cut a slit around circumference of apple to retain shape.
Fill centers with:
    2 tablespoons brown sugar
    1/4 teaspoon cinnamon
    1 tablespoon raisins
    1 teaspoon margarine
    1 teaspoon red cinnamon candies
Place in 2 (10-oz.) custard cups.
Cover with vented plastic wrap.
Microcook on high 3 to 5 minutes.
Hint: Time depends on size and variety of apple.

> - *2 large Rome apples*
> - *2 tablespoons brown sugar*
> - *1/4 teaspoon cinnamon*
> - *1 tablespoon raisins*
> - *1 teaspoon margarine*
> - *1 teaspoon red cinnamon candies*

Variation

Add 2 tablespoons caramel /butterscotch fudge topping to each apple center

Fruit Dessert

Chilling overnight allows a marriage of the flavors.
Serves 6. Microcook Time: 12 minutes.
Calories: 218. Fat: 4 g. Carbohydrates: 47 g. Protein: 1 g. Sodium: 58 mg.

- 2 tablespoons margarine
- 1/2 cup brown sugar
- 1/2 teaspoon cinnamon
- 1/4 teaspoon grated lemon peel
- 2 tablespoons grated orange peel
- 2 tablespoons orange juice
- 1 (8 1/2-oz.) can apricot halves, drained
- 1 (8-oz.) can pineapple chunks, drained
- 1 (8 1/2-oz.) can pear pieces, drained
- 1 (8 1/2-oz.) can sliced peaches, drained
- 5 maraschino cherries, halved

Combine in a 2-quart glass casserole:
    2 tablespoons margarine
    1/2 cup brown sugar
    1/2 teaspoon cinnamon
    1/4 teaspoon grated lemon peel
    2 tablespoons grated orange peel
    2 tablespoons orange juice
Microcook on high 2 to 3 minutes.
Add . . .
    1 (8 1/2-oz.) can apricot halves, drained
    1 (8-oz.) can pineapple chunks, drained
    1 (8 1/2-oz.) can pear pieces, drained
    1 (8 1/2-oz.) can sliced peaches, drained
    5 maraschino cherries, halved
Cover with vented plastic wrap.
Microcook on high 5 to 6 minutes.
Chill overnight.

Easy Bars

Good for an after-school treat.
Serves 12. Microcook Time: 8 minutes.
Calories: 334. Fat: 19 g. Carbohydrates: 39 g. Protein: 2 g. Sodium: 236 mg.

Place in an 8x12x2" glass baking dish:
    12 graham crackers
Set aside.
Place in a 4-cup glass measure:
    1/2 cup butter
    1/2 cup brown sugar
Microcook on high 1 1/2 to 2 minutes.
Stir once.
Add . . .
    1 (6-oz.) pkg. chocolate chips
    1 (6-oz.) pkg. butterscotch chips
    1/2 cup coconut
Microcook on high 2 to 3 minutes.
Stir once.
Spread chip mixture over graham crackers and **cool.**

- *12 graham crackers*
- *1/2 cup butter*
- *1/2 cup brown sugar*
- *1 (6-oz.) pkg. chocolate chips*
- *1 (6-oz.) pkg. butterscotch chips*
- *1/2 cup coconut*

Jim's Valentine Mousse

For my husband, Jim. An enchanting Valentine Treat!
Serves 6. Microcook Time: 10 minutes.
Calories: 541. Fat: 42 g. Carbohydrates: 49 g. Protein: 6 g. Sodium: 99 mg.

- 1 (10-oz.) pkg. frozen raspberries
- 1 pint whipping cream
- 1 (16-oz.) can chocolate fudge topping

Microcook on high 3 minutes:
  1 (10-oz.) pkg. frozen raspberries
Hint: Be sure to cut a slit in the plastic covering and place on a paper plate on a microwave-safe plate.
Drain juice.
Whip in a mixing bowl:
  1 pint whipping cream
Add and **mix** well:
  1 (16-oz.) can chocolate fudge topping
Stir in raspberries.
Spoon into 6 sherbet glasses; chill
Top with Chocolate Hearts, if desired (see below).

Chocolate Hearts

Such fun to eat and pretty, to boot!
Serves 6. Microcook Time: 16 minutes.
Calories: 168. Fat: 41 g. Carbohydrates: 18 g. Protein: 1 g. Sodium: 65 mg.

- 1 (6-oz.) pkg. chocolate chips
- 1 tablespoon vegetable shortening

Place in a 4-cup glass measure:
  1 (6-oz.) pkg. chocolate chips
  1 tablespoon vegetable shortening
Microcook on medium 2 minutes.
Stir.
Microcook at 30-second intervals until smooth.
Spread on a foil-lined cookie sheet.
Freeze 10 minutes.
Press a heart-shaped cookie cutter into chocolate and carefully **remove** hearts with spatula.
Hint: Decorate mousse or other desserts.

Bread Pudding

Serve with Sauce for Bread Pudding page 208. Delectable!
Serves 4. Microcook Time: 23 minutes.
Calories: 280. Fat: 8 g. Carbohydrates: 46 g. Protein: 9 g. Sodium: 259 mg.

Pour into a 4-cup measure:
    2 cups milk
Microcook on high 3 to 4 minutes.
Combine in a 2-quart glass casserole:
    2 cups bread cubes
    2 eggs
    dash salt
    1/2 cup golden raisins
    1/3 cup sugar
    dash nutmeg
Pour hot milk over mixture.
Stir.
Cover with waxed paper.
Microcook on high 2 minutes.
Rotate.
Microcook on medium 5 to 7 minutes.
Stand, covered, 5 minutes.

- *2 cups milk*
- *2 cups bread cubes*
- *2 eggs*
- *dash salt*
- *1/2 cup golden raisins*
- *1/3 cup sugar*
- *dash nutmeg*

Poached Pears with Lemon/Apricot Sauce

A Heart-watcher's dessert. Serve with Lemon/Apricot Sauce (page 240).
Serves 3. Microcook Time: 15 minutes.
Calories: 176. Fat: 1 g. Carbohydrates: 36 g. Protein: 1 g. Sodium: 6 mg.

Place in a 2-quart casserole:
    3/4 cup white wine
    1 tablespoon lemon juice
    2 tablespoons sugar
    1/2 teaspoon cinnamon
    dash nutmeg
    3 fresh pears, peeled and cored
Cover with plastic wrap.
Microcook on high 6 to 9 minutes.
Chill.

- *3/4 cup white wine*
- *1 tablespoon lemon juice*
- *2 tablespoons sugar*
- *1/2 teaspoon cinnamon*
- *dash nutmeg*
- *3 fresh pears, peeled and cored*

Lemon/Apricot Sauce

Serve with Poached Pears (page 239).
Serves 3. Microcook Time: 16 minutes.
Calories: 159. Fat: 2 g. Carbohydrates: 55 g. Protein: 6 g. Sodium: 63 mg.

Place in a 4-cup glass measure:

    1 cup skim milk
    1 tablespoon cornstarch

Stir.
Add . . .

    1/3 cup sugar
    1 egg, beaten

Microcook on medium high 5 to 6 minutes.
Stir 3 times.
Add . . .

    2 tablespoons fresh lemon juice
    1 teaspoon vanilla

Stir.
Place in a food processor:

    1 (16-oz.) can unsweetened apricots,
      drained

Pulse to puree apricots.
Add to thickened mixture.
Serve warm over pears.

`70%` ⚠

- 1 cup skim milk
- 1 tablespoon cornstarch
- 1/3 cup sugar
- 1 egg, beaten
- 2 tablespoons fresh lemon juice
- 1 teaspoon vanilla
- 1 (16-oz.) can unsweetened apricots, drained

Blueberry Crescent Dessert

I like to make this for my son, Mike, who loves blueberries.
Serves 8. Microcook Time: 28 minutes.
Calories: 485. Fat: 29 g. Carbohydrates: 49 g. Protein: 8 g. Sodium: 854 mg.

- 1 (8-oz.) pkg. refrigerator crescent rolls
- 2 (8-oz.) pkgs. cream cheese
- 2 tablespoons lemon juice
- 1 tablespoon grated lemon peel
- 2 tablespoons milk
- 1 (21-oz.) can blueberry pie filling, fresh blueberries or favorite fresh fruits
- 1 cup fruit juice (pineapple, orange, apricot)
- 1 tablespoon cornstarch

Preheat round microwave browning skillet according to manufacturer's directions.
Unroll . . .
    1 (8-oz.) pkg. refrigerated crescent rolls
Arrange triangle-shaped rolls to form a circle on preheated browner.
Hint: Use pot holders when handling browning skillet.
Microcook on high 4 minutes.
Stand on skillet 45 minutes.
Transfer crust to a serving plate; **set** aside.
Place in a 4-cup glass measure:
    2 (8-oz.) pkgs. cream cheese
Microcook on medium 45 to 60 seconds until softened.
Add . . .
    2 tablespoons lemon juice
    1 tablespoon grated lemon peel
    2 tablespoons milk
Stir until well combined.
Spread cream cheese mixture over crust.
Top with:
    1 (21-oz.) can blueberry pie filling, fresh blueberries or favorite fresh fruits
Hint: If fresh fruit is used, prepare a glaze as follows:
Combine in a 4-cup glass measure:
    1 cup fruit juice
    1 tablespoon cornstarch
Microcook on high 3 to 5 minutes or until thickened.
Stir 3 times.
Pour over fresh fruit.

Cherry Cheese Tart

A Valentine's charmer. You'll feel like the Queen of Hearts!
Serves 8. Microcook Time: 25 minutes.
Calories: 392. Fat: 23 g. Carbohydrates: 40 g. Protein: 4 g. Sodium: 322 mg.

- 1 refrigerated ready to bake pie crust
- 1 (8-oz.) pkg. cream cheese
- 1/4 cup sugar
- 1 teaspoon almond extract
- 1 (8-oz.) carton sour cream
- 1 tablespoon sugar
- 1 teaspoon vanilla
- 1 (21-oz.) can cherry pie filling

Preheat microwave browning skillet according to manufacturer's directions.
Place on heated browner:
    1 refrigerated ready to bake pie crust
Turn edge in to fit grill.
Hint: Use pot holders when handling hot browning grill.
Microcook on high 3 to 4 minutes.
Remove crust to a flat plate.
Place in an 8-cup glass measure:
    1 (8-oz.) pkg. cream cheese
    1/4 cup sugar
Microcook on medium 1 minute.
Add . . .
    1 teaspoon almond extract
Stir well.

Spread cream cheese mixture over crust.
Combine in a mixing bowl:
    1 (8-oz.) carton sour cream
    1 tablespoon sugar
    1 teaspoon vanilla
Stir well.
Spread over cream cheese mixture.
Top with:
    1 (21-oz.) can cherry pie filling
Chill.

Fresh Fruit Tarts

My cousin Nancy Henning loves this dessert almost as much as her son, Troy, does.
Serves 8. Microcook Time: 18 minutes
Calories: 304. Fat: 13g. Carbohydrates: 28g. Protein: 4 g. Sodium: 108 mg.

Preheat microwave browning skillet according to manufacturer's directions.
Place on browner:
  1 refrigerated ready to bake pie crust
Turn edge inward to form a lip and fit the browner-exactly. Be careful, browner is hot!
Microcook on high 4 minutes.
Place in a 2-cup glass measure:
  1 (8-oz.) pkg. light cream cheese
Microcook on medium 30 seconds.
Add . . .
  1 (3 1/2-oz.) pkg. almond paste
Stir well.
Spread cream cheese mixture over crust.
Transfer to serving plate.
Place fresh fruits of your choice over cream cheese mixture and top with glaze as follows:
Combine in a 4-cup glass measure.
  1 cup fruit juice
  1 tablespoon cornstarch
Microcook on high 3 to 5 minutes or until thickened.

- 1 refrigerated ready to bake pie crust
- 1 (8-oz.) pkg. light cream cheese
- 1 (3 1/2-oz.) pkg. almond paste
- 1 cup fruit juice
- 1 tablespoon cornstarch

Variation: 4th of July Pie

Top with whole strawberries and sprinkle with fresh blueberries.
Place in 4-cup glass measure:
  1 (4 3/4-oz.) pkg. Danish dessert mix
  3/4 cup cold water
  1/2 cup cassis syrup*
Cover with waxed paper.
Microcook on high 5 to 6 minutes.
Stir every 2 minutes.
Carefully top strawberries with thickened mixture.
Refrigerate.
Hint: Try kiwi with strawberries and blueberries, bananas and grapes or apples and peaches.
*Or try 3/4 cup water (total liquid 1 1/2 cups).

- 1 (4 3/4-oz.) pkg. Danish dessert mix
- 3/4 cup cold water
- 1/2 cup cassis syrup*

Bananas Foster

Sublime for an after-dinner treat.
Serves 4. Microcook Time: 10 minutes.
Calories: 464. Fat: 23 g. Carbohydrates: 60 g. Protein: 5 g. Sodium: 246 mg.

- *1/4 cup margarine*
- *1/4 cup brown sugar*
- *1 tablespoon cinnamon*
- *3 large bananas, sliced*
- *1 tablespoon coconut cream*
- *1 tablespoon liqueur**
- *New York vanilla ice cream*

Place in an 8" round glass dish:
    1/4 cup margarine
    1/4 cup brown sugar
    1 tablespoon cinnamon
Microcook on high 3 minutes.
Add . . .
    3 large bananas, sliced
    1 tablespoon coconut cream
    1 tablespoon liqueur*
Microcook on high 2 minutes.
Pour over:
    New York vanilla ice cream
*Try: Creme de banana, pina colada, coconut, amaretto or rum.

Candy Hints

- Candy is easy to make in a microwave oven.
- Large-size recipes may boil over and should not be used.
- Lower power settings work better with smaller quantities.
- Be sure to use an accurate microwave candy thermometer. Have pot holder ready to use because containers get very hot.
- Caramel and chocolate melt well, but watch carefully as they retain their shape when melted and can easily be overcooked.
- Avoid the use of glass containers with chips or cracks; the extreme heat may cause breakage.

Peanut Brittle

Crisp and sweet, nice to have on hand.
Serves 24. Microcook Time: 21 minutes.
Calories: 91. Fat: 4 g. Carbohydrates: 14 g. Protein: 2 g. Sodium: 70 mg.

- *1 cup sugar*
- *1/2 cup light corn syrup*
- *1 cup salted roasted peanuts*
- *1 tablespoon butter*
- *1 teaspoon vanilla*
- *1 teaspoon baking soda*

Place in an 8-cup glass measure:

    1 cup sugar
    1/2 cup light corn syrup

Microcook on high 4 minutes.
Stir in:

    1 cup salted roasted peanuts

Microcook on high 3 to 5 minutes until brown.
Stir in:

    1 tablespoon butter
    1 teaspoon vanilla

Microcook on high 2 minutes.
Hint: Peanuts should be light brown.
Add . . .

    1 teaspoon baking soda

Stir quickly until light and foamy.
Pour IMMEDIATELY onto cookie sheet that has been greased well.
Cool 1/2 to 1 hour.
Break into small pieces when cool.
Hint: If raw peanuts are used, add them to the sugar-syrup mixture along with a dash of salt before microcooking.

Pralines

Held dear by the people of New Orleans.
Serves 24. Microcook Time: 24 minutes.
Calories: 74. Fat: 2 g. Carbohydrates: 13 g. Protein: 0 g. Sodium: 42 mg.

- 1 (3 1/2-oz.) pkg. butterscotch pudding & pie filling mix
- 3/4 cup brown sugar
- 1/4 cup white sugar
- 1/3 cup evaporated milk
- 1 tablespoon butter
- 1/2 cup chopped pecans

Place in an 8-cup glass measure:
>1 (3 1/2-oz.) pkg. butterscotch pudding &
> pie filling mix (be sure it is cooked type,
> not instant)
>3/4 cup brown sugar
>1/4 cup white sugar
>1/3 cup evaporated milk
>1 tablespoon butter
>1/2 cup chopped pecans

Microcook on high 12 to 14 minutes.
Stir every 3 minutes.
Pour onto well greased cookie sheet making circles
(1 1/2" diameter).

Sugar & Spice Nuts

Created by my friend, Jeanne Chiodo, as a wonderful holiday treat.
Serves 24. Microcook Time: 18 minutes.
Calories: 94. Fat: 7 g. Carbohydrates: 8 g. Protein: 2 g. Sodium: 3 mg.

- 1 egg
- 1 teaspoon water
- 1/2 cup white sugar
- 1/4 cup brown sugar
- 1 teaspoon cinnamon
- 1/8 teaspoon cloves
- 2 cups walnut pieces

Beat with a wire whisk in an 8-cup glass measure:
>1 egg

Add . . .
>1 teaspoon water

Beat.
Add . . .
>1/2 cup white sugar
>1/4 cup brown sugar
>1 teaspoon cinnamon
>1/8 teaspoon cloves

Add . . .
>2 cups walnut pieces

Stir to coat.
Microcook on high 5 to 6 minutes.
Stir every 2 minutes.
Microcook on high until sugar crystallizes.
Spread on plate to cool.

Creamy Fudge

Smooth and chocolaty.
Serves 24. Microcook Time: 16 minutes.
Calories: 212. Fat: 10 g. Carbohydrates: 30 g. Protein: 2 g. Sodium: 98 mg.

Combine in an 8-cup glass measure:
  2 cups sugar
  1 (5-oz.) can evaporated milk
  1/2 cup butter
Microcook on high 8 to 11 minutes.
Stir every 2 minutes.
Check temperature with candy thermometer; should be 235 to 240 degrees.
Add . . .
  2 cups miniature marshmallows
Stir until well combined.
Add . . .
  1 (12-oz.) pkg. chocolate chips
  1 teaspoon vanilla
Stir well.
Pour into a buttered 8x8x2" pan.
Chill.

- *2 cups sugar*
- *1 (5-oz.) can evaporated milk*
- *1/2 cup butter*
- *2 cups miniature marshmallows*
- *1 (12-oz.) pkg. chocolate chips*
- *1 teaspoon vanilla*

Mint Bark

Surprisingly easy!
Serves 36. Microcook Time: 9 minutes.
Calories: 87. Fat: 4 g. Carbohydrates: 13 g. Protein: 0 g. Sodium: 25 mg.

Place in an 8-cup glass measure:
  1 lb. almond bark
Microcook on high 2 minutes.
Stir.
Hint: Be sure bark is all melted.
Add . . .
  1 1/4 cups coconut
  3/4 cup crushed peppermint candy
  2 drops red food coloring
Stir.
Pour onto waxed paper to make a thin layer.
Break into pieces when cool.

- *1 lb. almond bark*
- *1 1/4 cups coconut*
- *3/4 cup crushed peppermint candy*
- *2 drops red food coloring*

Caramel Apples

Perfect for Halloween parties or any fall or winter night!
Serves 6. Microcook Time: 5 minutes.
Calories: 345. Fat: 7 g. Carbohydrates: 64 g. Protein: 3 g. Sodium: 144 mg.

- •1 (14-oz.) pkg. caramels
- •2 tablespoons water
- •6 medium apples

Place in an 8-cup glass measure, removing wrappers:
    1 (14-oz.) pkg. caramels
Add . . .
    2 tablespoons water
Microcook on medium 7 to 8 minutes until melted.
Stir twice.
Place sticks into:
    6 medium apples
Dip into caramel mixture, **turn** to coat.
Hint: If caramel mixture thickens, **microcook** on medium for 1 minute.
May be dipped in chopped peanuts after the caramel.
May also be dipped in melted chocolate chips after the caramel for a chocolate and caramel treat.

Cocoa Mix

Keep on hand for a quick warmer-upper.
Serves 12. Microcook Time: 5 minutes.
Calories: 37. Fat: 0 g. Carbohydrates: 8 g. Protein: 2 g. Sodium: 25 mg.

- •1/2 cup cocoa
- •1/4 cup nondairy creamer
- •3 cups powdered sugar
- •3 cups nonfat dry milk

Combine . . .
    1/2 cup cocoa
    1/4 cup nondairy creamer
    3 cups powdered sugar
    3 cups nonfat dry milk
Place in food processor to remove lumps.
For 1 cup cocoa:
Microcook on high 2 1/2 to 3 minutes:
    6 oz. water
Add 1 heaping tablespoon of cocoa mix to water.
Stir.

Jumbo Oatmeal Cookie - Convenience

"Jumbo" is the key word for this delicious cookie.
Serves 24. Microcook Time: 15 minutes.
Calories: 126. Fat: 5 g. Carbohydrates: 19 g. Protein: 1 g. Sodium: 86 mg.

Prepare according to microwave instructions:
    1 (1 lb. 15-oz.) pkg. oatmeal raisin cookie
        mix
Add . . .
    1/2 (6-oz.) pkg. almond brickle chips
    1/2 (6-oz.) pkg. butterscotch chips
Tear and **fit** a sheet of waxed paper large enough to cover the sides and extend over the edge of an 8" round glass baking dish.
Grease waxed paper.
Pour 1/3 of mixture into dish.
Microcook on high 2 1/2 to 3 1/2 minutes.
Rotate 3 times.
Remove and cool on rack.

- *1 (1 lb. 15-oz.) pkg. oatmeal raisin cookie mix*
- *1/2 (6-oz.) pkg. almond brickle chips*
- *1/2 (6-oz.) pkg. butter-scotch chips*

Monster Crunch Cookie

This monster definitely won't "scare" anyone away.
Serves 12. Microcook Time: 5 minutes.
Calories: 75. Fat: 3 g. Carbohydrates: 12 g. Protein: 1 g. Sodium: 59 mg.

- 1 (1 lb. 15-oz.) pkg. sugar cookie mix
- 1/2 (6-oz.) pkg. almond brickle chips
- 1/4 teaspoon cinnamon

Prepare:
> 1 (1 lb. 15-oz.) pkg. sugar cookie mix according to microwave instructions

Add . . .
> 1/2 (6-oz.) pkg. almond brickle chips
> 1/4 teaspoon cinnamon

Tear and **fit** a sheet of waxed paper large enough to cover the sides and extend over the edge of an 8" round glass baking dish.

Grease waxed paper.

Pour half of batter into dish.

Microcook on high 2 1/2 to 3 1/2 minutes.

Remove and **cool** on rack.

Microcook on high 4 minutes.

Variation

Candy-coated chocolate candies may be sprinkled on or pushed into the cookie as it is removed from the oven.

Richfield's Awesome Cookie

Always Awesome.
Serves 16. Microcook Time: 10 minutes.
Calories: 285. Fat: 17 g. Carbohydrates: 28 g. Protein: 5 g. Sodium: 92 mg.

Combine in a mixing bowl:
>1 cup quick-cooking oats
>3/4 cup all-purpose flour
>3/4 cup brown sugar
>1 teaspoon cinnamon
>1/2 teaspoon baking powder
>1/4 cup chunky peanut butter

Stir.
Add . . .

>1/2 cup almond brickle chips
>1/4 cup chocolate chips
>2 tablespoons butterscotch chips
>1/4 cup sunflower nuts

Stir.
Add . . .

>1 egg
>1/4 cup oil
>1 tablespoon vanilla

Stir well.

Tear and **fit** a sheet of waxed paper large enough to cover and extend over the edges of a greased 9" round glass pie plate.
Grease waxed paper.
Pour 1/2 of the dough into pie plate.

Microcook on high 3 to 3 1/2 minutes.
Remove and **cool** on rack 15 minutes.
Repeat.

- 1 cup quick-cooking oats
- 3/4 cup all-purpose flour
- 3/4 cup brown sugar
- 1 teaspoon cinnamon
- 1/2 teaspoon baking powder
- 1/4 cup chunky peanut butter
- 1/2 cup almond brickle chips
- 1/4 cup chocolate chips
- 2 tablespoons butterscotch chips
- 1/4 cup sunflower nuts
- 1 egg
- 1/4 cup oil
- 1 tablespoon vanilla

Chocolate Fondue

Perfect for getting the party rolling.
Serves 9. Microcook Time: 5 minutes.
Calories: 291. Fat: 18 g. Carbohydrates: 32 g. Protein: 5 g. Sodium: 66 mg.

•2 (8-oz.) bars milk chocolate
•1 (5-oz.) can evaporated milk
•1 teaspoon vanilla

Place in a 4-cup glass measure:
    2 (8-oz.) bars milk chocolate
    1 (5-oz.) can evaporated milk
Microcook on high 1 1/2 to 2 minutes, or until chocolate melts.
Stir.
Add . . .
    1 teaspoon vanilla
Dip fruits into chocolate.
Hint: Ideas for dippers: Apples, pineapple, oranges or bananas.

Quick Onion Fondue

Use mini bread sticks or toasted cheese bread to dip.
Serves 8. Microcook Time: 5 minutes.
Calories: 26. Fat: 1 g. Carbohydrates: 2 g. Protein: 1 g. Sodium: 226 mg.

•1/2 cup low-fat sour cream
•1 tablespoon dry onion soup mix

Combine in a 2-cup glass measure:
    1/2 cup low-fat sour cream
    1 tablespoon dry onion soup mix
Stir.
Microcook on high 1 to 1 1/2 minutes until bubbly.

Popcorn Hints

- Popcorn, because of its low moisture content, will not pop in ovens below 600 watts.
- Always use microwave popcorn poppers, follow manufacturer's directions.
- Brown paper bags should not be used.
- Be sure popcorn is fresh.
- Gourmet-type works best.
- The average amount of unpopped kernels for popcorn prepared in microwave is 1 1/2 to 2 tablespoons.

Popcorn Mixers

Mexican Popcorn

For that south of the border zest!.
Serves 8. Microcook Time: 10 minutes. Includes popping time.
Calories: 160. Fat: 15 g. Carbohydrates: 7 g. Protein: 1 g. Sodium: 357 mg.

Place in a 1-cup glass measure:
  1/2 cup butter
Microcook on high 30 seconds.
Combine melted butter with:
  1 teaspoon chili powder
  1/2 teaspoon garlic powder
  1/2 teaspoon onion powder
  1/8 teaspoon cumin
Pour over:
  8 cups popped corn
Toss.

- 1/2 cup butter
- 1 teaspoon chili powder
- 1/2 teaspoon garlic powder
- 1/2 teaspoon onion powder
- 1/8 teaspoon cumin
- 8 cups popped corn

Dijon Popcorn

Gives popcorn a tangy flavor.
Serves 4. Microcook Time: 10 minutes. Includes popping time.
Calories: 161. Fat: 15 g. Carbohydrates: 7 g. Protein: 1 g. Sodium: 386 mg.

- *1/4 cup butter*
- *2 teaspoons Dijon mustard*
- *1 teaspoon dill weed*
- *8 cups popped corn*

Place in a 1-cup glass measure:
    1/4 cup butter
    2 teaspoons Dijon mustard
    1 teaspoon dill weed
Microcook on high 30 seconds.
Pour over:
    4 cups popped corn

Toss.

Fruit & Nuts Popcorn

Healthy party or anytime treat.
Serves 8. Microcook Time: 10 minutes. Includes popping time.
Calories: 174. Fat: 10 g. Carbohydrates: 23 g. Protein: 2 g. Sodium: 297 mg.

- *1/4 cup butter*
- *2 tablespoons sunflower nuts*
- *1 (6-oz. pkg.) chopped dried fruits and raisins*
- *8 cups popped corn*

Place in a 1-cup glass measure:
    1/4 cup butter
Microcook on high 30 seconds.
Combine melted butter with:
    2 tablespoons sunflower nuts
    1 (6-oz. pkg.) chopped dried fruits and
      raisins
Pour over:
    8 cups popped corn

Toss.

Lollipops

I loved these as a child.
Serves 12. Microcook Time: 17 minutes.
Calories: 99. Fat: 0 g. Carbohydrates: 26 g. Protein: 0 g. Sodium: 9 mg.

Combine in an 8-cup measure:
    1 cup sugar
    1/2 cup light corn syrup
    1/3 cup water
Caution: Be sure glass measure is free of cracks; extreme temperature may cause breakage.

Insert microwave candy thermometer.
Microcook on high 8 to 14 minutes or until temperature is 300 degrees.
Stir every 2 minutes.
Stir in carefully:
    1/4 teaspoon flavoring
    food coloring
Pour into greased lollipop molds.*
Stand 1 hour.
*Use pot holders! Handle gets hot!

- *1 cup sugar*
- *1/2 cup light corn syrup*
- *1/3 cup water*
- *1/4 teaspoon flavoring*
- *food coloring*

Pita Bread

Healthy and fun to make.
Serves 8. Microcook Time: 22 minutes.
Calories: 98. Fat: 1 g. Carbohydrates: 18 g. Protein: 4 g. Sodium: 195 mg.

- 1 loaf frozen whole grain bread dough
- cornmeal
- 1 cup fresh broccoli
- 1 cup sliced carrots
- 1 cup sliced zucchini
- 1 cup sliced fresh mushrooms
- 1/4 cup chopped green pepper
- 1/4 cup water
- 2 cups alfalfa sprouts
- 1 cup plain yogurt
- 1/2 teaspoon dill weed
- 1/4 teaspoon garlic powder
- 1/4 teaspoon instant onion flakes

Place on waxed paper:
    1 loaf frozen whole grain bread dough
Microcook on medium low 5 to 6 minutes.
Cut into 8 sections.
Roll 4 sections flat between 2 sheets waxed paper which has been sprinkled with:
    cornmeal
Remove top layer of waxed paper.
Microcook on medium low 10 to 30 seconds.
Hint: Dough will be warm.
Rotate.
Microcook on high 8 seconds.
Hint: You may press dough to make thinner, if desired.
Place on a small cookie sheet.
Bake in conventional oven 450 degrees 10 to 15 minutes (on bottom rack).
Repeat for 8 pitas.
Cool.

Filling

Combine in a microwave steamer:
    1 cup fresh broccoli
    1 cup sliced carrots
    1 cup sliced zucchini
    1 cup sliced fresh mushrooms
    1/4 cup chopped green pepper
    1/4 cup water
Microcook on high 6 to 8 minutes.
Fill pita with vegetables and top with:
    2 cups alfalfa sprouts
    1 cup plain yogurt
    1/2 teaspoon dill weed
    1/4 teaspoon garlic powder
    1/4 teaspoon instant onion flakes
Hint: Use filling with any pitas.

Pizza That Kids Love

And believe me, they do love it!
This recipe requires special equipment: A 12" microwave browning grill and cover.
Serves 8. Microcook Time: 20 minutes.
Calories: 165. Fat: 9 g. Carbohydrates: 14 g. Protein: 8 g. Sodium: 497 mg.

Thaw overnight:
    1/2 loaf frozen white bread dough
Roll on floured surface to fit browning grill.
Place in 12" microwave browning grill.
Place in a 4-cup glass measure:
    1 (8-oz.) can tomato sauce
    2 tablespoons chopped onion
Microcook on high 2 minutes.
Add . . .

    1/2 teaspoon oregano
    1/8 teaspoon garlic powder
    dash pepper
Pour over dough.
Top with:
    1 cup shredded mozzarella cheese
    1/2 cup sliced pepperoni
    1/4 cup grated Parmesan cheese
Add if desired . . .
    4 fresh mushrooms, sliced or 1 (4-oz.) can
      mushrooms, drained
    6 to 8 green pepper strips
    1 (2 1/4-oz.) can chopped ripe olives,
      drained
Cover.

Microcook on high 13 to 15 minutes.
Rotate 3 times.

Hint: Use a teflon spatula to remove pizza before cutting to avoid scratching the nonstick oven surface. For thicker crust use whole loaf.

- 1/2 loaf frozen white bread dough
- 1 (8-oz.) can tomato sauce
- 2 tablespoons chopped onion
- 1/2 teaspoon oregano
- 1/8 teaspoon garlic powder
- dash pepper
- 1 cup shredded mozzarella cheese
- 1/2 cup sliced pepperoni
- 1/4 cup grated Parmesan cheese
- 4 fresh mushrooms, sliced, or 1 (4-oz.) can mushrooms, drained
- 6 to 8 green pepper strips
- 1 (2 1/4-oz.) can chopped ripe olives, drained

Broccoli Pizza

A great pizza recipe; especially for those who avoid red meat.
This recipe requires special equipment: A 12" microwave browning grill and cover.
Serves 8. Microcook Time: 25 minutes.
Calories: 193. Fat: 9 g. Carbohydrates: 20 g. Protein: 10 g. Sodium: 409 mg.

- 1 (10-oz.) pkg. refrigerated buttermilk flaky biscuits
- 1 small onion, minced
- 2 ribs celery, chopped
- 1 (10-oz.) pkg. frozen chopped broccoli, thawed and drained
- 1 (8-oz.) can water chestnuts, drained and chopped
- 1 (6 1/2-oz.) can chicken chunks
- 6 drops hot pepper sauce
- 1 (10 3/4-oz.) can low-sodium cream of chicken soup
- 3/4 cup cubed process cheese

Cover microwave browning grill with:
> 1 (10-oz.) pkg. refrigerated buttermilk flaky biscuits

Press all the biscuits except 2 onto bottom.
Set aside.
Place in an 8-cup glass measure:
> 1 small onion, minced
> 2 ribs celery, chopped

Microcook on high 3 to 4 minutes.

Add . . .
> 1 (10-oz.) pkg. frozen chopped broccoli, thawed and drained
> 1 (8-oz.) can water chestnuts, drained and chopped
> 1 (6 1/2-oz.) can chicken chunks
> 6 drops hot pepper sauce
> 1 (10 3/4-oz.) can low-sodium cream of chicken soup

Stir.
Pour over biscuits.

Top with:
> 3/4 cup cubed process cheese

Place cover on microwave browning grill.
Microcook on high 11 to 13 minutes.
Stand 5 minutes before cutting.

Cajun Pizza

A lively recipe to be eaten with gusto!
This recipe requires special equipment: A 12" microwave browning grill and cover.
Serves 8. Microcook Time: 30 minutes.
Calories: 330. Fat: 14 g. Carbohydrates: 43 g. Protein: 12 g. Sodium: 1186 mg.

Place in a 4-cup glass measure:
    1 small onion, chopped
    1/2 green pepper, chopped
    1 cup frozen whole kernel corn
    1 clove garlic, minced
Microcook on high 4 to 5 minutes.
Add . . .
    1 (4-oz.) can chopped chilies, drained
    10 drops hot pepper sauce
Set aside.
Prepare as directed:
    1 (15-oz.) pkg. corn bread mix
Pour into 12" microwave browning grill.
Top with vegetable mixture.
Top with:
    1 cup cubed process cheese
    1/2 cup imitation bacon bits
Cover.
Microcook on high 15 minutes.

- 1 small onion, chopped
- 1/2 green pepper, chopped
- 1 cup frozen whole kernel corn
- 1 clove garlic, minced
- 1 (4-oz.) can chopped chilies, drained
- 10 drops hot pepper sauce
- 1 (15-oz.) pkg. corn bread mix
- 1 cup cubed process cheese
- 1/2 cup imitation bacon bits

Individual Pizza

Try making this with kids. You'll all be delighted.
Serves 12. Microcook Time: 10 minutes.
Calories: 143. Fat: 8 g. Carbohydrates: 13 g. Protein: 6 g. Sodium: 441 mg.

Combine . . .
    1 (6-oz.) can low-sodium tomato paste
    2 tablespoons chopped onion
    1/2 teaspoon oregano
    2 drops hot pepper sauce
    dash garlic powder
Spread on
    6 toasted hamburger buns
Top with:
    3 1/2-oz. sliced pepperoni
    1/2 cup sliced olives
    1 cup shredded mozzarella cheese
Microcook on medium; 4 halves take 3 1/4 minutes.

- 1 (6-oz.) can low-sodium tomato paste
- 2 tablespoons chopped onion
- 1/2 teaspoon oregano
- 2 drops hot pepper sauce
- dash garlic powder
- 6 toasted hamburger buns
- 3 1/2-oz. sliced pepperoni
- 1/2 cup sliced olives
- 1 cup shredded mozzarella cheese

Heart-watcher Pizza

Created for Dr. Malcolm Blumenthal; allergist, educator and friend.
This recipe requires special equipment: A 12" microwave browning grill and cover.
Serves 8. Microcook Time: 15 minutes. Thaw bread overnight.
Calories: 87. Fat: 2 g. Carbohydrates: 15 g. Protein: 4 g. Sodium: 134 mg.

- 1/2 loaf frozen whole grain bread dough, thawed
- 1 (6-oz.) can low-sodium tomato paste
- 2 tablespoons chopped onion
- 2 cloves garlic, chopped
- 2 zucchini, sliced
- 6 stalks fresh asparagus, sliced into 1/2" pieces
- 1/2 teaspoon oregano
- 1/4 teaspoon basil
- four drops hot pepper sauce
- 6 fresh mushrooms, sliced
- green pepper strips
- 1/4 cup chopped fresh parsley
- 1/4 cup freshly grated Parmesan cheese

Roll out to 12" on a floured surface:
> 1/2 loaf frozen whole grain bread dough, thawed

Place in a 12" microwave browning grill.

Top with:
> 1 (6-oz.) can low-sodium tomato paste
> 2 tablespoons chopped onion
> 2 cloves garlic, chopped
> 2 zucchini, sliced
> 6 stalks fresh asparagus, sliced into 1/2" pieces

Add . . .
> 1/2 teaspoon oregano
> 1/4 teaspoon basil
> four drops hot pepper sauce
> 6 fresh mushrooms, sliced
> green pepper strips
> 1/4 cup chopped fresh parsley

Top with:
> 1/4 cup freshly grated Parmesan cheese

Cover.

Microcook on high 13 to 15 minutes.

Rotate 3 times.

Hint: For thicker crust use whole loaf.

Fast & Fun Pizza

Pizza in a flash.
Serves 10. Microcook Time: 15 minutes.
Calories: 133. Fat: 8 g. Carbohydrates: 9 g. Protein: 6 g. Sodium: 470 mg.

Preheat microwave browning skillet according to manufacturer's directions.

Open . . .
    1 (10-oz.) pkg. refrigerated buttermilk flaky biscuits

Place 8 biscuits between 2 sheets of waxed paper and **press** to form a circle.

Hint: There may be holes in between; they will fill in during cooking.

Pull off top layer of waxed paper.

Remove browner from microwave with pot holders. Be careful, browner is very hot!

Flip rolls onto hot grill.

Microcook for 1 minute.

Spread over center top:
    1 (8-oz.) can tomato sauce

Add . . .
    10 pepperoni slices
    1/2 cup shredded mozzarella cheese
    1/2 cup grated Parmesan cheese

Microcook on high 4 to 5 minutes.

Cool on browner at least 3 minutes.

Transfer to a serving plate.

> - *1 (10-oz.) pkg. refrigerated buttermilk flaky biscuits*
> - *1 (8-oz.) can tomato sauce*
> - *10 pepperoni slices*
> - *1/2 cup shredded mozzarella cheese*
> - *1/2 cup grated Parmesan cheese*

Tex-Mex Pizza

A thrilling, spicy pizza.
Serves 8. Microcook Time: 10 minutes.
Calories: 221. Fat: 13 g. Carbohydrates: 19 g. Protein: 8 g. Sodium: 443 mg.

- *1/2 cup chopped onion*
- *1/2 cup chopped green pepper*
- *1 (15-oz.) can chili without beans*
- *1 (4-oz.) can chopped green chilies*
- *2 cups frozen whole kernel corn*
- *1 (2 1/2-oz.) can sliced ripe olives, drained*
- *1 cup crushed corn chips*
- *dash cumin*
- *1/2 cup cubed process cheese*
- *1 (10") flour or corn tortilla*
- *1/4 cup shredded Cheddar cheese*

Place in an 8-cup glass measure:
>1/2 cup chopped onion
>1/2 cup chopped green pepper

Microcook on high 1 1/2 to 2 minutes.
Add . . .
>1 (15-oz.) can chili without beans
>1 (4-oz.) can chopped green chilies
>2 cups frozen whole kernel corn
>1 (2 1/2-oz.) can sliced ripe olives, drained
>1 cup crushed corn chips
>dash cumin
>1/2 cup cubed process cheese

Mix well.
Microcook on high 4 minutes.
Place a on a glass 12" plate:
>1 (10") flour or corn tortilla

Spread mixture over tortilla.
Top with:
>1/4 cup shredded Cheddar cheese

Microcook on high 2 to 3 minutes.

Tostada Pizza - Convenience

Lusciously easy!
Serves 8. Microcook Time: 10 minutes.
Calories: 213. Fat: 12 g. Carbohydrates: 19 g. Protein: 9 g. Sodium: 393 mg.

Place on a 12" glass plate:
    1 super-size (10" diameter) soft tortilla
Spread with:
    1 (16-oz.) can refried beans with green
       chilies
Place in a microwave-safe colander on a 1 1/2-quart casserole:
    3/4 cup ground beef
Cover with waxed paper.
Microcook on high 3 to 4 minutes.
Drain fat.
Place meat in casserole.
Stir in:
    1 tablespoon chili powder
    1 teaspoon garlic powder
    1/2 teaspoon cumin
Pour meat mixture over beans.
Top with:
    1 (4-oz.) can chopped green chilies
    1/2 cup shredded Cheddar cheese
Microcook on high 3 to 4 minutes, until cheese has melted.
Top with:
    3/4 cup plain yogurt
    3/4 cup shredded lettuce
    1 tomato, chopped
    1 (2 1/2-oz.) can sliced ripe olives, drained
    1/3 cup taco sauce

- *1 super-size (10" diameter) soft tortilla*
- *1 (16-oz.) can refried beans with green chilies*
- *3/4 cup ground beef*
- *1 tablespoon chili powder*
- *1 teaspoon garlic powder*
- *1/2 teaspoon cumin*
- *1 (4-oz.) can chopped green chilies*
- *1/2 cup shredded Cheddar cheese*
- *3/4 cup plain yogurt*
- *3/4 cup shredded lettuce*
- *1 tomato, chopped*
- *1 (2 1/2-oz.) can sliced ripe olives, drained*
- *1/3 cup taco sauce*

Tostada

Fabulous and informal. You'll want to eat the whole thing yourself.
Serves 8. Microcook Time: 15 minutes.
Calories: 282. Fat: 16 g. Carbohydrates: 27 g. Protein: 10 g. Sodium: 416 mg.

- 1 cup all-purpose flour
- 2 tablespoons cornmeal
- 1/2 teaspoon baking powder
- 1/4 cup skim milk
- 3 tablespoons oil
- 1 tablespoon cornmeal
- 1 (16-oz.) can refried beans with green chilies*
- 3/4 cup ground beef
- 1 tablespoon chili powder
- 1 teaspoon garlic powder
- 1/2 teaspoon cumin
- 1/2 cup shredded Cheddar cheese
- 3/4 cup plain yogurt
- 3/4 cup shredded lettuce
- 1 tomato, chopped
- 1 (2 1/2-oz.) can sliced ripe olives, drained
- 1/3 cup taco sauce

Combine in an 8-cup glass measure:
> 1 cup all-purpose flour
> 2 tablespoons cornmeal
> 1/2 teaspoon baking powder
> 1/4 cup skim milk
> 3 tablespoons oil

Mix well, then "squeeze" several times to form a ball.
Place between 2 sheets of waxed paper.
Roll out to form a 9 to 10" circle.
Sprinkle 12" glass plate with:
> 1 tablespoon cornmeal

Remove top piece of paper and turn onto the 12" glass plate.
Microcook on high 4 to 5 minutes.
Spread with:
> 1 (16-oz.) can refried beans with green chilies*

Place in a microwave-safe colander on a 1 1/2-quart casserole.
> 3/4 cup ground beef

Cover with waxed paper.
Microcook on high 3 to 4 minutes.
Drain fat.
Place meat in casserole.
Stir in:
> 1 tablespoon chili powder
> 1 teaspoon garlic powder
> 1/2 teaspoon cumin

Pour meat mixture over beans.
Top with:
> 1/2 cup shredded Cheddar cheese

Microcook on high 3 to 4 minutes, until cheese has melted.
Top with:
> 3/4 cup plain yogurt
> 3/4 cup shredded lettuce
> 1 tomato, chopped
> 1 (2 1/2-oz.) can sliced ripe olives, drained
> 1/3 cup taco sauce

*Hint: Or try 1 (9-oz.) can bean dip with jalapenos and 1 teaspoon chili powder.

Veggie Pizza

You must try it to believe it.
Serves 8. Microcook Time: 10 minutes.
Calories: 396. Fat: 31 g. Carbohydrates: 32 g. Protein: 10 g. Sodium: 562 mg.

Unroll:
    1 (8-oz.) pkg. refrigerated crescent rolls
Preheat round microwave browner skillet according to manufacturer's directions.
Arrange triangle-shaped rolls to form a circle on preheated browner. They do not have to fit exactly. Be careful, browner plate is hot!
Microcook on high 4 minutes.
Place in a 4-cup glass measure:
    2 (8-oz.) pkgs. cream cheese
Microcook on medium 1 minute to soften.
Stir.
Add . . .
    1 tablespoon dill weed
    1 1/2 teaspoons garlic powder
    1/4 cup milk*
Stir until well combined and spread over crust.
Transfer crust to a serving plate.
Top with:
    1/2 cup cauliflower flowerettes
    1/2 cup broccoli flowerettes
    2 carrots, sliced
    1 green pepper, sliced
    6 mushrooms, sliced
    6 black olives, sliced
    1/2 cup cashew nuts
May be eaten immediately or chilled.
*Up to 1/2 cup light mayonnaise may be used in place of milk. This will add calories.

- 1 (8-oz.) pkg. refrigerator crescent rolls
- 2 (8-oz.) pkgs. cream cheese
- 1 tablespoon dill weed
- 1 1/2 teaspoons garlic powder
- 1/4 cup milk*
- 1/2 cup cauliflower flowerettes
- 1/2 cup broccoli flowerettes
- 2 carrots, sliced
- 1 green pepper, sliced
- 6 mushrooms, sliced
*6 black olives, sliced
- 1/2 cup cashew nuts

Peppermint Candy

Very pretty, very tempting.
Serves 16. Microcook Time: 10 minutes.
Calories: 245. Fat: 14 g. Carbohydrates: 29 g. Protein: 4 g. Sodium: 59 mg.

- 1/2 (20-oz.) pkg. almond bark
- 1 cup crisp rice cereal
- 20 crushed peppermint candies
- 20 chocolate candy kisses

Place in an 8-cup glass measure:
 1/2 (20-oz.) pkg. almond bark
Microcook on high 2 1/2 to 3 minutes until soft.
Stir in:
 1 cup crisp rice cereal
 20 crushed peppermint candies
Pour onto a 9" greased round glass plate.
Place in a 10-oz. custard cup:
 20 chocolate candy kisses
Microcook on high 45 to 60 seconds.
Drizzle over candy.
Stand.

White Candy Pizza

Chef Dick Hildebrand enlarged this recipe to make "almost the world's largest pizza."
Serves 20. Microcook Time: 10 minutes.
Calories: 132. Fat: 7 g. Carbohydrates: 16 g. Protein: 2 g. Sodium: 60 mg.

Place in an 8-cup glass measure:
  1/2 (20-oz.) pkg. or 6 squares white almond bark

Microcook on high 1 1/2 to 2 1/2 minutes until soft.

Stir.

Add . . .
  2 cups crisp rice cereal
  1/2 cup miniature marshmallows
  1/2 (6-oz.) pkg. almond brickle chips*

Stir until marshmallows melt.

Pour the candy onto a greased 12" glass plate.

Place in a 10-oz. custard cup:
  16 chocolate candy kisses

Microcook on high for 45 to 60 seconds until soft.

Stir.

Drizzle over candy in a circular pattern or spread evenly.

Top with:
  6 maraschino cherries, cut in half
  6 miniature marshmallows, cut in half

Chill.

  *1/2 cup peanuts may be added.

- 1/2 (20-oz.) pkg. or 6 squares white almond bark
- 2 cups crisp rice cereal
- 1/2 cup miniature marshmallows
- 1/2 (6-oz.) pkg. almond brickle chips*
- 16 chocolate candy kisses
- 6 maraschino cherries, cut in half
- 6 miniature marshmallows, cut in half

Cheese Pretzels

My students like these with mustard or Parmesan cheese.
Serves 12. Microcook Time: 20 minutes.
Calories: 141. Fat: 2 g. Carbohydrates: 27 g. Protein: 6 g. Sodium: 120 mg.

- 1 pkg. active dry yeast
- 1 1/3 cups very warm water (105 to 115 degrees)
- 1 tablespoon sugar
- 1/2 teaspoon salt
- 2 1/2 cups all-purpose flour
- 1/4 cup grated Parmesan cheese
- 1 cup whole wheat flour
- 1/4 cup grated Parmesan cheese
- 1 egg, beaten

Place in a large mixing bowl:

> 1 pkg. active dry yeast
> 1 1/3 cups very warm water (105 to 115 degrees)

Stir well.
Stir in:

> 1 tablespoon sugar
> 1/2 teaspoon salt
> 2 1/2 cups all-purpose flour
> 1 cup whole wheat flour
> 1/4 cup grated Parmesan cheese

Stir and form a large ball.
Place on floured surface.
Knead 5 to 7 minutes.
Add up to 1/2 cup more flour until ball is smooth.
Cut ball in half; **divide** each half into 6 pieces.
Make 12 "snakes" by rolling each piece between your hands.
Hint: Each snake should be 15" long.
Shape into pretzel form.
Enlarge hole in pretzel with thumb.
Place on a greased microwave baking dish.
Brush with:

> 1 egg, beaten

Hint: May top with sesame seed or wheat germ.
Microcook on medium 5 to 6 minutes.

50%

Stand 5 minutes.
Hint: A microwave-safe browning skillet may be used. It will brown the bottom crust.

Sugar Cookie Tart

Scrumptious and very dainty.
Serves 8. Microcook Time: 10 minutes.
Calories: 178. Fat: 4 g. Carbohydrates: 34 g. Protein: 2 g. Sodium: 115 mg.

Prepare:
    1/2 (15-oz.) pkg. sugar cookie mix using
      microwave instructions
Spread mixture on a greased 9" glass pie plate.
Microcook on a rack on high 3 to 4 minutes.
Place in a 2-cup glass measure:
    1 (8-oz.) pkg. cream cheese
Microcook on medium 30 to 45 seconds.
Stir.
Add . . .
    1/2 cup powdered sugar
    2 teaspoons almond extract
Stir.
Spread over cooled crust.
Top with fresh or canned fruits.
Serve.
Hint: Use leftover dough for a monster cookie.

- *1/2 (15-oz.) pkg. sugar cookie mix*
- *1 (8-oz.) pkg. cream cheese.*
- *1/2 cup powdered sugar*
- *2 teaspoons almond extract*

Sugar Cookie Tart Glaze

The finishing touch for a tasty tart.
Serves 8. Microcook Time: 7 minutes.
Calories: 17. Fat: 0 g. Carbohydrates: 4 g. Protein: 0 g. Sodium: 0 mg.

Combine in a 4-cup glass measure:
    1 cup cold water
    1 1/2 teaspoons cornstarch
Stir.
Microcook on high 3 to 4 minutes.
Stir 3 times.
Hint: Should thicken.
Add . . .
    1 banana, mashed
    1/4 cup lemon juice*
Stir well.
Pour over fruits.
*try 1/2 cup raspberry preserves, 1/3 cup cassis
syrup.

- *1 cup cold water*
- *1 1/2 teaspoons cornstarch*
- *1 banana, mashed*
- *1/4 cup lemon juice**

Caramel Corn

Perfect for cheering up the cold winter season.
Serves 12. Microcook Time: 10 minutes.
Calories: 299. Fat: 19 g. Carbohydrates: 30 g. Protein: 6 g. Sodium: 334 mg.

- *2 quarts of popped corn*
- *1 cup peanuts*
- *1/2 cup sunflower nuts*
- *1 cup brown sugar*
- *1/2 cup butter*
- *1/4 cup corn syrup*
- *1/2 teaspoon baking soda*

Place in a large mixing bowl that has been greased with vegetable shortening:

> 2 quarts of popped corn

Add . . .

> 1 cup peanuts
> 1/2 cup sunflower nuts

Set aside.

Place in an 8-cup glass measure:

> 1 cup brown sugar
> 1/2 cup butter
> 1/4 cup corn syrup

Microcook on high 3 to 4 minutes or until mixture boils.

Stir twice.

Add . . .

> 1/2 teaspoon baking soda

Stir.

Hint: Mixture will foam and turn light. Very hot!

Pour quickly over popped corn mixture while tossing.

`100% !`

Pumpkin Seeds

Save seeds from your Halloween pumpkin.
Serves 16. Microcook Time: 10 minutes.
Calories: 85. Fat: 18 g. Carbohydrates: 2 g. Protein: 4 g. Sodium: 0 mg.

- *2 cups pumpkin seeds*
- *1 tablespoon oil*

Place on a plate that has been lined with a paper towel:

> 2 cups pumpkin seeds

Sprinkle with:

> 1 tablespoon oil

Season to taste.

Cover with paper towel.

Microcook on high 6 to 8 minutes.

Stir every 2 minutes.

Sloppy Josies

Always greeted with smiles.
Serves 8. Microcook Time: 13 minutes.
Calories: 155. Fat: 8 g. Carbohydrates: 8 g. Protein: 11 g. Sodium: 487 mg.

Place in a microwave-safe colander over a 2-quart
casserole:
    1 lb. ground beef, crumbled
    1 onion, chopped
Cover with waxed paper.
Microcook on high 4 to 6 minutes.
Drain fat.
Place meat into casserole.
Stir in:
    1 cup chili sauce
    1 teaspoon Worcestershire sauce
    dash pepper
Cover with waxed paper.
Microcook on high 4 to 5 minutes.
Stir twice.
Serve on hamburger buns.

- *1 lb. ground beef, crumbled*
- *1 onion, chopped*
- *1 cup chili sauce*
- *1 teaspoon Worcestershire sauce*
- *dash pepper*

Macaroni & Cheese

Every kid's basic favorite.
Serves 6. Microcook Time: 13 minutes.
Calories: 247. Fat: 8 g. Carbohydrates: 34 g. Protein: 11 g. Sodium: 290 mg.

Place in a 8-cup glass measure:
    1 (7-oz.) pkg. macaroni, cooked
Add . . .
    1 cup cubed process cheese
    1/4 cup grated Parmesan cheese
    1/2 teaspoon onion powder
    1/2 teaspoon dry mustard
Cover with vented plastic wrap.
Microcook on high 6 to 8 minutes.
Stir 3 times.
Stand 5 minutes.

1 (7-oz.) pkg. macaroni, cooked
1 cup cubed process cheese
1/4 cup grated Parmesan cheese
1/2 teaspoon onion powder
1/2 teaspoon dry mustard

Candy Rolls

I bet you never thought you could make this old-time favorite at home!
Serves 24. Microcook Time: 10 minutes.
Calories: 53. Fat: 1 g. Carbohydrates: 11 g. Protein: 0 g. Sodium: 12 mg.

- 1 square unsweetened chocolate
- 1 tablespoon margarine
- 1/4 cup dark corn syrup
- 1/4 teaspoon vanilla
- 1 1/2 cups powdered sugar
- 2 tablespoons instant nonfat dry milk

Place in a 4-cup glass measure:
> 1 square unsweetened chocolate
> 1 tablespoon margarine

Microcook on high 1 minute, until melted.

Stir in:
> 1/4 cup dark corn syrup
> 1/4 teaspoon vanilla

Microcook on high 1 minute.

Sift . . .
> 1 1/4 cups powdered sugar

Add . . .
> 1 cup ONLY powdered sugar to mixture

Mix . . .
> 1/4 cup powdered sugar + 2 tablespoons nonfat dry milk

Add . . .
> 1/4 cup powdered sugar + 2 tablespoons nonfat dry milk

Stir well.

Place on waxed paper that has been dusted with powdered sugar.

Knead.

Add . . .
> remaining 1/4 cup powdered sugar, if needed, to make a stiff ball

Divide ball into 4 parts.

Roll into pencil strips and cut into individual pieces.

Wrap pieces in waxed paper.

Refrigerate.

Yogurt Pops

My grandson Jon's favorite treat.
Serves 12. Microcook Time: 5 minutes.
Calories: 12. Fat: 1 g. Carbohydrates: 1 g. Protein: 1 g. Sodium: 9 mg.

Pour in a 4-cup glass measure:
>   1 cup water

Microcook on high 2 1/2 to 3 minutes:
Add . . .
>   1 (3-oz.) pkg. sugar-free gelatin dessert
>   1/2 cup cold water

Add and stir:
>   1 cup plain or flavored yogurt

Stir well.
Hint: Fruits may be added to complement the gelatin dessert.
Pour into 5 1/2-oz. paper cups and **top** with foil.
Push a stick through the foil into mixture and **place** in freezer for 1 hour or until hard.
Hint: Try strawberry gelatin, add strawberries and/or bananas; orange gelatin, add orange segments; lime gelatin, add crushed pineapple; raspberry gelatin, add frozen raspberries.

- *1 cup water*
- *1 (3-oz.) pkg. sugar-free gelatin dessert*
- *1/2 cup cold water*
- *1 cup plain or flavored yogurt*

Chocolate Pudding Pop

A delightful, summertime refreshment.
Serves 1. Microcook Time: 6 minutes.
Calories: 314. Fat: 8 g. Carbohydrates: 54 g. Protein: 5 g. Sodium: 126 mg.

- 1/2 cup skim milk
- 2 tablespoons semisweet chocolate chips
- 2 teaspoons cornstarch
- 2 tablespoons sugar
- 2 tablespoons cold water
- 1/2 teaspoon vanilla

Place in a 2-cup glass measure:
    1/2 cup skim milk
    2 tablespoons semisweet chocolate chips
Microcook on high 1 to 2 minutes.
Combine in a 6-oz. custard cup:
    2 teaspoons cornstarch
    2 tablespoons sugar
    2 tablespoons cold water
    1/2 teaspoon vanilla
Stir until mixed and **add** to hot mixture.
Microcook on high 30 to 45 seconds.
Stir until thick.
Pour into a paper cup and **cover** with foil.
Place wooden stick in the center.
Freeze.

Yogurt Dip

Great for topping on baked potatoes, and much better for you than sour cream.
Serves 8. Prep Time: 5 minutes.
Calories: 21. Fat: 1 g. Carbohydrates: 2 g. Protein: 1 g. Sodium: 18 mg.

- 1 (8-oz.) carton plain yogurt
- 2 teaspoons grated Parmesan cheese
- 1 teaspoon dill weed
- 3/4 teaspoon instant chopped onion
- 1/4 teaspoon garlic powder
- 1/4 teaspoon onion powder
- 6 drops hot pepper sauce

Combine in an 8-cup glass measure:
- 1 (8-oz.) carton plain yogurt
- 2 teaspoons grated Parmesan cheese
- 1 teaspoon dill weed
- 3/4 teaspoon instant chopped onion
- 1/4 teaspoon garlic powder
- 1/4 teaspoon onion powder
- 6 drops hot pepper sauce

Cover with plastic wrap.
Stand.
Refrigerate to intensify flavor.
Serve over vegetables or as a topping for baked potatoes.

Banana Pops

A year-round treat for kids of all ages.
Serves 12. Microcook Time: 3 hours, includes time to freeze.
Calories: 288. Fat: 21 g. Carbohydrates: 24 g. Protein: 3 g. Sodium: 33 mg.

Peel . . .
    6 bananas
Cut crosswise in half; **place** wooden stick in the wide end.
Freeze on foil for 1 hour.
Place in 9" glass pie plate:
    1 (6-oz.) pkg. semisweet chocolate chips*
    1/4 cup shortening
Microcook on high 2 1/2 minutes until chocolate is melted.
Stir.
Dip each banana half in chocolate mixture.
Coat with:
    8 oz. crushed walnuts or pecans
Wrap each banana in foil and **freeze:**
*Butterscotch chips may be substituted for chocolate chips, or try 3 oz. chocolate and 3 oz. butterscotch chips.

- *6 bananas*
- *1 (6-oz.) pkg. semisweet chocolate chips*
- *1/4 cup shortening*
- *8 oz. crushed walnuts or pecans*

100%

The Following Foods Are High in Dietary Fat

High Fat

- avocado
- bacon
- cream
- cheese
- chocolate
- nuts
- olives
- whole milk
- whole milk yogurt
- salad dressing
- sour cream
- ice cream

Saturated Fat

- coconut oil
- palm oil
- coconut oil
- palm kernel oil
- hydrogenated oil
- shortening
- chicken fat
- butter
- lard

Hidden Fat

- bars and brownies
- biscuits
- chips
- cookies
- cakes
- croissants
- doughnuts
- muffins
- pastry

Instead try to include these

- low-fat cheeses - farmer's, pot
- sherbet & sorbet
- fresh fruits and vegetables
- rice
- pasta
- skim or low-fat and nonfat dry milk
- fish
- lean meat
- poultry without skin
- dried beans and peas
- spices and herbs for flavor
- marinated meats, fish and poultry in lemon, lime, orange or tomato juice or plain low-fat yogurt
- Poly-unsaturated vegetable oil (safflower, corn, soybean)

A P P E N D I X

To cut down on Sodium, watch the following foods

- nitrite-cured foods
- salt-cured foods
- smoked foods
- ham and sausage
- cereals
- cheese
- all processed foods
- bouillon cubes
- catsup
- mustard
- pickles
- soy sauce
- tomato juice
- Worcestershire sauce
- salt
- meat tenderizer
- canned soups
- sauerkraut
- olives
- crackers

To cut down on Sugars, watch the following foods

- gum
- candy
- pastry
- doughnuts
- soft drinks
- fruit canned in syrup
- ice cream
- flavored yogurt
- jam and jelly

Instead try to include these

- fresh fruits and vegetables
- pasta
- rice
- fish
- poultry
- cereals - oatmeal, puffed wheat, shredded wheat
- potatoes
- dried peas and beans
- foods seasoned with spices and herbs

Potassium foods

- apricots
- bananas
- cantaloupe
- oranges
- raisins
- dried fruits
- artichokes
- avocados
- lima beans
- broccoli
- carrots
- greens
- potatoes
- squash
- yams
- mushrooms
- onions

Fiber foods

- fresh fruits
- fresh vegetables
- whole grains
- whole grain breads
- whole grain cereals
- dried beans and peas
- nuts
- seeds

Cruciferous Vegetables
- broccoli
- Brussels sprouts
- cabbage
- cauliflower

Vitamin A foods

- apricots
- cantaloupe
- nectarines
- peaches
- asparagus
- avocados
- broccoli
- Brussels sprouts
- carrots
- corn
- greens
- peas
- green peppers
- squash
- sweet potatoes/yams

Vitamin C foods

- cantaloupe
- honeydew
- watermelon
- citrus fruits
- kiwis
- raspberries
- strawberries
- asparagus
- broccoli
- Brussels sprouts
- cabbage
- cauliflower
- peppers
- potatoes
- spinach
- tomatoes
- turnips

INDEX

I N D E X

I N D E X

INDEX

INDEX & INFORMATION

For information about cancer & heart disease contact the following:

American Cancer Society
3340 Peachtree Road NE
Atlanta, Georgia 30026

National Cancer Institute
9000 Rockville Pike
Bethesda, Maryland 20892

American Heart Association
7320 Greenville Ave.
Dallas, Texas 75231

Microwave Mastery Ordering Information

- To order additional copies of Microwave Mastery send $12.95 plus $2.00 {U.S.A. funds} postage & handling per book to Mic•it Publishing, Inc. Cookbook Order, Department 1111 P.O. Box 23148 Minneapolis, Minnesota 55423 {Minnesota residents add 6% sales tax}

Please send _____ "Microwave Mastery" Cookbook(s)
Send to:
Name_____
Address_____
City/State/Zip_____
Master or Visa #_____Exp. Date_____
Signature_____

- School discounts of 20% on approved school orders of 5 books or more may be made by sending orders prepaid.

- Full nutritional printouts for each recipe in this book may be ordered by sending $2.50 per recipe or $10.00 for 10 recipes (includes postage & handling). Include recipe name and page number. Send inquires to: Mic•it Publishing, Inc. Nutritional Analysis, Department 5151 P.O. Box 23148 Minneapolis, Minnesota 55423

Send to:
Name_____
Address_____
City/State Zip_____
Master or Visa #_____Exp. Date_____
Signature_____